TREASURES OF THE SAKYA LINEAGE

TREASURES OF THE

SAKYA LINEAGE

TEACHINGS FROM THE MASTERS

Migmar Tseten

David,

With prayers,

Shambhala
Boston & London
2008

Shambhala Publications, Inc.
Horticultural Hall
300 Massachusetts Avenue
Boston, Massachusetts 02115
www.shambhala.com

9 8 7 6 5 4 3 2 1

First Edition

Printed in the United States of America

♾ This edition is printed on acid-free paper that meets the
American National Standards Institute z39.48 Standard.

Distributed in the United States by Random House, Inc.,
and in Canada by Random House of Canada Ltd

Interior design and composition: Greta D. Sibley & Associates

Library of Congress Cataloging-in-Publication Data
Treasures of the Sakya Lineage; teachings from the masters /
[compiled by] Migmar Tseten.
p.   cm.
ISBN 978-1-59030-488-4 (pbk.: alk. paper)
1. Sa-skya-pa (Sect). I. Tseten, Migmar.
BQ7672.T74 2008
294.3'923 22
2007033817

CONTENTS

Contents

THE SAKYA TRIZIN

Words of great masters are like water to the thirsty, medicine to the sick, and a guiding star to the lost. The teachings sow the seeds. Understanding and reflecting back upon them nurtures the sapling. But it is only by incorporating the essence of the words in daily living that many have been able to reap the sweet fruit of enlightenment.

It gives me much pleasure to introduce this compilation of short teachings by various Sakyapa masters and scholars. I appreciate Lama Migmar Tseten's endeavor to bring Dharma to laypeople in the form of this compact collection.

I am sure the contents of this book will benefit many seekers of the profound truth.

With my blessings for the success of all the noble efforts made toward propagating the peerless doctrine of the Enlightened One. By this merit, may all sentient beings achieve deliverance from suffering.

The Sakya Trizin
April 2007

PREFACE

The Sakya monastery in Tibet is the oldest continuously operating institution among the four lineages of Tibetan Buddhism today. Founded by Khon Konchog Gyalpo in the late eleventh century, it became home primarily to the lineage of teachings brought to Tibet from India by the famed translator Drogmi Lotsawa, and codified by the five founding masters of Sakya. Detailed information about the Sakya school and its origin and doctrines may be found in chapter 25. The central teaching of the Sakya school, the path and result (*lamdre*), is based on the practice of the deity Hevajra and the view of the inseparability of samsara and nirvana.

This collection covers a vast range of Buddhist topics within the three *yanas,* and is representative of the Sakya school's method of presenting the Dharma.

The Sakya school has long been known for its balanced approach to study and practice, never emphasizing one at the expense of the other. Another feature of the Sakya school is its commitment to preserving the Indian Sutra and Tantra traditions as fully as possible. The writings of Sakya scholars have been deeply influential in every school of Tibetan Buddhism, and they continue to be now.

This collection is important because it features the teachings of both contemporary and ancient Sakya masters, showing a thousand years of lineage continuity. The Sakya masters of the past are Jetsun Dragpa Gyaltsen, Sakya Pandita, Chogyal Phagpa, and Ngorchen Kunga Zangpo. The texts of Jetsun Dragpa Gyaltsen are translated from a collection of his mystical songs found in his collected works. The longest and most comprehensive of these songs is the *Great Doha*. Likewise, the texts by Sakya Pandita, Chogyal Phagpa, and Ngorchen Kunga Zangpo are taken from their collected works.

The contemporary masters included here are His Holiness Sakya Trizin, His late Eminence Chogye Trichen, Khenpo Appey, and Lama Migmar Tseten. The texts by H.H. Sakya Trizin and H.E. Chogye Trichen are edited from talks and teachings. The series of texts by Khenpo Appey are drawn from his teachings on Sakya Pandita's masterpiece, *Clarifying the Buddha's Intent*. Lama Migmar Tseten's text is drawn from his teachings on the *Abhidharmakosha* of Vasubandhu.

The texts in this collection were selected from four anthologies privately published in a series called *Visions*.

ACKNOWLEDGMENTS

First of all, with profound respect, I would like to acknowledge H.H. Sakya Trizin and H.E. Ludhing Khenchen Rinpoche for their enlightened guidance, and to thank Khenpo Appey Rinpoche and Geshe Tashi Namgyal for their concise clarification of some critical points during the compilation of this text.

Next, I recall with gratitude the kindness of my teachers at the Tibetan Institute in Varanasi, India, who shaped my education in Buddhist philosophy: Gen Thupten Tsering (Gaden), Gen Yeshe Thapkhe (Drepung Loseling), Gen Tsultrim Gyatso (Drepung Gomang), and Gen Jampa Dhonyo (Sera), as well as Sakya Khenpo Tashi Sangpo and Sakya Tritso Khenpo.

I am grateful for my association with the Tibetan Institute and with Samdhong Rinpoche (the present prime minister of the Tibetan government in exile), who inspired me to dedicate my life to the Tibetan wisdom culture through the preservation of a distinct school of the Tibetan Buddhist tradition.

I also want to thank Shabdrung Rinchen Paljor Rinpoche, Thartse Rinpoche, Dzongsar Kyentse, Traleg Khyabgon, Tulku Thondup, Khenpo Gyatso, Lama Pema Wangdak, Lama Kalsang, Lama Jamyang Legshe, Professor Tashi Tsering, and Geshe Jamyang Tsultrim for their encouragement and support.

With deep appreciation, I give thanks to Kunga Namdrol and Ani Jamyang for their dedication during the various preparatory stages of this book.

Acknowledgments

The creation of this work would not have happened had it not been for Sam Bercholz, Hazel Bercholz, Sara Bercholz, Emily Bower, Ben Gleason, and Shambhala Publications, who originally conceived the idea for this edition. To them I am very grateful.

My sincere thanks goes to Jim Wilton for his legal advice and Tom Hlas for his help in creating and managing my website, www.lamamigmar .com.

I acknowledge the support of my colleagues Raymond A. Kahng, Dr. Bernard Steinberg, Greg Epstein, and the other chaplains at Harvard University. Working together is a joy.

To the Schaffer Foundation I extend heartfelt gratitude for their continued support of my translations and publications.

With profound devotion, I dedicate this book to the memory of His late Eminence Chogye Trichen Rinpoche and the late Khenpo Rinchen, without whom I would not have made a connection to the profound and vast lineage of the Sakya tradition.

Finally, I dedicate this book to the long life of His Holiness the Fourteenth Dalai Lama.

TREASURES OF THE SAKYA LINEAGE

Jetsun Dragpa Gyaltsen (1147–1216)

The Great Song of Experience

Namo gurubhadraya.
To the gurus and personal deities residing inseparably,
who join all qualities to the mind stream,
I prostrate with pure body, speech, and mind;
I make an offering free from both grasper and grasped;
I praise with mind, beyond the activity of speech, free from
    proliferation;
I make a confession untouched by the sins of the three times;
I go for refuge without an object, free from fear;
I create limitless *bodhichitta* without objects,
the nature of which is *dharmata*,[1] like space;
the root of virtue not gathered is dedicated to enlightenment;
accept this mandala of empty phenomena;
please bestow blessings upon me, the fortunate one.

When only the view was established,
it was said by the Buddhas,
"All views of emptiness are a source of faults,"
therefore, the view cannot be viewed.
For one with wisdom, there is no view;
for one with sharp intelligence, it is beyond words;
for one with diligence, nothing is to be meditated on;

for one with faith, there is no cause and result;
for one with compassion, there are no sentient beings;
for the gatherer of the accumulations,[2] there is no buddhahood.
Freedom from extremes is beyond knowledge, expressions, and objects;
Madhyamaka,[3]
Chittamatra,[4] and so on,
expressions in words are proliferations.
Thoughts in the mind are concepts,
the nature[5] is inexpressible and unthinkable.
For as long as views continue to exist,
there is no liberation from all suffering.
Conceptuality is great ignorance;
it is said one sinks into the ocean of samsara.
Without the mind stream being liberated by hearing,
do not express the view in words!
With scripture, reason, and *upadesha,*
the view is determined, mind is at ease.
When only the practice of meditation was done,
there was no meditation, and also no meditator.
That meditation free from extremes is without an object,
so leave one's activities and practice.

With the mind without mind, look into the mind;
if seen, that is not mind itself.
With seeing without seeing, mind itself is seen;
remain undistracted in unseeing mind.
If attached, make a connection with clarity;
if scattered, hold with the iron hook of recollection.
Meditation is clarity without concepts.
Do not express meditation in words
without being connected with the nectar of experience!
Begin with developing compassion and bodhichitta;
at the end, dedicate merit to enlightenment.

When only practicing the conduct,
one experienced view and meditation.
Having sealed the appealing things,

perform conduct without accepting and rejecting.
Do not leave such naturally unfabricated conduct
on the side of misconduct.
Do not leave that conduct of visiting friends
on the side of wild behavior.
Do not leave that conduct of nongrasping one taste
on the side of desire and anger.
Do not leave that conduct of relaxing without activity
on the side of nonvirtue!
Do not leave that conduct of completely purifying the three wheels[6]
to defiled virtue.
Do not leave that conduct without virtue and nonvirtue
in neutrality.

When only buddhahood was established,
aside from mind there were no dharmas.
When mind itself is comprehended, that is Buddha,
do not seek elsewhere for Buddha.
Please do not leave that *dharmakaya* possessing two purities[7]
on the side of the basis.[8]
Do not grasp the essence of Buddha
in the *rupakaya*, which appears to those
[sentient beings] to be tamed.
In the basis, there is no Buddha;
do not hope for attainment.
In the ultimate, there are no sentient beings;
do not fear suffering.

In the view without thought or expressions,
one is deluded by the activity of hearing and
contemplating sutras and tantras.
In the meditation free from extremes,
one is deluded by making physical and mental effort.
In that ceaseless natural activity of conduct,
one is deluded by becoming lost in misconduct and wild behavior.
In that result, the inseparability of samsara and nirvana,
one is deluded by becoming lost on the side of hope and fear.

That view of Great Madhyamaka
is bliss without delusion because that is not a proposition.
That meditation relaxing body and mind
is bliss without delusion because that is without effort.
That conduct, the causal ground of desire and anger,
is bliss without delusion because it is without accepting and rejecting.
That result, *mahamudra,*[9]
is bliss without delusion because that is without hope and fear.
If there is no proliferation, that is the view.
If there is no distraction, that is meditation.
If activity is abandoned, that is conduct.
If mind itself is comprehended, that is the result.
If doubt is cut, that is the view.
If there is no distraction, that is meditation.
If there is no clinging and attachment, that is conduct.
If the qualities are complete, that is the result.

Generally, for a being who has realized the view,
if there is no object of meditation,
that great meditator is without a practice.
If there is no conduct to perform,
that is yoga free from conduct.
If there is no result,
[At this point a line is missing in the original Tibetan text.]
the supreme view is without views,
philosophical conclusions are not needed here;
the supreme meditation is without meditation,
grasping mind is not needed here;
the supreme conduct is not conduct,
misconduct is not needed here;
the supreme result is not a result,
hope and fear are not needed here.

Generally, there is no object to see in Reality,[10]
now, also, the view is not a view.
There is no object of meditation in the original nature,[11]

now, also, meditation is not meditation.
In the natural state,[12] there is no conduct,
now, also, conduct is not conduct.
If the view has no center or limits,
surely one might think it is space.
If there is no movement or wavering in meditation,
surely one might think it is a mountain.
If there is no obscuration of clarity in experience,
surely one might think it is the sun and moon.
If there is no acceptance and rejection in conduct,
surely one might think it is the ground of the earth.
If there is no hope and fear in the result,
surely one might think one has turned away from grasping.

Meditation may or may not have been integrated into the view,
but when meditation is integrated into the view,
there is no distraction in the ultimate original nature.
View may or may not have been integrated into meditation,
but when the view is integrated into meditation,
there is no grasping to the taste of *dhyana*.[13]
View and meditation may or may not have been integrated into
     conduct,
but when view and meditation are integrated into conduct,
the experiential realization of meditation and postmeditation arises.
Because realization does not arise in the mind,
what is the benefit of a high view?
Because it does not become an antidote to the defilements,
what is the benefit of good meditation?
Because wisdom is not connected with compassion,
what is the benefit of precise conduct?
Because one's faults are undiminished even on the surface,
what is the benefit of primordial buddhahood?[14]
If the meaning of nonarising is realized,
one has arrived at the limit of the view.
If both meditation and postmeditation do not exist,
one has arrived at the limit of meditation.

If destruction and protection are neutralized,[15]
one has arrived at the limit of conduct.
If one obtains both dharmakaya and rupakaya,[16]
one has arrived at the limit of the result.

Examine one's mind for the view;
is the existence or nonexistence of permanence and annihilation seen?
Examine one's mind for meditation;
is the existence or nonexistence of distraction seen?
Examine one's mind for conduct;
is the existence or nonexistence of vulgarity seen?
Examine one's mind for the result;
is the existence or nonexistence of the ability to endure hardship seen?
View is the guide of the mind,
meditation is the path of the mind,
conduct is the friend of the mind,
the result is the host of the mind.
The sky of the view is considered to be high,
the ocean of meditation is considered to be deep,
the field of conduct is considered to be tilled,
the crop of the result is considered to be ripened.

Although I do not possess the best understanding,
yet by studying with learned gurus,
by accumulating the knowledge of hearing and contemplation,
this is how my understanding of realization arose.
Similar to the yoke and the neck of an ocean tortoise,[17]
understand that a human body is difficult to obtain.
Similar to the jewel of Takshaka's crown,[18]
understand that it is difficult to find a guru.
Understand the changes of the body through the four seasons
as the secret sign of death.
Similar to a person being exiled to an enemy country,
understand everything is left behind in passing away.
Similar to the colors of a peacock's feathers,
understand everything is born from karma.

If emptiness by nature is realized,
understand there is no birth in samsara.
Similar to a reflection in a mirror,
understand the nature of appearances is emptiness.
Similar to a display seen in a dream,
understand the nature of emptiness is appearances.
Similar to the golden luster of whey,
understand the nature[19] is completely pure.
Similar to clouds, dirt, or rust,
understand conceptuality as adventitious.
Understand conceptuality as samsara,
understand nonconceptuality as nirvana.
Understand samsara as suffering,
understand liberation as bliss.
Understand both happiness and suffering do not exist,
understand primordial emptiness as free from origin.[20]

Generally, if comprehension arises in the mind, bliss;
if the view is realized, bliss again.
The ripened illusory body[21] is bliss;
if there is no disease, bliss again.
Relying on seclusion of retreat is bliss;
if activities are abandoned, bliss again.
Livelihood agreeing with Dharma is bliss,
if wrong livelihood is abandoned, bliss again.
The desire objects of the youthful body and mind are bliss,
if one is connected with the method,[22] bliss again.
Friends with agreeable view and conduct are bliss,
practicing in solitude is bliss.
Food and wealth without grasping and attachment are bliss,
no definite residence is bliss.
Friendship free of obligation is bliss,
if one obtains freedom, bliss.

I am not someone who possesses merit,
but my obtaining the complete human birth and

spreading buddhadharma;
both of those occur at the same time.
Turning away from clinging to worldly dharma and
the arising of enthusiasm for spiritual Dharma;
both of those occur at the same time.
Leaving one's country abandoned and
meeting the guru in exile;
both of those occur at the same time.
Studying the scriptures and
understanding the words and meanings;
both of those occur at the same time.
Finding a Vajrayana guru and
obtaining the four *abhishekas* completely;
both of those occur at the same time.
Bestowing the oral transmission and instructions and
the arising of profound certain knowledge;
both of those occur at the same time.
Arousing devotion for the master and
the entry of blessings into the mind stream;
both of those occur at the same time.
Cutting doubts about the outer objects and
the arising of spontaneous wisdom;
both of those occur at the same time.
Having clarity in the creation-stage deity and
experiencing the realization of the completion stage;
both of those occur at the same time.
Having the heat of bliss[23] blazing in the body and
the arising of bliss and emptiness in the mind;
both of those occur at the same time.
Understanding delusion as relative and
understanding emptiness as ultimate;
both of those occur at the same time.
Losing awareness of the object
and being connected with the hook of recollection;
both of those occur at the same time.
Being robbed by misfortune and

the arrival of friends, the antidotes;
both of those occur at the same time.
Desire lost in objects,
and being connected with skillful means;
both of those occur at the same time.
Experiencing happiness and suffering
and understanding them as illusions;
both of those occur at the same time.
Seeing the suffering of sentient beings and
arousing profound compassion;
both of those occur at the same time.
Producing an argument with an opponent
and arousing proof inside oneself;
both of those occur at the same time.
Revealing the spring of merit
and turning away from attachment to food and wealth;
both of those occur at the same time.
Abandoning misconduct and
doing whatever conduct is pleasing;
both of those occur at the same time.

Please may hearing and wisdom also meet;
please may scripture and reason also meet;
please may the lineage and the guru also meet;
please may practice and oral instruction also meet;
please may diligence and faith also meet;
please may fame and qualities also meet.
No comprehension will arise
through hearing that lacks wisdom.
No certain knowledge will arise
through reason not connected with scripture.
No blessing will occur
through a guru without a lineage.
There will be no achievement
through faith without diligence.
There is no benefit for oneself

through an oral instruction without practice.
There is no benefit for others
through qualities without fame.

Without an egg, from where does the chicken originate?
Without a chicken, how does the egg originate?
Which is first, chicken or egg?
In the nonarising nature,
if there is no creation by conditions,
which is first, cause or result?
In the original purity of mind itself,
if both conceptuality and wisdom do not exist,
which is first, Buddha or sentient being?

Since dharmas[24] do not exist from the beginning,
if the result, buddhahood, never occurs,
which is first, dharmas or Buddha?
There is never anything in the ultimate;
if both delusion and nondelusion do not exist,
which is first, relative or ultimate?
Since in the ultimate there is no Buddha,
by whom was the Tripitaka[25] taught?
If no Dharma[26] was taught by the teacher,
how are there volumes of scriptures?
If it is said that "Cessation is nonexistent,
all of whatever will die and be born,
the conditioned, is ultimately nonexistent,"
how can it be that a result is produced from action?
If the nature does not arise from the beginning,
how will there be cessation?
Aside from the *dharmadhatu,*
nothing exists in any way.
In that immutable dharmata,
how can there be birth and death?
If all dharmas are false,
why do we think them reliable?

If all dharmas are true,
how is it that everything is deceptive?
If samsara is suffering itself,
performing nonvirtue is extremely deluded.

If there is no liberation to higher realms,
performing virtue to cause such a liberation is deluded.
If the result of karma itself is true,
the nature, emptiness, is deluded.
The moon in the water is not the moon in the sky,
but without depending on that [moon] that [reflection]
    does not appear;
similarly, the nature of all things
is taught as the two truths.
There will be no dharmas
not included in the two truths.
Because the nature is not true and not false,
grasping to the two truths is deluded.

Desire objects, the saltwater of craving,
can never satiate [craving] at any time;
similar to a leper looking in a mirror,
when one turns away from attachment, one is sated.[27]
The ripples of the river of *duhkha*[28]
can never be removed at any time;
similar to the smoke of an extinguished fire,
if one turns from nonvirtue by the method,
[one's duhkha] is removed.
From the river of birth, aging, sickness, and death,
one can never be freed at any time;
similar to constructing a bridge in a river,
if one realizes nonarising, one is liberated.
The great ocean of samsara
can never be dried up at any time;
similar to the arising of the seven suns of existence,
if one turns away from craving desire objects,

[one's own samsara] is dried up.
The difficult conditioned activities of work
can never be completed at any time;
similar to changing canals for irrigation
by leaving [the work] as it is, it is finished.
The dense darkness of ignorance
can never be removed at any time;
similar to a lamp in a dark room,
if the sun of wisdom arises, [ignorance] is removed.
The sun of the wisdom of selflessness
can never arise at any time;
similar to the dawn of sunrise,
if the supreme dharmas[29] arise in the mind stream, [wisdom] arises.
The painful defilement of concepts
can never be extracted at any time;
similar to an experienced doctor extracting a bullet,
if one possesses the powerful antidotes, it is extracted.
The knot of avaricious selfishness
can never be untied at any time;
similar to untying a knot of silk,
if one understands possessions are illusory, it is untied.
From the prison of samara's three realms
one can never be freed at any time;
similar to a prisoner being released from a cell,
if one is liberated from the iron chains of the grasper and grasped,
    one is freed.
The city of nirvana
can never be reached at any time;
similar to a guest entering onto a path,
if one is connected with the beginning of the path of liberation, one
    will arrive.
The guru, the spiritual friend,
can never be met at any time;
similar to Dharmodgata and Sadaprarudita,[30]
if a past accumulated karmic connection exists, [the guru] will
    be met.
The stream of nectar of oral instruction

can never be drunk at any time;
similar to finding a drink when one is thirsty,
if a suitable student abandons [mundane] activities, that student
    has drunk.
Nondual mahamudra
can never be realized at any time;
similar to a camel meeting with her calf,
if the mind is recognized, [mahamudra] has been realized.
The leaves of the words of conventions
can never be exhausted at any time;
similar to [closing] business activities due to exhausting one's
    merchandise,
if conceptuality is exhausted, [words] are exhausted.
The raw hide of one's mind stream
can never be tamed at any time;
similar to medicine for one with a disease,
if one practices according to Dharma, [the disease] is cured.
Possession of the three kayas and five wisdoms
can never be obtained at any time;
similar to a kingdom from gathered merit,
if the two accumulations are completed,
those [kayas and wisdoms] are obtained.

Do monks who have done hearing and contemplation
comprehend the intent of sutras and tantras?
It is dangerous not to cut doubts;
please do not fall on the side of convention.
Do all teachers who write and teach
have the benefit of definite knowledge?
Inquire into the sacred oral instruction!
There is a danger that scholars will die in an ordinary way.
All great meditators who practice,
please do not enjoy engaging in idle talk;
please do not yearn greatly for food and clothing;
please do not become attached to the taste of dhyana.
All Dharma practitioners who turn away from nonvirtue,
please comprehend the view of sutra and tantra a little,

occasionally follow the guru as an attendant,
always look into one's mind.
If one is lazy toward virtue,
[keep] the impermanence of death in mind!
If desire and anger arise toward objects,
[keep] the dharmata of dharmas in mind!
If connected with a circle of people and things,
[keep] the deceptions of Mara in understanding!
If, despite whatever one may do, there is no happiness,
[keep] the faults of samsara in mind!
With Dharma, this life and the next life are blissful,
the bardo existence is blissful,
rebirth is blissful—
[these are] very blissful because of birthlessness.
The practitioner is blissful, others are blissful, both are blissful,
therefore, please always practice Dharma.

At the time of obtaining complete human birth,
why is it that one does not practice spiritual Dharma?
Having been with a sacred guru again and again,
why is it that one has not pleased him?
Having requested the profound oral instruction again and again,
why is it that one has not done any practice?
Having aroused definite knowledge in the Dharma again and again,
why is it that one turns back again?

Generally, having abandoned one's country, one remains in exile;
although separated from one's country, one has no regret.
Direct the mind always to positive dharmas;
although born in hell, one has no regret.
Rely on the guru as the principal deity;
although one's resources are exhausted, one has no regret.
Do any devotional service to the guru;
although he is not interested in the disciple, the disciple has no regret.
Request the upadeshas in accord with scripture;
although one cannot practice, one has no regret.

The principal virtuous conduct is abandoning activities;
although *siddhi*[31] is not obtained, one has no regret.
Protecting one's promises is one's principal business;
although one is ridiculed by friends, one has no regret.

Spend one's life in the Dharma gathering accumulations;
although one has died, one has no regret.
Please do not create regret for oneself;
although blamed by others, one has no regret.
Reside alone without attachment to friends;
although one is without attendants, one has no regret.
Look into the mind as the principal realization of view;
although one's realization is small, one has no regret.
Rely on eating food to harmonize disease;
although one is ill, one has no regret.
Perform conduct that corresponds with the vows one has taken,
although it becomes misconduct, one has no regret.
Examine one's own faults, do not examine others' faults;
although affection is lacking, one has no regret.
Considering others' benefit is one's principal consideration;
although one's own benefit is lost, one has no regret.
Sing a small song agreeing with experience;
although lost to idle talk, one has no regret.
Apply the measure of thrift to possessions;
although celebrations are poor, one has no regret.

Similar to a stone thrown into an ocean,
please seek an irreversible Dharma!
Similar to cutting the head of a banana tree,
please seek a nonarising Dharma!
Similar to a light in a mass of darkness,
please seek an antidotal Dharma!
Similar to a disciple of a Vedic Brahmin,
please seek a scripturally valid Dharma!
Similar to applying vitriol to gold,
please seek a conducive Dharma!

Although those door protectors inside the temple
seem to be hitting, hitting, they do not hit.
Although those increasingly powerful laypersons
seem happy, happy, they are miserable.
Although those Dharma practitioners facing hardship
seem miserable, miserable, they are happy.
Although that wealth coming from generosity
seems to be dwindling, dwindling, it is increasing.

Sentient beings and Buddhas are equal,
yet happiness and sadness produce the great difference between them.
Self and others are equal,
yet the reason for grasping produces the great difference between them.
Enemies and children are equal,
yet loving-kindness and anger produce the difference between them.
Everyone obtaining a human body is equal,
yet victory or defeat produces the difference between them.

Beings who have obtained a human body,
do not rejoice in sinful activity;
Since the duhkha of this life is unbearable,
why mention the duhkha of lower realms?
All the virtue one performs,
perform connected with view and dedication;
please do not make it into defiled virtue.
"There is no happiness for samsaric beings"—
if that meaning does not exist for oneself,
what is the benefit of giving teachings?
Without turning away from this life's thinking,
what is the benefit of entering Dharma?
Without fear of birth and death,
what is the benefit of teaching the oral instructions?
Without cutting the hairy leaves of conceptuality,
what is the benefit of cutting the hair on one's head?
Without bringing change to ordinary perception,
what is the benefit of changing the color of a cloth?

Without relying on the sacred guru,
what is the benefit of abandoning one's country?
Without doing the practice of the oral instructions,
what is the benefit of hearing and contemplation?
When the time of death arrives, nothing helps aside from Dharma.

Generally, a greedy and deceitful guru
has no time to bestow the profound oral instructions;
a big liar misleading with provisional meaning
has no time to meet with the definitive meaning;
the great magnifier of samsara's duhkha
has no time to obtain nirvana.
The one of the great black darkness of ignorance
has no time for the dawn of the sun of wisdom.

If the meaning of the simile of illusion is realized,
one's search has found words of truth.
If the meaning of nonarising is realized,
one's search has found delusion.
If the meaning of cause and result is realized,
one's search has found provisional meaning.
If the meaning of the simile of space is realized,
one's search has found definitive meaning.
If the meaning of emptiness is realized,
one's search has found conceptuality.
If one is connected to the mind of the sacred guru,
one's search has found the oral instructions.

Further, however much of the Dharma is understood,
if one is not a suitable recipient of instructions,
the view will not be realized.
Do not be distracted by the worldly distractions
of not cutting off conventional proliferations.
If one is not able to live in solitude,
one will not obtain siddhi;
abandon and leave one's circle of people and things.

If the germ of the ultimate is not realized,
there is no essence in the husk of convention.
Not carried away by the distractions of the eight worldly dharmas,
abandon activities and take up practice.

See the connection between view and meditation;
see the connection between conduct and time;
see the connection between oral instruction and scripture;
see the connection between the person and Dharma practice;
see the connection between meditation and postmeditation;
see the connection between lineage and guru.

Generally, there is no end to the words of sutras and tantras;
right now, the important activity is to stop words.
Having cut doubt in the meaning,
now, the important activity is to stop looking.
[There is] no purpose in doing worldly activities;
now, the important activity is to abandon distractions.
One cannot depend on Yama,[32] the lord of death;
now, the important activity is to practice;
the time of death is uncertain, develop diligence.
If one is happy, it is the kindness of the guru,
if one is sad, it emanates from previous karma;
if one has loss, do not be discouraged,
and if one has gained, do not be arrogant.

The person of faith
in the eighty-four thousand gates of Dharma
may turn away from sinful actions.
One must engage in virtuous activity;
it is necessary to possess a mind without
[mundane] activity.
Further, abandon and leave Dharma activities.
Do not slander the Dharma;
also do not abuse the person.
Because a confusion between Dharma and person is perceived,

if asked how that is perceived,
a person is perceived to be misled with Dharma
because of [his] inferior intelligence and small learning.
Without possessing the goal of realization,
greatly exaggerating and disparaging Dharma and persons,
covered by the spittle of worms of conceptuality,[33]
grabbed by the hook of the mara,[34] of conceit,
without the point of many being of one taste,
also leave Kadampa[35] Dharma and go!
By not making a distinction between the acceptance and rejection of
     virtue and nonvirtue,
pretending to be knowledgeable without having understanding,
without heat,[36]
one performs wild conduct,
creating deceptions, filling the country with lies,
also leave Yogin[37] Dharma and go!
Having accepted Secret Mantra[38] as Dharma,
without possessing the ripening path of abhisheka[39]
and separated from points of the liberating path method[40]
because one does not meet a Lord of Secret Mantra,[41]
also leave Mahamudra Dharma and go!
Having accepted Mahayana as Dharma, separated
from compassion and bodhichitta,
action, Dharma, and person are not connected
in the dharma of the effortless basis[42];
also leave Dzogchen[43] Dharma and go!
Similar to the horns of a rabbit, the aggregates are without basis,
in particular, counting mouths, eyes, and wrinkles,
searching for a characteristic without a basis of a characteristic;
also leave Abhidharma[44] and go!
A reckoning that connects contradiction with contradiction
for the deceptive, unreal, deluded appearances is meaningless,
without benefiting the mind, one is deceived at the point of death;
also leave Logic Dharma and go!
Possessing an internal tumor of grasping truth in deluded
     appearances,

holding the acceptance of emptiness as the essence,
with the effort of establishing the pervasion of the minor premise[45];
also leave Madhyamaka and go!
Spending life on conventional words,
although knowledgeable, one does not understand the meaning
    of mind,
one dies in the body of delusion at the moment of death;
also leave Dialectical Dharma and go!
The master, not possessing qualifications, makes
Dharma connections[46] with the following three—
greedily giving a price for Dharma,
enjoying the consort of the guru without samaya,
attached to both union[47] and liberation[48] without the method[49];
also leave Vajrayana Dharma and go!
Held in the prison of misconduct of body and speech,
mind itself is without the view and meaning of meditation.
Duplicitous hardship is purposeless;
also leave Ordained Dharma and go!
Ignorantly meditating without hearing and contemplation,
doing construction or sewing when sitting,
behaving with misconduct if one goes to the village,
one's meditation session ends in foggy and sluggish sleep;
if one looks, one looks for gifts,
permitting someone with gifts in the gate,
stopping the one without gifts outside the gate,[50]—
supporting relatives by feeding them with devotional offerings;
also leave Great Meditators' Dharma and go!
Not understanding if profound Dharma is explained;
enjoying jokes, pointless idle talk, seductive dances and song;
one with deceit has Dharma and view only in the mouth,
creating calumny and dispute here and there,
if one can, robbing wealth from the neighbor's home,
throwing away family responsibilities with nothing else to do;
also leave Housewife Dharma and go!
Profit, fame, conflicts, arguments, livelihood, frustration,
    dissatisfaction,

a source of misfortune and suffering opposed to virtuous
	dharmas;
spending life in misery without any purpose,
there is no other place to go than the three lower realms;
leave Householder Dharma and go!
First, leave nonvirtuous activities;
in the middle, leave mundane activities;
finally, leave Dharma activities.
The mind of the yogin who has relinquished activities is happy;
the great meditator who gathers wealth is a layperson;
meditating with characteristics is conceptuality;
the virtuous actions of body and speech are misconduct.
Without activity, leave the six consciousnesses[51] relaxed.
If attached, attachment to the deity is also bondage.
If desirous, desire for buddhahood is also deluded.
If grasped, grasping at Dharma is also deceived.

Dissolve awareness into the natural state.
This is the oral instruction for those who understand;
awareness moves into the emptiness of mind,
characteristics of grasping and grasper are liberated at their
	own place[52];
even the term *biased opinion* does not exist;
the mind that confirmed the view is blissful.
Nondistraction moves into nonmeditation;
the characteristics of conceptuality are liberated at their own place;
even the terms *sluggishness* and *agitation* do not exist;
the mind that confirms meditation is blissful.
Naturally occurring [conduct] moves into ceaselessness;
the characteristics of misconduct are liberated at their own place;
even the terms *acceptance* and *rejection* do not exist;
the mind that confirms conduct is blissful.
Deathlessness moves into the state of nonarising;
the characteristics of hope and fear are liberated at their own place;
even the terms *present* and *future* do not exist;
the mind that confirms the result is blissful.

The view is produced without being eclipsed,
if the delusion is destroyed, it is destroyed by this;
because opinionated bias is not possessed,
the absence of the harm of grasper and grasped is amazing!
Unfabricated meditation occurs naturally,
if the paths and stages are reached, they are reached by this;
because the cause of focusing on objects is not possessed,
the absence of the harm of sluggishness and agitation is amazing!
Ceaseless conduct naturally occurs,
if grasping is turned away, it is turned by this;
because the thought of refutation and establishment is not possessed,
the absence of the harm of acceptance and rejection is amazing!
Not seeking the effortlessly produced result,
conventionally, dharmakaya is obtained by this,
because the thought of abandonment and achievement is not
    possessed,
the absence of the harm of hope and fear is amazing!

Sometimes there is bliss in the space of the sky;
there is bliss in the state without extremes or center.
Sometimes there is bliss in the depth of the ocean;
there is bliss in the state without movement or agitation.
Sometimes there is bliss in the sun and moon;
there is bliss in the state without obscured clarity.
Sometimes there is bliss in the middle of a river;
there is bliss in the unceasing state.
Sometimes there is bliss in the presence of the guru;
there is bliss in the oral instructions for eliminating proliferation.
Sometimes there is bliss residing in retreat;
there is bliss in practicing in solitude.
Sometimes there is bliss in the middle of the market;
there is bliss in carrying appearances onto the path.
Sometimes there is bliss in a row of yogins;
there is bliss in comparing experiential realization.
Sometimes there is bliss in the middle of begging lepers;
there is bliss in performing the conduct of one taste.

Sometimes there is bliss if the country is wide;
there is bliss in wandering aimless and alone.
There is bliss when permanently abiding in reality,
there is bliss in the state without bias or partiality.

In the beginning, a good consultation arose,
in the middle, enjoyment arose,
finally, mental bliss arose;
by leaving activities, one is connected to the
beginning of the path,
by relaxing, the paths and stages are reached,
by covering the head,[53] one can see clearly into the distance.

Even the deepest hell of sentient beings,
is the Dharma palace of Akanishtha.[54]
Even the suffering of both hot and cold,
is the dharmakaya free from proliferation.
Even philosophical conclusions of non-Buddhists
are the essential meaning of Madhyamaka.
Even the oral instructions of the holy gurus
are illusions deceived by illusions.
Even the experience of one's realization
is drawing pictures on the water.
Even the arising of the five paths and ten stages
is similar to counting the number of horns on a rabbit.
Even the accomplished Buddha
is just a name without ultimate existence.
Even dharmata established by awareness
is a banana tree without a heartwood.[55]
Because the realization of reality without activities
and the verbal view without certain knowledge
resemble one another, there is a danger of error.
Because the oral instruction of relaxing the sense organs
and losing the six sense consciousnesses to distraction
resemble one another, there is a danger of error.
Because intensely produced renunciation and

the behavior of a madman's coarse conduct
resemble one another, there is a danger of error.
Because the complete exhaustion of hope and fear
and the aversion of one who has an inner grudge
resemble one another, there is a danger of error.

This song of experience was sung by the upasaka Dragpa Gyaltsen. Based on both sutras and tantras, the song was composed in verse and beautified by the ornaments of poetry to decrease the arrogance of scholars and increase the enthusiasm of the faithful. Thus, the teaching of the song is completed.

Notes

1. *Dharmata* refers to the ultimate nature of dharmas, freedom from extremes.

2. The wisdom and merit accumulations.

3. Madhyamaka is the philosophical conclusion that emphasizes the freedom from extremes.

4. Chittamatra is the philosophical conclusion that emphasizes the ultimate reality of mind.

5. In this context, *nature* refers to the nature of reality that is free from extremes.

6. The three wheels are gift, giver, and receiver.

7. The two purities are dharmakaya's freedom from the obscuration of defilement and knowledge.

8. In this context, *basis* refers to the cause continuum, free from extremes, which contains all dharmas of samsara and nirvana.

9. *Mahamudra,* or "great seal," refers to realizing the union of clarity and emptiness in the form of the deity in the highest yoga tantra deity practice.

10. In the context of the view, *reality* means the nature of things free from extremes.

11. In the context of meditation, *original nature* is the basic nature of the mind when it is free from extremes.

12. In the context of conduct, the *natural state* means the nature of things free from extremes.

13. Dhyana is concentration meditation.

14. Primordial buddhahood is the unconditioned Buddha-nature that pervades all sentient beings.

15. *Destruction* means to destroy one's enemies and *protection* to protect one's followers.

16. Dharmakaya is the result of wisdom accumulation, the full realization of the ultimate nature of the mind. Rupakaya is the result of merit accumulation, physically appearing in buddha realms and samsara.

17. This line refers to the famous analogy of the wooden yoke floating on the surface of the ocean and the rare instance in which a sea turtle will surface with its head through the hole of the yoke.

18. Takshaka, one of the eight naga kings, is crowned with a precious jewel.

19. Here, *nature* refers to emptiness.

20. "Free from origin" means unconditioned.

21. The "ripened illusory body" refers to the human body as a result of the ripening of karma.

22. "The method" refers to Vajrayana practices.

23. The "heat of bliss" refers to the bliss that results from engaging in the completion-stage practice of inner-heat yoga.

24. Here, *dharmas* refers to things that possess characteristics.

25. The Tripitaka is the Buddhist canon comprising three sections: the Vinaya, Abidharma, and Sutra.

26. Here, *Dharma* refers to the doctrine of the Buddha.

27. The first two lines of each of these four-line stanzas refer to the general conditions of samsara; the second two lines refer to the methods of liberating oneself from those conditions.

28. *Duhkha* is Sanskrit for "suffering."

29. Supreme dharmas are the supreme mundane dharmas acquired as the fourth stage of the path of application, which immediately precedes the path of seeing.

30. This refers to the story of Sadaprarudita found in Edward Conze, trans., *The Perfection of Wisdom in Eight Thousand Lines and Its Verse Summary* (Bolinas: Four Seasons, 1973), Chapter 30.

31. *Siddhi* comprises both common siddhis (wealth and so on) and the uncommon siddhi (full enlightenment).

32. Yama is the king of the dead.

33. This metaphor refers to speaking about Dharma practices from a purely conceptual point of view that is not integrated with personal experience.

34. *Mara* refers to beings and forces that create obstacles to spiritual practice. They are commonly divided into four categories: the mara of the aggregates, the

mara of defilements, the mara of death, and the mara of the son of the god of the desire realm (Cupid).

35. The Kadampa lineage was founded in Tibet by the Indian master Jowo Atisha in the mid-eleventh century. This lineage is famous for its wide propagation of the Mind Training teachings, such as Seven Points of Mind Training and others.

36. Here, *heat* refers to the first level of realization of the path of application before realizing the firelike wisdom of the path of seeing.

37. A yogin is a spiritual practitioner.

38. "Secret Mantra" is a common name for tantric teachings in Tibetan Buddhism.

39. Abhisheka is the method for achieving enlightenment in the lifetime by creating a special dependant origination between the cause—aggregates, elements, and ayatanas—and the result—the kayas and wisdoms—and also introduces the student to Vajrayana.

40. The points of the liberating path method are the instructions and practices found in Vajrayana.

41. Here, a Lord of Secret Mantra is a deity; *meeting* refers to realizing a deity such as Vajrayogini as the union of clarity and emptiness, or mahamudra.

42. The "dharma of the effortless basis" refers to the nature of the mind, the union of clarity and emptiness.

43. Dzogchen, or ati yoga, is the highest teaching of the Nyingma school of Tibetan Buddhism.

44. Abidharma are those scriptures and commentaries concerned with wisdom training.

45. The minor premise is a term in a syllogism.

46. Making "Dharma connections" means creating disciples.

47. *Union* refers to the yoga of union with a qualified consort.

48. *Liberation* means the destructive rituals that liberate evil sentient beings.

49. Here, *method* refers to proper compassion and motivation.

50. This passage refers to those "great practitioners" who show favoritism to those who bring gifts and ignore those who cannot.

51. The five physical sense consciousnesses and mental consciousness.

52. "Liberated at their own place" means "freedom from dualistic extremes."

53. "Covering the head" refers to shading the eyes.

54. Akanishtha is the pure realm of the sambhogakaya.

55. In the same way that a banana tree has no heartwood, or center, dharmata has no inner substance.

☞ 2 ☜

Ngorchen Kunga Zangpo

A Prayer for the Happiness of All Living Beings

May the priceless teachings of the Omniscient One, the only door through which happiness ever appears to living beings, never decline in any place or time but spread forth to every direction's end.

May the span of life be lengthened and enhanced for our peerless teachers and spiritual friends who cherish the Buddha's religion more than their lives and whose compassion and wisdom are measureless.

May the assemblies of monks who practice his teaching always endure and their works pervade the ten directions, for they point out to beings the path of virtue and carry the great burden of teaching and meditation.

May all human beings be free from fears of old age, disease, and death, and live instead with right views of existence in this world. May their minds grow to love one another and limitless joys always increase for everyone.

May the cities of the earth be beautiful, strung with rows of prayer flags, white and rippling in gentle breezes; may their inhabitants not be poor but wear the fine clothes and jewels they long to have.

May the eyes of living beings be gladdened by skies made splendid by clouds that lightnings garland, while on earth below, the peacocks dance with joy as showers of rain, falling gently, approach.

May the mountains be adorned by rippling grasses, clusters of wildflowers, and falling waters, and may the valleys overflow with grains and commingling herds, while men sing songs that spring forth from joy, in freedom from pride, wars, and discord.

May the rulers govern well in peaceful ways and peoples heed their rulers with unfeigned respect so that, all inner and outer conflicts set at rest, well-being prevails as it did in the Age of Perfection.

May every temple be adorned by many images of the Enlightened One and by books of holy scripture; may the great rain of worship be increased there by infinite clouds of offerings from the gods.

May the chanting and study of scriptures increase in every monastery, each of them filled with spiritual friends and monks in saffron robes who uphold the teachings of the Sage and devote their days to discussing, explaining, and writing about his words.

May the holy teaching of the Blessed Enlightened One be enhanced by lay disciples, novices, monks, and nuns, each endowed with moral conduct that is flawlessly pure and diligent in study, reflection, and meditation.

May meditators who have given up every distraction be increased by those attainments of insight that follow renunciation; away from all bustle and harm, may they ever dwell in tranquil places of solitude.

May this, our own circle of meditators, whose prayers are offered with especial faith, be blessed with prosperity untainted by wrong livelihood, and may our life spans and our understanding of Dharma increase.

May there also arise within me spiritual qualities of learning and realization and the perfection of every principle that the enlightened ones have taught, through my own wholehearted performance of giving, moral conduct, patience, diligence, meditation, and highest wisdom.

For the sake of others, may I also grow in harmony with the holy teaching and gather others together through kind words and generous deeds; by the power of right explanation, may their actions and mine become attuned to the Way.

This prayer that I offer on behalf of all is that every obstacle to Dharma may vanish and every auspicious condition completely prevail; may every virtue that the Sage has praised increase always in every way!

This prayer for the happiness of all living beings was written by Venerable Master Ngorchen Kunga Zangpo, who established the famous hermitage of Ngor Evam in 1434.

⊰ 3 ⊱

An Interview with His Holiness Sakya Trizin

The Buddhist Essence Teaching

We Made Many Predictions, and
They All Said the Same Thing.

Q: *Your Holiness, would you give us an account of your life?*

HIS HOLINESS SAKYA TRIZIN: Perhaps I should begin by telling you what happened before my birth. The title Sakya Trizin means "holder of the throne of Sakya." My grandfather had been the last Trizin in our family. To ensure they would have a son, my parents went on a pilgrimage to Mount Kailash, to Nepal, to Lhasa, and to South Tibet, but there was never any sign that a son might be born. They had given up all hope when they reached Nalanda Monastery, an important Sakya monastery north of Lhasa, and told the abbots of their quest. The leaders were shocked and very worried, as our family lineage, the Dolma Palace line, held the tradition of the most esoteric Sakya teachings; moreover, most of the heads of the monastery had received these teachings from my grandfather, so to them, the continuation of our family was most important. They urged my parents not to give up hope and they allowed one of their best teachers, Lama Ngawang Lodro Rinchen, to leave and travel with my parents. This was something of a loss to the monastery, but he was a very powerful lama, who could perform all the different rituals, and in particular, his prayers had caused children to be born to women who had been unable to have children before. After this, he always traveled with my father, and together they performed many rituals and prayed for a son to be born. At last, it became clear that their prayers had been answered, and my parents halted at Tsedong, a small, pleasant town near Shigatse. It had been decided that it was a good place for a child to be born, partly perhaps for its reputation as the birthplace of many great Sakya teachers, such as Ngachang Chenpo Ngawang Kunga Rinchen. In fact, I was born in the same room as Ngachang Chenpo.

A further problem arose: a succession of astrologically inauspicious days. As my parents wanted me to be born on an auspicious day, many more prayers were said. And I was not born on a bad day: I was born on the first day of the eighth Tibetan month (September 7, 1945), which was considered quite good. It is said that rainbows were seen over our house and that an image of Guru Rinpoche was then offered to my father, which were good signs, but of course, I didn't know anything of this.

Q. *What happens when a child is born into Your Holiness's family?*

HHST: The very first thing, as soon as the child is born, is that the letter DHIH, the letter of Manjushri, who represents speech and wisdom, is written on the child's tongue with a special nectar made of saffron and many other things.

Q. *When did you first go to Sakya?*

HHST: That was later. I am told that my first birthday was celebrated in Tsedong, and that after this, our family went on a short pilgrimage to the famous shrine of Guru Rinpoche in the south of Tibet. After that, we returned to Sakya, where my second birthday was celebrated rather elaborately.

Q. *Your parents died when you were quite young, I think?*

HHST: Yes. I cannot remember my mother at all. She died when I was two or three, but I remember her sister, my aunt. She was like a mother to me. My father died in 1950 when I was five. That I remember very well.

Q. *How old were you when your studies started?*

HHST: This was when I was five. In that same year, Lama Ngawang Lodro Rinchen gave me my first lesson in the alphabet. We went to the special Manjushri shrine in Sakya, where he gave me the Consecrations of Manjushri and Achala, and then a very ancient copy of the Tibetan alphabet written in gold was produced. This was especially for the use of the sons of our family. Then Lama Ngawang read the letters in front of the Manjushri image, and I repeated them after him. This, of course, was the ceremony. After that, I had another teacher for reading.

Q. *Did your spiritual studies begin then too?*

HHST: Yes. I had to memorize and recite prayers to Manjushri. I remember all this very clearly. After the ceremony, I was taught spelling seven hours a days, six days a week, for nearly two years. We Tibetans say that the more you practice spelling, the faster you will be able to read.

Q. *Were you receiving religious teaching at this time too?*

HHST: I had received consecrations frequently. In fact, I am told that I received the blessings of Amitayus for long life from my father almost as soon as I was born. When I was four, I received the Consecration of Vajra Kila (Dorje Phurba) from my father. I remember that very clearly also. I was sitting in the lap of a very dear personal attendant, and I remember when my father gave the wrathful part of the consecration, he was wearing the hat and costume of a black hat dancer and performed the ritual dances. I even remember who played the musical instruments then!

Q. *Where did this all take place?*

HHST: In the Dolma Palace. It is a big palace with three main shrine rooms and many other rooms. Altogether it has about eighty rooms, and all the teachings were given in one of these shrine rooms.

Q. *Did you ever go out of the palace?*

HHST: Oh yes, but not often into town. There was a very extensive open area of fields around the palace, and the river ran quite near. I used to go out there with an attendant to play with other children when I was not studying.

Q. *When did your religious studies begin in earnest?*

HHST: I began to study reading in the summer of 1950, and in the autumn, I went to Ngor Monastery, where I received the Esoteric Path-Result (Lamdre) teaching. My guru for this was Lama Ngawang Lodro Shenphen Nyingpo, abbot of the Khangsar Abbey of Ngor.

Q. *How do you remember him?*

HHST: He was a very holy, very spiritually advanced lama, always very calm, very slow in movement, and he did everything very perfectly. He was then very old. He gave the teaching in his own room to a very few people, maybe thirty in all. At that time, I was very small and could barely read. I remember I sat in the lap of Khangsar Shabdrung, the successor to the abbot, who held out the pages in front of me so I could read the introductory prayers each day. While the abbot was teaching the Mahayana part, I could understand it quite well, but I could not understand the tantric section very well. I spent much time with the abbot, and in the meantime, I continued to practice spelling and reading by going through some biographies. I stayed about four months in Ngor for the teaching and then returned to Sakya.

The following year, I visited Lhasa for the first time and met His Holiness the Dalai Lama, who confirmed me as "the Sakya Trizin designate." I spent four months in Lhasa visiting many of the monasteries there and in central Tibet. We visited Nalanda and Samye also, then returned through south Tibet, where I visited many holy places and monasteries on pilgrimage.

During these visits, I was hard at work memorizing the *Hevajra-tantra*, which is the basic text for Sakya religious practice. Then, early in 1952, I was enthroned in a simple ceremony; I was too young for the full enthronement, which came later. I had to recite the full *Hevajra-tantra* in front of the monk officials and teachers of the Tantric Monastery in Sakya; this was considered a test of ability that all monks had to take. I was then only six, but I am glad to say that I passed by reciting it correctly.

After that, I attended the monthly recitation of that tantra by all the monks of the Tantric Monastery: it was the first ceremony I attended there. Later, I left Sakya to attend the enthronement of the Panchen Lama in Shigatse, which lasted for several weeks. This time, I traveled with the full dignity and entourage of a Sakya Trizin.

I returned to Ngor that summer to receive the Esoteric Path-Result teachings from Khangsar Khenpo, during which he stopped frequently to give other teachings, such as Vajra Yogini, the Zenpa Zidel, and many other important instructions. In all, the teaching lasted for a year, until I had to return to Sakya, at the request of the Chinese, for some talks. Early in 1953, I again returned to Ngor to resume studies there, but unfortunately, Khangsar Khenpo passed away just before he had finished the whole teaching, and it was concluded by his successor. I returned to Sakya before September, as that year I witnessed the yearly ceremony and ritual dance of Vajra Kila. It is always held in the seventh Tibetan month. Then I began the meditative retreat of Hevajra at the Dolma Palace.

Q. *Was this your first retreat?*

HHST: Not quite. During the time I received the first Lamdre teaching, I had performed the retreat of Amitayus, and then I gave the consecration to my guru, Khangsar Khenpo. Also, in the interval between the two Lamdre teachings, I performed the retreat of Bhutadamara, a special form of Vajrapani, for one month. But this was the first major retreat I performed. During the retreat, we had many difficulties. I had a very strict teacher, and I was allowed to see only my aunt, my two servants, and my teacher. Though I myself remained quite well throughout, my teacher got very ill following the first half of the retreat—very, very ill, and we had a difficult time because of his sickness. Nevertheless, the retreat ended successfully. I say "we" because my sister was performing the same retreat at the same time, but in a different room some distance away. Of course, we were not allowed to meet, but we communicated by writing notes.

After the retreat, my teacher remained ill for some months, and during this period, I had a long holiday! I became rather wild and took to wandering off and doing as I pleased. My aunt was a little worried and appointed a temporary teacher under whom I had to memorize the texts of the Vajra Kila, both for daily practice and for the long ritual.

Then that summer of 1954, Khangsar Khenpo's successor was invited to Sakya to give the Druthab Kuntu, a collection of tantric meditations and teachings collected and edited by the first Khyentse Rinpoche. This lasted for three or four months and was a very pleasant occasion. The entire teaching was held in the summerhouse in our park at Dolma Palace, and Khangsar Shabdrung taught in a very leisurely fashion. By this time, my teacher had recovered from his illness and taught me the ritual dances that go with the Kila practices. In September, I attended the month-long Kila ceremonies. I was not the master of ceremonies that year, but I took part in the dances and attended nearly every day of the ceremonies. Next, I received the Mahakala teachings from Lama Ngawang Lodro Rinchen and went straight into retreat to meditate on that Dharma Protector for one month. I received more Mahakala teachings from Lama Ngawang, and the Thangtong Nying-Gyud from Drupchen Rinpoche, a very great Nyingma yogi and an incarnation of the Tibetan saint, Thangtong Gyalpo. I then entered the retreat of Vajra Kila for three months. During this time, my sister, who was then sixteen, was giving the three-month teaching of Lamdre. She had never done the Kila retreat, so I was asked to give her the consecration when I finished my retreat. This was the first major consecration I gave. About sixty monks were to receive the Lamdre, but many other people arrived for the Kila Consecration—about one thousand, I think. That was all in my ninth year.

Q. *How do you remember Lama Ngawang Lodro Rinchen?*

HHST: He was the lama who caused me to have human birth. He was a very wonderful lama, very strict in his observance of Vinaya rules of discipline, and would never eat after lunch nor wear skins nor shirts with sleeves. His arms were always bare, no matter how cold it was, and no matter how cold it was in Sakya—and Sakya is really a very cold place—his room was always as warm as if centrally heated. In his house, we could keep flowers, we could keep water. Elsewhere, we could never keep water during the winter: if we put water in a bottle, it would freeze within a few minutes and crack the bottle!

Q. *Your Holiness had a strenuous childhood. What relaxations did you enjoy?*

HHST: I used to enjoy going out into the fields around the palace. The river ran quite near the palace, and I used to love going there. I remember when I attended the Kila ceremony, I would be escorted home by attendants from the town of Sakya itself. They left immediately, and as soon as they were out of sight, I would tear off all my ceremonial clothes and go down to the river in the simplest attire. I used to like to bathe, but even in September, the water was very, very cold—dreadfully cold. Then sometimes I would like to go out to the summerhouse in the park. We had an old gramophone, the kind that you wind up, and a pile of old records—mostly British military marches, but also some Tibetan folk songs—that we enjoyed listening to.

Q. *Did Your Holiness visit Lhasa again?*

HHST: Yes, in the summer of 1955, I received many esoteric teachings from Lama Ngawang Lodro Rinchen, and that autumn I went again to Lhasa. That winter, I received some short teachings from His Holiness the Dalai Lama. But Lhasa had changed. When I first visited it in 1951, I saw a beautiful, early traditional Tibetan capital. Even then the Chinese were arriving; a few Chinese were to be seen in the streets. But on my second visit in 1955, I drove into Lhasa from Shigatse by jeep—by Chinese jeep! And Lhasa itself was full of jeeps and lorries; there were Chinese people and goods everywhere.

I stayed about six months in Lhasa, giving some small teachings and performing a sacred dance as a prayer there. At this time, I first met Venerable Jamyang Khyentse Rinpoche and stayed quite near him, visiting him frequently. I received many Sakya teachings from him, but most of them were actually Nyingmapa. Early in the following year, I made another visit to south Tibet and then returned to Lhasa, where I had to sit on the Chinese Preparatory Committee, along with His Holiness the Dalai Lama, His Holiness Gyalwa Karmapa, and other prominent Tibetans. By then the Chinese intentions were becoming quite clear, but we felt that it was best to try to control the situation as best we could, without violence. In any case, our country was not a powerful one in any military sense.

I returned to Sakya in the summer, and later in the year, Khyentse Rinpoche came to Sakya. That winter, His Holiness the Dalai Lama went to India on a pilgrimage for the Buddha Jayanti celebrations, and I met him in Shigatse, on his way to India. A little later, I also went to India on a pilgrimage, visiting the four most holy shrines of Buddhist pilgrimage there: Bodh Gaya, Lumbini, Sarnath, and Kushinagara. I stayed in India about two months and then returned to Sakya. In the following year, 1957, I again performed the meditative retreat of Vajra Kila and again received the Lamdre teaching, this time from the abbot of the Tantric Monastery in Sakya, the Venerable Jampal Sangpo.

Q. *When did Your Holiness's full enthronement occur?*

HHST: That was after the New Year, early in 1959. It was an event requiring much preparation. At the end of 1958, the great sacred dance of the Protectors of Religion was held, at which I presided. Then, at the New Year, the enthronement was held.

Q. *How is this performed?*

HHST: In the Tantric Monastery, there is a big courtyard in front of a temple with golden roofs. The spiritual throne of Sakya Pandita is kept in this temple, and on that is placed the temporal throne of Chogyal Phagpa. I had to sit on top of these and teach a text called *The Sage's Intent,* written by Sakya Pandita. The teaching, which included a little explanation, lasted for three days. After this, offerings were made by representatives from His Holiness the Dalai Lama, the Panchen Lama, Sakya, many other Tibetans, and on this occasion, the Chinese. After this, a great procession is held.

Q. *This must have happened shortly before Your Holiness came to India.*

HHST: Yes, we left for India almost immediately afterward.

Q. *How did you get out of Tibet?*

HHST: It was very complicated. At that time, the tension in Tibet was very high and people talked of nothing but the Khampas and the Chinese, the Chinese and the Khampas. We made many predictions, and they all said the same thing: that Tibet would be lost and many dreadful things would happen. But we still waited, until one day, news came from an Indian broadcast that there had been a battle in Lhasa and His Holiness the Dalai Lama had escaped to the southeast of Lhasa. Then we hurried. I was unable to leave directly from Sakya because there were many Chinese spies. So I let it be known that I was going into retreat at the hermitage not far from Sakya. I arrived there safely and sent word to my aunt and sister to join me. From there, we left by night.

Q. *How long did it take?*

HHST: It is not far from Sakya to the Sikkimese border. We got there safely in five days. Our party was of only eight or nine people, and because of the circumstances, I was unable to bring any of the many precious and holy things we had in Sakya.

In Sikkim, I spent a month in Lachen, where I began to learn English, and soon after I could pick out simple words. Then a message came from Khyentse Rinpoche that he was very ill in Gangtok, so I went there. The message, in fact, was brought by a Tibetan doctor who is now my father-in-law, although then I didn't know him! Khyentse Rinpoche was very unwell, and I said many prayers for him, but he became weaker and passed away in July 1959.

After this, I went down to Darjeeling and that winter made a pilgrimage through India and Nepal, returning to Kalimpong and Darjeeling in early 1960. I spent that year and the next two studying philosophy under a very learned Sakya abbot called Khenpo Rinchen. You see, although I had received many teachings and performed many retreats in Tibet, I had never had time to study Mahayana philosophy very much, so in these three years, I learned Madhyamaka philosophy, logic, Prajnaparamita, Abhidharma, and other studies. Then at the end of 1962, there was a border war between India and China, so we left Darjeeling and went to Mussoorie.

The following year I spent recovering from tuberculosis, but at the end of 1963, I was able to attend the religious conference in Dharamsala, and in March 1964, we founded the Sakya Centre, located at the foot of Mussoorie, to function temporarily as our main monastery. I went back to Mussoorie to take up studies with the Venerable Khenpo Appey, a great Sakya teacher. Primarily, I studied the tantras under him and received the many profound explanations he had received from his own teacher, the first Deshung Ajam Rinpoche, the great Tibetan mystic. Later, I also studied some Madhyamaka philosophy, poetry, grammar, and arithmetic under him. In 1965, I attended the second religious conference in Bodh Gaya. In 1966, I went on a pilgrimage to Sanchi and the caves at Ajanta and Ellora, but otherwise, my studies continued uninterrupted until 1967 when Khenpo Appey went to Sikkim. In the winter of 1967, I gave the Lamdre for the first time at Sarnath; I was twenty-two. About four hundred monks and perhaps one hundred lay Buddhists attended. Early in the following year, we started our Sakya Rehabilitation Settlement at Puruwala for nine hundred refugees from Sakya. The place was chosen for its physical similarity to Sakya, although of course, it was much hotter.

Perhaps I should mention a succession of Western friends who had stayed with me during these years, helping with our rehabilitation work, and from whom I learned to speak English.

In 1970, a tragic motor accident deprived us of the Venerable Thutop Tulku, a young and very capable monk who had organized the center and the settlement practically single-handed. Since I now knew English fairly well, I took over the work of administration. That autumn, I moved to the Sakya Centre and have lived in Rajpur ever since. The next two years—1971 and 1972—were good, as the Venerable Chogye Trichen Rinpoche stayed with us in Rajpur, giving a major collection of consecrations and the Gyude Kuntu of Jamyang Khyentse Wangpo. In the spring of 1974, I married and soon after left on my first visit to the West and Japan. For four months, I visited Switzerland, England, Canada, the United States, and Japan, giving religious teachings and meeting Tibetan immigrants and Western Buddhists. On November 19, 1974, my son, Tungse Rinpoche, was born. The following spring, we went on a pilgrimage to Chogye Rinpoche's newly completed monastery in Lumbini, Nepal, after which I spent a month teaching at our Sakya monastery in Bodhnath, Kathmandu. That summer, my aunt, who had brought me up and upon whom all the decisions and work had rested during my childhood, passed away, to our great sorrow. In 1976, I taught in Darjeeling. I taught the Druthab Kuntu in Ladakh, Kashmir, and undertook a teaching tour of the settlements in southern India.

Q. *And next?*

HHST: I very much look forward to teaching in the West again.

Q. *Your Holiness, whom do you regard as your main gurus?*

HHST: My main guru was Khangsar Khenpo, from whom I received the Lamdre. Then my father, Khyentse Rinpoche, Khangsar Shabdrung Rinpoche, Lama Ngawang Lodro Rinchen, and Sakya Khenpo Jampal Sangpo. Then to a lesser degree, Phende Khenpo, Drupchen Rinpoche, and many others.

If You Want to Know the Future, Look for It in Your Present Actions

Q. *Your Holiness, why should we practice Buddhist teaching?*

HHST: I would like to answer this by describing the three types of persons who practice Buddhism. Generally speaking, from the smallest insect on up to the most intelligent human being, there is agreement: all want happiness and all wish to avoid suffering. The majority of human beings do not understand what the cause of suffering is or what the cause of happiness is, but in the teachings of Buddhism and in their practice, you will find the answers to these questions.

Q. *What are the causes of suffering and happiness?*

HHST: The *Ratnavali* of Nagarjuna says, "Every action arising from desire, aversion, and ignorance produces suffering; every action arising from the absence of desire, aversion and ignorance produces happiness."

Now, as I said, there are three kinds of people. Like all other beings, the lowest person wants happiness and not suffering or rebirth in the lower realms of existence, so he practices Buddhism to create the causes of rebirth in the human realm or in the heavenly realms of the gods. He does not have the power or the courage to leave worldly existence completely. He only wants the best parts of worldly existence; he wants to avoid the worst parts, and that is why he practices the Buddhist religion—to gain a higher rebirth.

The middling sort of person understands that the whole of worldly existence, no matter where one is born, is suffering by its nature, just as fire is hot by its nature. He wants to get out of it altogether and attain nirvana, the state that is entirely away from suffering.

The highest person realizes that just as he himself does not want to suffer and does want happiness, so also do all living beings have the same fears and wishes. He knows that since we have been born again and again from beginningless time in worldly existence, there is not a single sentient being who has not been our mother and father at one time or another. Since we are that close to all sentient beings, the best person is one who practices Buddhism in order to remove all these countless beings from suffering.

q. *How should we practice?*

hhst: At the beginning of all Buddhist practice come two very important things: meditation of the four recollections and taking refuge. The four recollections are of the difficulty of attaining human birth; of the impermanence of all samsaric things; of the sufferings of worldly existence; and of the law of karma, or cause and effect.

Generally speaking, it is very difficult to be born as a human being. We think that there are many human beings, but if we compare our numbers to those of other beings, we realize how few we are. For instance, in each of our bodies, there are millions of germs, microbes, viruses, and so on. So statistically, the chances of attaining a human life are very poor. In any case, there are many places of rebirth that are of no use to a being, as he will be unable to meet with the Buddha's teachings in them. There are eight unfavorable places of birth, including the realms of hell, hungry ghosts, animals, and barbarians; places where religious teaching is incorrect; places where there is no Buddha; and certain god realms. Yet even if we attain human rebirth, there are ten necessary preconditions, such as it is necessary to be born in a place to which the Buddha has come, where the Buddha actually taught the religion, where the teaching is still alive, where the teachers are kind enough to teach, and where there are still Buddhist followers such as monks and lay followers. There also are five external circumstances required of oneself: one must not have committed any of the five limitless downfalls, as this would create a great obstruction.

This difficulty is explained in other ways also. The cause of human birth is the performance of virtuous acts and keeping correct moral conduct, and since very few people are aware of this, human birth is rare by its cause. By nature, it is much easier to be born elsewhere. The difficulty is illustrated by an example: imagine a blind tortoise living in the ocean. Floating on the surface of the ocean is a yoke. The tortoise comes to the surface only once a century, yet he stands a better chance of putting his neck in that yoke than we do of being born in human form.

The second recollection is of impermanence. The Buddha said, "The three realms of existence are like a cloud in autumn. The birth and death of beings is like a dancer's movement. A being's life is like a waterfall, like a flash of lightning in the sky; it never stops even for a single moment, and once it starts, it goes inevitably to its conclusion." Everything is changing—outside the seasons change; spring gives way to summer, to autumn and winter. Children grow into adults, adults become old; hair turns from black to white, the skin shrivels and life fades. Isn't that so? Everything changes constantly. There is not one single place where we can escape impermanence. Since everything changes constantly, we never know when the end will come. We may be in perfect health today and yet die tomorrow. We know only two things about death: it is certain to come, and we have no idea when it will. It could come at any moment, and many internal and external things can cause it. Thus, if we want to practice Buddhism, we must realize that it is necessary to start immediately. We can never be sure of a tomorrow in which to do anything.

Q. *How does this help us? The practice of Buddhism will not make us less impermanent.*

HHST: It will not make us less impermanent, but it will give us the certainty that, in our coming lives, we will have less suffering. The practice of Dharma, of religion, means avoiding nonvirtuous acts and performing virtuous acts. When we behave in this way, it is obvious that we will be happier in the future.

Q. *Does it mean that since we expect less from this life, we will also suffer less?*

HHST: Yes, that too. But more important, by thinking about impermanence, we will be moved to practice Dharma quickly. The thought of impermanence helps us to speed up our path a great deal.

Q. *What are the six realms and their sufferings?*

HHST: As I said before, no matter where we are in worldly existence, we are suffering. Suffering is of three kinds: the suffering of suffering, the suffering of change, and the suffering of conditioned existence. The suffering of suffering is when we have a headache or something like that. It is simply suffering that everyone accepts and thinks of as suffering. The suffering of change is the suffering undergone through perception of change. We are with friends today, but we have to depart; when we go, we meet enemies. Nothing stays, and seeing this, we experience the suffering of change. The suffering of conditioned existence refers to the inadequacy of worldly activity. We do many things in the world but are never really satisfied. There are always more things to be done, which we cannot do, and this is the frustration that is suffering.

The lowest of the six realms are the hell realms of excessive heat and cold and the "neighboring hells," which are also states of great suffering and last for incredible periods of time. The cause of these states of suffering is hatred. Then there is the realm of hungry spirits who are tantalized by food and drink they cannot swallow. This is the result of desire and stinginess. The animal realm is well known to us, and birth there is caused by ignorance. We know the human realm too. The fifth realm is of the demigods, who are constantly engaged in war with the gods out of jealousy and who will thus naturally suffer in their next lives. The gods seem very comfortable. They enjoy great pleasures and immensely long lives, but sooner or later, they experience old age and death. As they have done nothing but enjoy themselves, they will not have created the merit to achieve high rebirth and will fall into states of great suffering. The three lower worlds' beings experience the suffering of suffering exclusively; humans experience all three but chiefly the first two; while the gods suffer mainly the last two.

The last of the four recollections is of karma, the law of cause and effect. In the Buddhist view, everything we have and do today has a cause in the past. In fact, it is said that if we want to know what we did in the past, we should look at our present situation; whether we are rich or poor, ugly or beautiful, this is the result of past actions, as the future, happy or otherwise, depends on what we do today. If a tree's root is medicinal, the flowers, the leaves, the bark, and everything that grows on the tree will be medicinal; like this, an act that grows out of the opposite of desire, aversion and ignorance will produce happiness. If the root of the tree is poisonous, then everything that grows on the tree will be poisonous, just as acts of desire, aversion, and ignorance produce suffering.

Q. *Is there a practice based on the law of cause and effect?*

HHST: The law of cause and effect, karma, is one of the main teachings of Buddhism. It means that we should always practice virtuous things, since nonvirtuous acts will always bring suffering in this life as well as in the next. If we don't want suffering, we should avoid its cause; if there is no cause, there will be no result, just as if the root of the tree is removed, there will be no fruit. If we want happiness, we must be very careful about the cause of happiness, just as if we want the tree to grow, we must take care of its root. If the root is defective, the tree will not grow.

So before we begin any meditation, we should contemplate these four recollections very carefully and then take refuge. Taking refuge marks the difference between Buddhists and non-Buddhists; it means that we have surrendered, taken asylum.

Q. *In what way do we surrender?*

HHST: We surrender ourselves. As I said, worldly existence is full of sufferings. There are many obvious sufferings and also many that are less obvious and that common people do not notice. We wish to be free from these sufferings, but we don't have full knowledge or full power to do this, so there is nothing much that we can do about it for the present. Now, when we undertake an important act, we seek help from a powerful person: if we are sick, we consult a doctor, and if we have trouble with the law, we go to a lawyer. So when we want to be saved from the sufferings of worldly existence, we have to take refuge in the Triple Gem, which is the real helper in this undertaking. The Triple Gem consists of the Buddha, who is the guide; the Dharma (or religion), which is our Path; and the Sangha, which comprises our spiritual companions. However, the final refuge is only the Buddha. The Dharma has two parts: the teaching and the realization. The teaching is the Tripitaka (Sutra, Abhidharma, and Vinaya discourses), but this is like a boat you use to cross a river: when you get to the other side, you simply leave it behind. The realization also has two parts: the truth of cessation and the truth of the Path. The first of these is void (*shunyata*), so it cannot be a final refuge, while the Path, being itself impermanent, also cannot be the final refuge. As for the Sangha, even its very highest members are still on the Path, so they cannot be a final refuge. The refuge is only in the Buddha, but we always take refuge in the Buddha, Dharma, and Sangha.

Q. *Does this mean that the Buddha is permanent?*

HHST: Yes, yes. The Buddha is, of course, permanent. The *dharmakaya* ("body of reality") is beyond permanence and impermanence, and the *sambhogakaya* ("bliss body") always exists. The *nirmanakaya* ("apparent body") is the form the Buddha takes on earth, which has the appearance of impermanence, although it is always present somewhere, if not here.

Q. *What is the actual practice of taking refuge?*

HHST: Taking refuge is performed differently according to the intentions of the three types of persons who perform it, although the three causes—fear, faith, and compassion—are the same. The actual practice is the recitation of the prayer of refuge. The simplest prayer says, "I take refuge in the Buddha. I take refuge in the Dharma. I take refuge in the Sangha." A more elaborate prayer says, "I take refuge in the Buddha,

Dharma, and Sangha until I obtain enlightenment; by the merit of doing this, may all beings attain Buddha's stage."

But mere recitation of the prayer with the voice is not sufficient; it must be recited from the heart. If we want to take refuge from the rain, it won't help to say "house, house" or "umbrella, umbrella." We have to find a house or go and get an umbrella; if we do this, we will undoubtedly be saved from the rain. So it is necessary to take refuge very seriously, with full belief, and moreover, we must think that, no matter what happens, we will seek the refuge only of the Triple Gem and that we will always remain under it. Reciting the prayer in this way and with this intention is the first practice of Buddhism and one of the foundations of all practice. Taking refuge like this distinguishes the Buddhist from the non-Buddhist.

Although recitation like this is sufficient to make someone a Buddhist, it is common for a short ceremony to be performed in front of a spiritual guide. The guide will say the words of the prayer, which the disciple will repeat after him and also promise to uphold the basic moral teachings of Buddhism. From that time onward, the disciple should continue to recite the prayer daily and with great devotion.

Q. *Is animal rebirth really possible for a human?*

HHST: Yes, definitely. There are many stories of animals being reborn as humans as a result of good actions and of humans being reborn as animals as a result of bad actions. Some animals are extremely kind, especially to their offspring, and by working very hard, they can create enough causes to achieve human birth.

Q. *Why is human birth so important?*

HHST: Human birth is extremely precious because, through human life, we can not only achieve higher rebirth and nirvana, but also practice Dharma and attain enlightenment.

Q. *Does it really help us to think a great deal about impermanence? We always know we are impermanent, and thinking about it too much might make us miserable.*

HHST: Yes, it does help. Tsongkhapa said, "A prisoner has only one thought: 'When can I get out of this prison?' This thought arises constantly in his mind. Your thought on impermanence should be like this; meditate on impermanence until this state of mind arises."

Q. *Are we really in the position of prisoners? We often do find things pleasant in worldly existence.*

HHST: But that pleasure isn't permanent, is it? That very pleasure can lead to disaster, can't it? So we are happy now, but we never know what might happen in the next hour. There may be a complete disaster. Since pleasure is impermanent, since it is very uncertain, we are not actually happy, because our pleasure is colored with anxiety. In fact, we are never happy, because we don't know what will come, so anxiety is inevitable.

Q. *Are the hells metaphors for states or amounts of suffering, or do they really exist as described in the Buddhist sutras?*

HHST: Something really exists, I think. Actually, it says in the sutras that the hells are really much more terrible than they are described, because the Buddha didn't fully explain them. If he had, people would have fainted.

Q. *How real are they?*

HHST: They are as real as the life we have today. Yes, many people think they are not real, like a dream. But actually, we are happy and unhappy in dreams, just as we are when we are awake. This present experience also is not real, but we think everything around us is real. Hell is as real as this. Of course, hell is not real in reality either. This is also not real. What is this then?

Q. *Do the Buddhas suffer?*

HHST: No, they never suffer. They are absolutely free from sufferings.

Q. *Do they see suffering?*

HHST: They don't see suffering either.

Q. *Then how can they help people who are suffering?*

HHST: They don't suffer. This answer is one of the differences between the Sakya and Gelugpa orders: the Gelugpas say that the Buddhas do see suffering, and we say that they do not. The man who has awakened from sleep doesn't have dreams. This impure samsaric scene of suffering is like a dream, it's like an illusion. So the man who has awakened from this illusion can never dream again. But due to his bodhichitta (enlightenment mind) and his compassion, help for others spontaneously arises. But the Buddha himself never sees suffering. For him, all things are transformed into pure appearance.

Q. *Is the Buddha involved in karma?*

HHST: He has achieved the final karmic result, the highest and best possible results of karma.

Q. *Can anything happen to us that is not the result of our own actions?*

HHST: No, never.

Q. *Can the Buddha perceive the results of his or others' acts?*

HHST: Yes. For instance, there have been many prophecies, but I don't think the Buddha sees or perceives the results. Where there is a need for a prophecy, it just arises spontaneously.

Q. *Can we modify the results of past acts?*

HHST: Certainly. The Vajrasattva meditation can purify many of our past bad actions, but in any case, the creation of good causes and merit is very helpful and necessary.

The Bodhisattva Is Born Out of Love and Compassion.

Q. *In the Small Way of mere personal salvation (Hinayana), nirvana (liberation) is one of the four noble truths, but it seems less important in the Great Way (Mahayana).*

HHST: Yes. There are two extremes: worldly existence and liberation. The first is completely involved in suffering, and the other has gone completely beyond it. The Great Way teaches that we should enter neither. Instead, we should follow the Middle Way, which means that through the power of wisdom, we do not remain in worldly existence, and through the power of compassion, we do not remain in liberation. If we are in liberation, we cannot be active, we cannot help other beings. We will be completely free from suffering, but there is nothing we can do for others. By attaining enlightenment, which we call the Great Liberation, we are not only free from suffering, but we can also help all sentient beings immensely. That is the main difference.

Q. *What are the principle practices of Mahayana?*

HHST: There are three main practices: love, compassion, and enlightenment mind. Love means that you wish every sentient being in all six realms of existence to be happy, and compassion is the wish that all beings in suffering should part from suffering. The enlightenment mind means, generally speaking, the wish to attain enlightenment for the sake of all sentient beings. These three are very important. Without love and compassion, the enlightenment mind will not arise, and without the enlightenment mind, you cannot attain enlightenment; therefore, love and compassion are necessary. But of these, compassion is of particular importance. It is the seed of the Great Way in the beginning; the water that makes the crops grow in the middle; and finally, the ripening of the fruit. Since compassion is in the beginning, the middle, and the end, it is clearly very important. Thus, when Chandrakirti wrote the *Madhyamakavatara*, he preceded it with homage to compassion. "The Buddha," he said, "arises from the Bodhisattva, and the Bodhisattva is born out of love and compassion, but especially out of compassion." The main cause of the Great Way is compassion.

Q. *How should we practice these?*

HHST: First, study is required and then meditation. Visualize those who are dear to you and wish them to be happy and free from suffering; then pray that you may have the power to accomplish this for them, that you will be able to do this. Then meditate on those who are not near to you and finally on all sentient beings. In fact, you should start by thinking of the four recollections, then taking refuge, then visualizing your mother and thinking very clearly on the most elaborate details of her kindness to you and the care she had for you. Then realize that she is still suffering and creating the causes for the suffering. At this, the wish to help her will arise, and when you want to help her out of suffering, the enlightenment mind will arise. Finally, pray to the guru and Triple Gem that she may be happy and without suffering. Then think of your father, of other beings, and of your worst enemy. If this is difficult, remember that hatred is your real enemy, as it will create states of great suffering. Then meditate upon all beings in the six realms until natural love for them arises without a single reservation. Finally, wish that any merit accumulated through this may benefit all sentient beings equally; this sharing of merit concludes every meditation.

Compassion is of the greatest importance and should be practiced as much as possible. It should be completely instinctive. Avalokiteshvara, the Lord of Compassion, said in a sutra, "One who wishes to gain enlightenment should not practice many things, but just one, and that one is compassion." The practice of compassion is of three kinds. Compassion to beings is the wish that first your mother and then all other limitless sentient beings should be free from suffering and that you may be able to help them. Compassion to dharmas (conditioned phenomena) is the wish that sentient beings should abandon the root of suffering, for the root of suffering is ignorance. The third practice is called objectless compassion. You must realize that all sentient beings are not really there, but nevertheless, through ignorance of what is real, they are tied to the ego, and this causes them suffering.

Q. *Sentient beings are not really there?*

HHST: No, actually sentient beings are not really there, but through attachment to ego, there arises illusory appearances. Since you desire certain of these appearances, you may also have many aversions to others, and so long as you ignorantly believe them to really exist, you remain caught in the closed circle that is worldly existence.

The third practice is of enlightenment mind, which is a very important practice. Generally speaking, there are two enlightenment minds: the relative one and the absolute one. The relative enlightenment mind also has two parts, called "wishing" and "entering." The wishing enlightenment mind is the aspiration, the wish to gain enlightenment for all those sentient beings, and this is like the wish to make a journey. The entering enlightenment mind is like making that journey. Everything you actually do to achieve the aim of getting enlightenment is the entering enlightenment mind; so in fact, this entering enlightenment mind includes all the Buddhist practices, such as the six paramitas of giving, moral conduct, patience, vigor, meditation, and wisdom. Then the absolute enlightenment mind is the understanding of the true nature of all things, which is emptiness. To realize this is absolute enlightenment mind.

Q. *How should we understand emptiness?*

HHST: Emptiness is actually only a name. It doesn't mean that all things are empty or void. Every religion tries to explain the true nature of phenomena, but all have come to the conclusion of something existing, either positively or negatively. Ordinary people do not think much about phenomena and their origins, but the more spiritual people do and wonder why things exist and where they come from. Christianity concluded that all things are created by God. An early Buddhist school, Sarvastivada, concluded that, although gross things do not really exist, atoms—so minute that they can have no sides facing different directions—do exist as basic elements. A more advanced Buddhist school, the Vijnanavada, decided that ultimately nothing exists externally and that the things we seem to perceive are only projections of mind. However, when the Madhyamika philosophers examined phenomena, everything seemed to disappear and they could find nothing. They were not satisfied by the explanation that God created everything or that tiny atoms existed, and they reasoned that it was impossible for subjective mind to exist if objects did not exist, as mind and objects are as interdependently inseparable as are right and left. So if there was no external matter, there could be no mind. The Madhyamika concluded, after a very scrupulous examination, that there was nothing, ultimately, that could be clung to as really existing. Positive things could not be found; negative things could not be found; nothing could be found that could be accepted as really existing, because the true nature of all things is beyond existence and nonexistence, beyond thought, and inexpressible. Shantideva said, "The Absolute is not an object of mind; it lies beyond mind. It is something you cannot describe; it is the wonder of the incomprehensible." However, when we talk about such things, we have to name them, so we call it "emptiness," but emptiness is not really something that can be named, it is inexpressible.

Of course, this is all "ultimately speaking." Relatively speaking, the Madhyamika accept whatever ordinary people accept, but the writings of this school do show an experience of the inexpressibility of all things.

Q. *Isn't this critique of phenomena merely a logical paradox? Can it have any bearing on daily life?*

HHST: Of course it does. When you realize the ultimate truth, you are free from suffering. We are in suffering because we haven't awakened from the relative illusion. We are wrapped up in this relative illusion, and due to this, we hold things as real; holding them as real, we act and hence suffer and create many more causes of suffering.

Q. *So the real point is attachment?*

HHST: When you are no longer attached to things as real, you create no further causes of suffering.

Q. *Is this a subject of meditation?*

HHST: There are many meditations on this in the Great Way, and especially the Tantric Way. You have to realize that sufferings come from bad karma, which comes from the defilements, and that the defilements arise from ego. If you are deluded, you may think a coil of rope is a snake; you do this in supposing that a self exists. When you have "self," there must be "other"; when there is other, there is a desire for self and an aversion to other, and this leads further into delusion and the obscuration of the true nature. The enlightenment mind is the best way to uproot the mistaken notion of a self. In what way are other beings different from you? Try first to see them as equal to yourself and to love them as much as you love yourself, until finally you can love other beings more than yourself. Try to wish constantly, however much you are suffering, that even so, all the sufferings of all sentient beings may come to you and that all your causes of happiness may be given to them. And you should always wish that the merit gained through this should be of benefit to all beings.

The practice for realizing emptiness, the absolute enlightenment mind, has two parts: the practice of concentration and the analysis of experience, which shows us clearly the Madhyamaka experience. These practices need some lengthier explanation, and I cannot deal with them adequately here. But before and after every practice, you must take refuge and share the merit.

Q. *If things and mind don't exist, what are appearances? Where do they begin and where do they end?*

HHST: They have no beginning. There is an end, though, when you achieve enlightenment. This is all illusion, unreal, like a dream. Where does the dream arise? Where does it go? It is like that. This is a long dream.

Q. *So what are appearances?*

HHST: They are a long dream.

Q. *Love and compassion are good, but doesn't there come a point when it is better to be angry with people? Is anger ever justified?*

HHST: Maybe, if the intention is white, even though the action is black. Even if you are angry, if it is with the thought of benefiting a being, your anger arises from compassion, and whatever arises out of compassion is good. If the root is medicinal, even if the fruit appears bad, it will be medicinal.

Q. *Buddhism is often thought of as leading to negative and passive behavior.*

HHST: This is true if you enter and abide in liberation. But if you enter the Great Way, instead of selfish desire for liberated quiescence, you have compassion, which is the active desire for the benefit of all beings.

Q. *Buddhism is sometimes said to be atheistic because it holds that there is no God.*

HHST: Buddhism does not believe in a God as the creator of the world, and in that sense, you might say it is atheistic. If, however, God is something else, a divine compassion or a divine wisdom, manifest in the form of a deity, you might say that Buddhism is not atheistic but polytheistic.

Q. *If there really is no self, then what is reborn?*

HHST: The continuum of mind, the serial mind stream of a person and the results of his deeds give rise to a new being. In any case, rebirth is a relative truth. The interpretation of relative truth differs from school to school, from religion to religion. The Madhyamika believe the relative to be whatever we see, without examination—the view of ordinary people. Relatively, there is rebirth, but not ultimately.

Q. *How did the Madhyamaka philosophy arise? Isn't it later than the Buddha's time?*

HHST: Of course, it is Buddhist: it is the actual meaning of the Prajna-paramita sutras, where it is clearly said that anyone who follows extremes will never be free from suffering. The extremes are of positive and negative, of belief in existence and nonexistence, and the like. The philosophy is developed from the sutras, which were taught by the Buddha.

Q. *If we don't accept the existence of beings, since all things are emptiness, what reason do we have for being compassionate?*

HHST: Everything is not just emptiness; emptiness is also a wrong view, an extreme—the true nature of things is away from extremes. In order to realize this, you have to accumulate a great deal of merit, and the best way to do this is to practice love and compassion for all sentient beings. Until this merit has been accumulated, the understanding of emptiness will not arise.

The Guru Has a Tremendous Responsibility.

Q. *What is Mantrayana, Your Holiness?*

HHST: Mantrayana, or tantra, is actually method. The first intentions and the final goal are exactly the same as they are in Mahayana, but since the Mantrayana is direct, more intelligent, and has more methods, it reaches the same destination from the same starting place much more quickly; the difference is as between traveling by train and by airplane. The Mahayana practices consist mainly of meditation through thinking about things, but in the Mantrayana, our bodies are also used extensively. By knowing and using our bodies, we can reach our destination much more quickly. Now, many things are required for an airplane to fly, such as fuel, wind, the design of the machine, and so on, and in the same way, when we try to attain realization in the Mantrayana, we practice not only in thought. We visualize different mandalas, repeat mantras, and so on. You can say that if these practices are followed correctly, realization will automatically arise.

Q. *Is this the only difference between Mahayana and Mantrayana?*

HHST: The Mahayana is called the "Cause Yana," or the Causal Path, and the Mantrayana is called the Result Path. In the Mahayana, you work only to create the right causes by practicing giving, moral conduct, and so on. These practices are very valuable and correct, but they are still very different from the immense qualities of the Buddha. But in Mantrayana, you imagine yourself right from the beginning in the form of the result—the Buddha, in one form or another. By this practice, the result—which is the same as the practice—will arise, and consequently Mantrayana is called the Result Path. Right from the beginning, you think of yourself as the Buddha with all the qualities, the thirty-two major signs, the eighty minor signs, and so on.

Q. *Is it not wrong to think of ourselves as the Buddha?*

HHST: Indeed not. It is said in Mahayana too, of course, that the nature of our mind, of our entire organism, is actually Buddha and always has been. However, we have not realized this and we are wrapped up in an illusion, so consequently we suffer. If the obscurations and defilements were intrinsically part of our mind, purification would not be possible. Coal will not become white, however much we wash it, but since the nature of mind is pure, it can be purified. Since other beings have attained enlightenment, it is clear that it is possible for us too, that our minds can also be purified.

The way Mantrayana deals with this problem is as follows: there are five races, or types, of persons. Actually there are hundreds and thousands of different types, but they can all be included in five categories. In fact, these five can all be included in one, which is Vajradhara, but, in general, it is convenient to think of five. These five we imagine in a mandala, which is a celestial mansion of certain proportions and decorations, surrounded by fire. The Buddha in the center is dark blue and is called Akshobhya ("the Unshakable One"). In the east is the white Buddha Vairocana ("the One Who Creates Appearances"); in the south is the yellow Ratnasambhava ("the One Who Has the Nature of the Gem"); in the west is the red Amitabha ("Limitless Light"); and in the north is the green Amoghasiddhi ("the One Who Is Skilled in Accomplishing all Possible Works"). They all look like Shakyamuni Buddha except they have different mudras, or hand gestures. Akshobhya touches the earth in the bhumisparsha mudra; Vairocana's hands are in the gesture of teaching; Ratnasambhava displays the gesture of giving and Amitabha, the gesture of meditation; Amoghasiddhi holds up his hand to show the crossed vajra, the mudra of fearlessness. Each of these five has specific qualities, but each is also related to the five most common defilements we are afflicted with: the blue Akshobhya to anger, red Amitabha to passion and desire, green Amoghasiddhi to envy, white Vairocana to ignorance, and yellow Ratnasambhava to pride and avarice. The colors are clearly related to the corresponding defilements. In English, we say "green with envy," while passion is associated with red and anger with dark blue. We can clearly see the characteristics of these five races in individuals: an individual who is dark in complexion, who may have a mark on his person resembling a vajra, and who is often angry is of the Akshobhya race. (The vajra is the sign of Akshobhya). Since there is a complete link of cause and effect, that person will succeed particularly easily if he practices the path related to Akshobhya. You see, the Buddha Akshobhya represents the complete transformation of anger. In Mantrayana, we never regard any defilement, such as anger or desire, as something to be repressed. Instead, the energies tied up in the defilement are purified and result in one of the five Buddhas, each of whom is characterized by a certain type of wisdom. This is another reason why the Mantrayana is the Result Path.

In fact, there is no impurity. The impurities appear because we have not realized the truth and we are still thinking in terms of subject and object. So we can say that impurities also come from delusion.

Q. *How do we practice this path?*

HHST: Although this path is obviously superior, it is not easy to understand correctly. For a start, we must be certain of our practice of pure resolve, the bodhichitta, and only then can we receive the teachings of the five Buddhas, in one of the many forms they take to suit our own individual nature. This teaching is given in the form of an empowerment which is called a *wang* in Tibetan. It means "consecration" or "initiation." This empowerment is a transmission, and it is necessary to receive it from a guru and then to study, think about it, and meditate on it in order to achieve the final result. After receiving the consecrations, one must carry out the daily practice without fail and learn to think very clearly and completely of oneself as identified with the final result. Then, because of the connection between cause and result, the result will naturally arise.

Q. *This transmission is important?*

HHST: Transmission from the guru is particularly important in Mantrayana. The guru transmits the teaching to you, and he is part of an unbroken succession of teachers that goes right back to the original Buddha, Vajradhara, from whom the teachings arose in the first place. Even in the Mahayana, you cannot practice without guidance, and this is particularly true of Mantrayana.

Q. *Does this mean that we will not get the result unless we receive the teaching in this way?*

HHST: Of course you will not. No one can get anything merely by studying a text. You must first receive the teaching in an oral tradition that goes right back to Vajradhara, and this direct, unbroken blessing of the teaching line must be received first; without this special blessing, no ripening will occur. Although most of the teachings have now been written down, you must first receive them orally; then you can study them.

Q. *So the guru is essential?*

HHST: It is said in the tantras that the guru is the source of all *siddhis,* or spiritual accomplishments. So it is important to find a guru, and generally, it is necessary to find the right guru, the one who has all the qualifications to teach tantra. In particular, it is necessary for you to find the lama with whom you have a particular connection by karma. For instance, when Milarepa first heard of Marpa, he felt a particularly urgent desire to meet him immediately. Or when Tsarchen heard of the great Sakya teacher, Doringpa, he felt a special urge to meet him as quickly as possible. When you find this guru, you must receive a transmission and explanation from him. In tantra, it is necessary to receive the wang, meaning the empowerment, transmission, or consecration. Wang is the door to tantra. Without wang, there is nothing you can do. Wang is like fertilizing the ground and planting the seed; it creates the right conditions. After receiving the wang, it is only a matter of looking after the seed to see that the crop grows.

Q. *How can you recognize the guru with whom you have a karmic link?*

HHST: In some cases, there is a clear sign. In Tsarchen's case, a woman appeared to him while he was meditating in a cave. At that time, he was a Gelugpa monk. She gave him a book and told him to find Doringpa. He found Doringpa in Sakya and discovered that the book he had been given had come from Doringpa's library. The woman had been a manifestation of Vajra Yogini, a female deity. Tsarchen practiced her meditation, in particular, after receiving it from Doringpa, and achieved great realization. Generally, however, if you feel a particular urge to meet or communicate with a certain lama, a feeling of something happening when you meet him, this is a good indication.

It can also be discovered by prediction. When I was very young, my aunt asked some monks to do a form of prediction involving a mirror. They saw a strange lama in the mirror and myself in front of him. The lama had long ears, and the space between his upper lip and nose was very wide. He had a scar. We didn't know who it could be but later discovered it was Khyentse Rinpoche.

Q. *Does this mean that we can only get good results with a lama with whom we have a karmic link?*

HHST: No, not necessarily. In my case, I was unable to receive a great deal of teaching from Khyentse Rinpoche. Any qualified guru is good, but there is a special one who can help you more than any other.

Q. *Is it right for a guru to make extraordinary demands on his disciples?*

HHST: Yes. For instance, when Marpa was teaching Lama Ngog, he asked him if he had brought all his wealth. Ngog replied that he had left behind only one lame old goat. Marpa sent him back to fetch it. Marpa said that although an old lame goat made no difference to him, he had demanded it only to uphold the dignity of the teaching. If you have to offer everything, you must hold back nothing. But the relationship of guru and disciple is not the relationship of a master and a servant. It is the relationship of a father and a son. It is a spiritual relationship, but it must be as warm and close as the relationship of a father and his son. The guru has a tremendous responsibility to care for his sons, who in their turn must follow all the teachings they are given and keep all their vows.

Q. *What are the vows involved?*

HHST: They are far from simple. After receiving the wang, there are many vows to keep, in addition to daily practice and study. If you have already received the pratimoksha vows of the Hinayana code, you must keep these, and then in addition to the Mahayana vows, you must keep the tantric vows, which are very important. Without keeping these, no practice will be effective. The vows are given to create the right conditions for caring for the seed planted during consecration. The vows must be kept properly, and daily practice must be performed with its visualizations and mantra recitations and meditation on the two stages of kyerim (process of creation) and dzogrim (process of completion).

Q. *What is a tantric deity?*

HHST: There are limitless living beings with different tastes, backgrounds, ideas, and dispositions, so in order to suit different types, the Transcendental Wisdom—or Buddha or whatever you prefer to call it—has taken different shapes. For instance, people who have much desire meditate on deities embracing, and people who have much hatred meditate on deities in a wrathful, angry form. People who have much ignorance meditate on very elaborate deities with many jewels and ornaments. But actually they are all the same Transcendental Wisdom appearing in different forms to suit different types of people.

Q. *What is the connection between tantric teaching and the historical Buddha?*

HHST: We call the historical Buddha the "common" Buddha and the tantric Buddhas are "uncommon," but many of the tantras were recited by the historical Buddha. The *Hevajra-tantra* is one of these.

Q. *What is Mahamudra?*

HHST: Mahamudra is the Transcendental Wisdom you realize after practicing kyerim and dzogrim. Kyerim is the process of creation: you visualize a mandala arising out of a letter, you visualize it peopled with deities. Dzogrim means the stage of completion. This is usually at the end of the practice. You imagine everything being absorbed back into the original letter and then that too disappears. Actually, kyerim purifies birth, and dzogrim purifies death.

Q. *What are the main Sakya practices?*

HHST: The main Sakya practice is Lamdre, or Result Path, which covers the Hinayana, Mahayana, and Mantrayana. It comes to us through Virupa, a great Indian saint who lived in 650 A.D., and it was brought to Tibet by the translator Drogmi, who died in 1072. It is based on the consecration and practices of the *Hevajra-tantra* and includes the philosophy of tantra as well as all the yogic practices such as inner-heat, breathing yoga, bodily positions, the yoga of dreams, phowa ("transference of consciousness"), bardo practices, and so on. The entire teaching takes three months to give. Then we practice on a very special, very esoteric teaching of Naropa, a Vajrayogini teaching with eleven yogas. Then we have many teachings of Mahakala; Vajra Kila, which comes from the original Nyingma tradition of my family; Sarvavidya, which is particularly helpful for the dying and the dead; Vajrabhairava, a wrathful form of Manjushri; the Thirteen Golden Teachings that belong only to the Sakya order; and many others. But the Lamdre contains everything.

Q. *In the Western concept of morality, sexual energies are usually regarded as a hindrance to the spiritual path. Does tantra mean the acceptance of these energies, and can they really help us along the Path?*

HHST: If they are rightly used; if used by the right persons, at the right time and correctly, they can be a very great help. The story is often told of King Indrabhuti, who told Shakyamuni Buddha that he would rather be reborn as a wolf in the jungle than undertake a spiritual path that demanded the renunciation of worldly things, so the Buddha gave him a special teaching—the Guhyasamaja teaching—of which we still have the transmission. Mere external renunciation is, of course, of little use; one can renounce something externally and still be very attached to it! True renunciation is the renunciation of attachment. In any case, King Indrabhuti was of the very highest type of person, and he and his entire court actually attained enlightenment while the Buddha was giving them the teaching.

However, most tantric practitioners are, of course, monks who are not allowed worldly pleasures and who must be celibate. King Indrabhuti attained enlightenment immediately, but we have only to read the story of Milarepa to see the difficulties that even gifted individuals undergo.

Q. *What dangers are there in incorrect practice?*

HHST: "If something goes wrong in tantra, there is only one direction: down to hell." Practicing tantra is like being a snake in a bamboo tube—it can only go up or down. It is necessary to find a good guru and practice the teaching very carefully.

Q. *Why does tantra involve so much secrecy?*

HHST: I think that, generally, it is to avoid creating disbelief in or even aversion to tantric teachings. If people hear things at the wrong time or without proper explanation, they may be shocked and think that tantra is a bad thing and lose faith in the Tantric Path. Also, if people see mandalas and perhaps read mantras in books, they may be tempted to try and practice by themselves, which is a very serious mistake. In tantra, one cannot do anything by oneself. Everything must be handed on by the guru.

Q. *Is tantra more than just ritual?*

HHST: Ritual is only a small part of tantra. The main practice is one's daily meditation, visualization and recitation; the practice of physical yogas, breathing yogas, and so on.

Q. *What is the result?*

HHST: Generally, the result is the three, four, or five bodies (kayas) of the Buddha. There are three kayas: two are rupakayas ("form bodies"), and one is a spiritual body. The latter is called the dharmakaya (the "body of reality"); it is the continuation of the mind that has been completely transformed and has become inseparable from shunyata. The sambhogakaya ("bliss body") is the body that dwells permanently in the Akanishtha buddhafield, giving teaching to the great Bodhisattvas.

The nirmanakaya ("illusory body") has different types, but the excellent nirmanakaya is one like the historical Buddha who appeared among us in India. These bodies result from the transformation of our present organism. Our present body becomes the rupakaya, and our present mind becomes the dharmakaya.

Buddha Sees That Ego Does Not Exist Anywhere.

Q. *It is said that the most important quality needed for successfully practicing Dharma is great faith. What kind of faith is needed? Why is faith so important?*

HHST: Of course faith is very important, but it is not the only important thing. It is the beginning. Without it, you cannot achieve good results. For instance, if the seed is burnt, you cannot grow a good crop. No matter how much you practice Dharma, you will not get any result without faith. But it is not a blind faith that is required. Generally, there are said to be three types of faith: first, "voluntary faith," which means that you perceive so many excellent qualities in the Triple Gem that you wish to accept it in order to benefit all sentient beings; second, "clear faith," which means that, seeing the great, good qualities of the Buddha, your mind becomes clear and certain; and third, "faith of confidence," which means that you accept the Buddhist teachings, such as the four noble truths and so on, as valid— you study these teachings and conclude that they are correct.

Q. *So faith is not just a matter of accepting certain dogma?*

HHST: No, no, certainly not.

Q. *The teaching of rebirth is unfamiliar to the West. Can one practice Dharma effectively if one does not accept rebirth?*

HHST: According to our definition of the practice of Dharma, no. We say that whatever you practice, however high or good it may be, it is not Dharma if it is just intended for this life. Dharma is what you practice for the next life, so the idea of rebirth cannot be separated from the idea of Dharma. The law of karma is an intrinsic part of Dharma, and future rebirth is the result of present causes.

Q. *Many people in the West might deny the universality of suffering.*

HHST: Buddhists, however, say that wherever you are in worldly existence, there is suffering. It is wrong to ignore the continual presence of suffering. You should not hide from it; you should know its causes and try to avoid creating them.

Q. *What is the* anatman, *or "egolessness," doctrine taught by the Buddha?*

HHST: The Buddha sees that ego does not exist anywhere. Mind is not ego, body is not ego; ego is just a name given to a grouping of things: form, perception, feeling, impulses, and consciousness all together. So in reality, when you examine in order to find what it is we call ego, there is nothing. *Ego* is just a name given to a collection of things.

Q. *Even though we have no immortal soul, doesn't ego exist in some way?*

HHST: No, ego never exists, but the continuity of mind exists.

Q. *From where does our strong sense of ego arise?*

HHST: Since beginningless time, we have been born in worldly existence with a very strong habit of thinking that the continuum of mind is our own ego, and we have lived with a very strong attachment to it.

Q. *So ego is only a habit of thought?*

HHST: Yes.

Q. *Some Westerners think that death is complete annihilation.*

HHST: That is not right. When you die, your body ends, but your mind still continues.

Q. *If there is no real ego, what continues?*

HHST: The continuum of the mind. It is like a rosary—all the beads are different, but it is the same rosary.

Q. *What is mind?*

HHST: There are many parts to it, but there is a very basic aspect that we call *Kun-Shi* (*Alaya*). Literally, this means "foundation of all," and it is a luculent "self-seeing." It is the base from which worldly existence and liberation arise. It is actually unobstructed mind, that part of mind that doesn't grasp at outer objects. It is lucid and continues right from beginningless time until enlightenment is reached.

Q. *This mind is also nonexistent in the Absolute?*

HHST: It exists relatively, of course. Ultimately, it is shunyata, but relatively, it exists. In reality, you cannot say it exists or doesn't exist.

Q. *Is it individual, or is it a kind of collective consciousness, a common basis of all individual minds?*

HHST: It is individual.

Q. *What distinguishes followers of the Mahayana from followers of Hinayana?*

HHST: There are seven differences, but the main thing is that one who wishes to get enlightenment for the benefit of all sentient beings belongs to the Mahayana.

Q. *Is compassion for all living beings just a matter of feeling sorry for them?*

HHST: No. Compassion is a thought, the wish for beings to be free from suffering.

Q. *Does compassion have to involve understanding the cause of suffering, or is it just a matter of feeling?*

HHST: I think both are involved. Compassion has three phases: the wish that the cause of their suffering be removed, and the wish that beings should be freed from suffering by understanding the true nature of all things. The practice of compassion clearly involves an understanding of the cause of suffering.

Q. *The meditation for arousing compassion is based upon a reflection of the kindness of our mother. What should we do if our mother was not kind?*

HHST: Every mother can be considered kind. It is a great kindness that she gave you a human body. That is enough for you to think of her as kind. If the meditation is difficult, you should always try to think of her kind actions and good qualities until the feeling of love arises.

Q. *Your Holiness has said that our sense of "I" is really an illusion. If this is so, why is it difficult for us to see this?*

HHST: As I said earlier, from beginningless time through lives, we have built up propensities that are reinforced by every act that assumes "I" is real; these propensities make it very difficult for us to realize the illusory nature of "I."

Q. *Seeing the unreality of ego is like breaking a bad habit?*

HHST: Yes.

Q. *Your Holiness has said that the teaching of rebirth is a relative truth and that many things exist relatively but not ultimately. What is this distinction between relative and ultimate truth?*

HHST: Yes, there are two truths, relative and ultimate. Relatively, we suffer; relatively, there is cause, path, and result. But in the experience of ultimate truth, nothing can be said to exist or not exist or both together or neither. These are what we call the four objectionable extremes; they are objectionable in the sense that valid, logical objections can be raised to all four possibilities.

Q. *Can ultimate truth be expressed in words?*

HHST: No, although it can be described to some extent. However, it can actually only be realized and experienced.

Q. *Is the Madhyamaka doctrine of emptiness taught by all schools of Tibetan Buddhism, and is their teaching the same?*

HHST: Yes, they all teach the same thing, but their ways of teaching differ. They all have their own qualities, and all achieve the same result.

Q. *Do followers of Mantrayana accept all the Mahayana teachings?*

HHST: Yes, Mantrayana accepts all Mahayana teachings. It is distinguished by the greater variety of methods, the use of more direct methods to attain the truth.

Q. *What is the significance of the vajra and bell used in tantric meditations and ceremonies?*

HHST: Each has many facets, but they are mainly symbolic of method and wisdom, which are of equal importance on our path; they also represent masculine and feminine qualities.

Q. *Ritual is important in Tibetan Buddhist practice. What is its use?*

HHST: Ritual is very important, and through its practice, much progress may be made. However, it is not necessary for everybody to perform elaborate rituals. Only the vajra and bell are necessary—and mudras.

Q. *Why are mudras important?*

HHST: They are very significant, externally and internally, and are very helpful in visualization practices. They also have much power in themselves to protect, to receive blessings, to heal.

Q. *What qualities are required before one can give wangs?*

HHST: Three types of gurus are described in the tantras. The highest type is one who has really seen the deity as clearly as we would see another person. The second type is one who has received at least some sign of spiritual accomplishment, perhaps in a dream. The third type, which is usual these days, is the guru who has received all the necessary wangs and teachings from a proper guru; who has performed the retreats of certain major deities; who has learned all the rituals, the mudras, the arrangement of the mandala, and so on. Only then can he give wangs.

Q. *Is it good enough to receive the teaching from a guru of the third type?*

HHST: Yes, it makes some connection, even if it is not as close as the first type. The first type of guru can introduce you to the deity as he would to a friend!

Q. *What is a meditation retreat?*

HHST: There are many different kinds. You can have a simple retreat, where you practice the meditations on love, compassion, and the resolve to win enlightenment. In tantric meditation, you visualize the deities, recite the mantras, concentrate on seeing the deities' form very clearly, or simply meditate on shunyata. There are many practices.

Q. *Why are retreats so important?*

HHST: Through meditative retreats, you attain enlightenment. Without performing many retreats, it is not possible to attain enlightenment. It is well known that in Tibet many yogis spent years in solitary retreat for this purpose; some still do so in India. Unless you had the very highest qualities, it would not be possible to attain enlightenment in this life without performing long retreats.

Q. *In Mantrayana practice, does it matter which deity one meditates on?*

HHST: It is best to meditate on a deity with which one has a karmic connection. This type of deity is called a *yidam,* or a "patron deity."

Q. *Can every deity be a yidam?*

HHST: Not all. The Protectors cannot be yidams. There is a class of deities which are yidams, and among these will be one with whom you have a particular connection.

Q. *Can Bodhisattvas like Manjushri and Avalokiteshvara be yidams?*

HHST: Yes, they have forms as both Bodhisattvas and yidams.

Q. *What qualities are required of us before we can take wangs?*

HHST: Many different qualities of the worthy disciple are described, but the main qualities are faith, compassion, and bodhichitta. People without a developed bodhichitta are not allowed to take major consecrations, the consecrations of deities like Hevajra.

Q. *Is it still a matter of luck, even if one has developed bodhichitta, to find a guru?*

HHST: No, one has to search. One can always find a guru from whom to receive teachings.

Q. *What should a person do if he doesn't find a guru?*

HHST: He should search more!

Q. *What is the* Anuttarayoga-tantra?

HHST: There are four classes of tantra of which *Anuttarayoga-tantra* is the very highest. Briefly, it is the practice in which every act of one's life—even eating, bathing, and so on—everything that you do, every action in worldly existence both during your meditation and while you are not meditating, everything, every action is transformed into the Path.

Q. *Does Buddhist practice mean we have to renounce the material world?*

HHST: According to Hinayana and Mahayana, yes. But according to Mantrayana, not necessarily.

Q. *By renunciation, you mean going to the mountains and living like a hermit? Can we continue to live in cities and still practice?*

HHST: Certainly, in Mantrayana. This is why the Lord Buddha taught the Mantrayana to King Indrabhuti.

Q. *Why then is monasticism important?*

HHST: Monasticism is important to keep the tradition alive, to keep the teaching properly. When you stay in the world, you can still practice, perhaps very effectively, but generally there is too much potential for distraction in the material world, and laypeople don't have the time to practice properly or to study the teachings effectively. They have too many other things to attend to. Monks have a much better opportunity to practice and study Dharma, as they have nothing else to attend to.

4

His Eminence Chogye Trichen Rinpoche

The History of Buddhism

A Buddhist Aeon

To put the Buddhist tradition into context and understand how a fully enlightened being appears in this world, it is important to know about *kalpas,* which are aeons or cycles of time. Within a given cycle, a physical environment of "outer elements" is always formed, and this environment is inhabited by sentient beings such as ourselves. A kalpa is divided into three phases. First, there is the process of coming into being, or creation; next, the time span during which the environment and beings abide; and finally, the phase of cessation, where the cosmos and the beings within it disappear. A kalpa in which a fully enlightened being appears is called an aeon of light, or a fortunate aeon. It is fortunate because a fully enlightened one appears in the world and bestows the light of spiritual intelligence on the other beings there. In contrast, there are the dark aeons, those cycles of creation in which no enlightened being will appear. It is said that the dark aeons are more numerous than the aeons of light.

A Fortunate Aeon

The particular cycle in which we now live is of a very special type, known as a fortunate aeon. At the beginning of this aeon, there was a chakravartin, a universal monarch of great power, known as Tsibkyi Mugyu (Arenemi). As ruler at an early stage in the formation of this aeon, King Arenemi enjoyed a reign of great prosperity, harmony, and well-being. This was true not only for the realm of the gods, but also for the human worlds. Although officially King Arenemi may not have had many queens, as a great universal regent, he had thousands of queens. We are told that these queens bore him more than one thousand princes. Due to his vast merit, he could merely gesture to one of these women and call her his queen for her to be able to bear him a son. King Arenemi gave rise to the wish that each of his sons could share in the rulership of his kingdom.

In those times, there lived a Buddha known as Mahavairochana—the historical Buddha of that era, just as the historical Buddha of our era is Shakyamuni. Such fully enlightened Buddhas display the twelve great deeds of an enlightened one. The king approached Buddha Mahavairochana, saying that he had fathered more than one thousand sons and asking how he might bless each son to enjoy a worthy and meaningful reign as king. He asked if he might offer the services of these princes to Buddha Mahavairochana, so that his sons might bear even greater fruits of virtue. The Buddha accepted King Arenemi's request, taking the princes as his disciples. The king had great aspirations for his sons, wondering in his heart when they would become equal to the Buddha. He asked Mahavairochana, "When will they be like you?" The Buddha assured the king that as his disciples, all of the princes would one day become fully enlightened.

Over the progression of the kalpas, it is said that an aeon of light is generally followed by a dark aeon. The aeon in which we dwell is known as a Bhadrakalpa, an extremely auspicious aeon. It is said that at the beginning of the formation of this aeon, a golden lotus flower with one thousand petals blossomed in the middle of the universal ocean. This wondrous lotus sprang up with such force that it reached to the heights of the realms of the gods, or devas. The appearance of the golden lotus caused the gods to exclaim, "What a wonder it is to witness the blooming of the thousand-petaled golden lotus! It is an auspicious omen, signifying the coming of one thousand Buddhas in this aeon." Thus the blossoming of the lotus foretold the birth of the thousand princes destined for buddhahood. Previous Buddhas were delighted by Mahavairo-chana's prediction.

Arenemi asked the Buddha in what order his sons would become enlightened. Mahavairochana ordered that the name of each prince be written out, and the names were gathered in a cloth and placed in a vase. Then the Buddha drew names, one by one, unfolding the sequence in which each of the princes would reach buddhahood. The first name selected, the one who would become the first Buddha of our fortunate aeon, was the one we know as Buddha Krakucchanda.

The second name drawn was the one who became Buddha Kanakamuni, the second Buddha of our kalpa. The third name drawn was the prince who would be born as the Buddha Kashyapa, the third Buddha of our fortunate aeon. The fourth was the name of the individual who was to become the enlightened one of our present era, Buddha Shakyamuni. Hence Shakyamuni is known as the Fourth Great Emancipator, or the Liberating One. The fifth name drawn was that of our next Buddha, Lord Maitreya. The sixth will come as Buddha Simhanada. In this way, the names of each of the thousand princes was drawn. Mahavairochana further prophesied that the prince whose name was drawn last, upon taking birth as the final Buddha of this fortunate aeon, was to be an extraordinarily enlightened one. He would embody the realization, qualities, and activities of all the previous Buddhas united. Our present era is that of the fourth prince, known to us as Buddha Shakyamuni.

The Coming of the Buddha of This Age

Prior to Shakyamuni's descent into our world, he reigned in the realm of the gods known as Tushita. Whoever ruled in the Tushita Heaven assumed the name of Svetakirti, so this was Shakyamuni's name when he dwelt there. While reigning in the Tushita Heaven, Svetakirti received many requests from gods as well as humans, beseeching him to appear in our world and manifest the twelve deeds of a supremely enlightened one. In response, he made five careful and specific observations regarding the circumstances of his future birth. These included the place in our world in which he would be born, the time and date, whose child he would be, and so forth. From these five careful observations, Svetakirti determined that he would appear in this world as a prince, the son of King Suddhodana and Queen Mayadevi in the kingdom of Kapilavastu. The remains of Kapilavastu are found in southern Nepal, not far from the border with India.

Lumbini Garden

In those ancient times, just to the east of Kapilavastu, there was a small kingdom whose capital was Devadaha. The two kingdoms enjoyed prosperous matrimonial bonds, with frequent marriages occurring between them. The woman who was to be the grandmother of Shakyamuni Buddha was named Lumbini and was the queen of the country. While she dwelled in Devadaha, she used to visit a very beautiful garden nearby, which was owned by a wealthy family. She went there frequently and grew to wish that she could have the garden as her own. Her husband, the king, told her, "Although I may be the lord of this land, it would not be right for me to claim someone else's garden for you. Still, if you so wish, I shall build for you just such a garden." So it was that the king built a most unique and splendid garden in the countryside between Devadaha and Kapilavastu. He named the garden in honor of his queen, and that place is known to this day as Lumbini.

Queen Lumbini became the mother of two beautiful princesses. As was the custom, she consulted the astrologers and soothsayers, so that she might know what future best suited her daughters. The seers unanimously predicted that both girls had the great merit either to marry a powerful ruler or to become the mother of a mighty being who would become a supreme enlightened one. In light of these predictions, Suprabuddha, the king of Devadaha, wished to form a bond with the king of Kapilavastu, a man of great fame and reputation, and the king of Kapilavastu harbored a similar wish. Thus Queen Lumbini's eldest daughter, Mayadevi, was chosen to marry Shuddodhana, the prince of Kapilavastu. Their wedding was a grand celebration.

The Birth of Shakyamuni

In due course, the future Buddha Shakyamuni entered into this world. It is said that Queen Mayadevi conceived her son on the night of the full moon in the sixth lunar month in the earth sheep year. The legends of the Buddha's birth tell us that from the day he entered Mayadevi's womb, all the devas and gods from the golden celestial realms watched over and protected him. On the seventh day of the fourth lunar month of the following year, the year of the iron monkey, she gave birth to a son. A normal pregnancy is nine months, yet traditional histories say that Mayadevi's was almost ten.

Mayadevi stayed away from the social activities of the royal court for most of her confinement. But as the time to give birth grew near, she wished to withdraw to somewhere more peaceful. When asked what place she would find pleasing, she proposed a visit to her mother's garden park, Lumbini, to relax and rest. As she strolled in the Lumbini grove, the time for the Buddha's birth suddenly came upon her. Just as Queen Mayadevi reached out to grasp the branch of a plaksha tree, the Buddha miraculously issued forth from under her right arm in the form of shimmering, scintillating golden light. Thus his appearance in this world was not by means of an ordinary birth, but by a miraculous event.

Immediately upon emerging from his mother, the Buddha walked seven steps in each of the four directions and uttered four profound statements. In the Tibetan language, these statements reflect a play on the words for *east, south, west,* and *north*. As the Buddha took his first steps to the east, he said, "From here I arrive to attain nirvana, enlightenment." The word for *east* in Tibetan also means "to arrive." Stepping to the south, he said, "I will be in harmony with worldly understanding." As he moved to the west, the direction of the setting sun, he said, "This is my final birth." And with seven steps to the north, Buddha said, "I have purified all my deeds in samsara, worldly existence," playing on the word for *north,* which also means "to purify." Naturally, a child born in the ordinary way would never be able to walk and speak with such eloquence and dignity. Yet at his birth, the Buddha strode forth in each of the four directions, heralding the event of his birth to all the world as he fearlessly proclaimed, "I am unexcelled by anyone ever to appear in this world." The child was raised as Prince Siddhartha, and all people held great hopes for him as the future leader of the Shakya clan.

The Spiritual Growth of the Buddha

Marriage

When his time of maturity had come, two fair princesses were proposed who might serve as his future queens. They were called Yasodhara and

Gopaka. Both princesses belonged to highly respected and wealthy families, and there were many princes in the surrounding kingdoms who eagerly sought their hands in marriage. And so a competition was arranged, and all their suitors had to display their skills and sportsmanship in hopes of winning such widely coveted brides. Prince Siddhartha defeated every rival and had the honor of claiming both princesses as his queens. In this way, he prepared to succeed his father as ruler. Having married, he reigned as prince of the Shakya kingdom.

One day, the prince went on his first excursion outside of the palace and into the city of Kapilavastu. On this journey, he witnessed four events that changed him forever. These events brought Siddhartha face-to-face for the first time with human suffering, from which he had so far been carefully shielded by his father. Having never in his life seen such conditions, Siddhartha immediately understood that all living beings are subject to the inevitable sufferings of illness, old age, and death. As the full force of this understanding struck his mind, he wondered how anyone could pretend that all was fine in the world and carry on as if such suffering did not exist. This experience quickly caused Prince Siddhartha to have a powerful sense of renunciation, and it forced him to recognize the futile nature of this world. All the activities of this life were ultimately meaningless, since all who inhabit this world must one day experience the same pains and pass away, leaving the experiences of this world to fade away like a dream. Having come to this realization, Siddhartha resolved to leave palace life and wander in search of the truth. He sought to extract from life its essential meaning.

Leaving the Palace

The young prince had a faithful attendant known as Chanda and an excellent horse called Kanthaka. Siddhartha summoned his attendant and ordered him to prepare his mount. Bidding his wife and infant son farewell as they lay asleep, he stole from the palace in secrecy, under cover of night, lest his subjects learn of his departure.

Prince Siddhartha ordered his attendant to grasp the tail of Kanthaka; the horse then miraculously bounded over the walls of the palace compound and into the city. It is said that the four great guardian deities of the directions offered their services to the prince, each lifting one hoof of his horse and spiriting him off through the air, until at last they brought him to the place known as Vishuddha Stupa, the "Stupa of Great Purity." It was there that the prince formally abandoned the life of a householder and adopted one of total renunciation. Seizing a blade, he cut off the length of his hair as a sign that he had parted from all attachment to this world. Siddhartha discarded his princely garb. It is said that hosts of gods and devas magically appeared all about him, offering him the robes of a spiritual mendicant. Donning the garments bestowed upon him by the gods, he declared, "I have renounced worldly life in order to seek the path to enlightenment."

Early Asceticism

Now Siddhartha carefully pondered the nature of the path he sought. He understood that all the Buddhas of the past had reached enlightenment through ascetic practice. He knew with certainty that he had to follow the same path. Siddhartha resolved to practice the ascetic way, making a solemn vow of fasting, and abstained from all food for six years. He further determined to remain motionless in meditation, and so it was that he sat continuously for six years without moving. This period of Siddhartha Gautama's life has come to be known as the six years of asceticism, of unbroken, solitary meditation practice. This is how penances led him to the threshold of enlightenment on the banks of the river Niranjana. During his six years of fasting, Siddhartha also kept a vow of noble silence. He did not speak to anyone but remained absorbed in the silence of meditation. Once, as he sat motionless and speechless, some local cowherds came upon him and wondered whether he was a human being or a statue. They went so far as to poke burning irons into his ears, but Siddhartha showed not the slightest reaction. In this way, he demonstrated the greatest determination to succeed in his meditation and austerities.

Enlightenment

Siddhartha Gautama's mother had passed away seven days after giving birth to him, and she was reborn in the land of the gods known as the realm of the thirty-three. As a deva of this realm, she possessed some limited clairvoyance and was able to see that her son from her previous life was undergoing great hardships. As the former Mayadevi wept for Siddhartha, her tears miraculously fell from the celestial world, forming a small pool in front of the meditating Buddha. In response to this, the great meditator broke his silence just one week before he was to attain enlightenment. He spoke out reassuringly to his mother, saying, "Although I have gone through these ascetic practices of unimaginable difficulty, yet I still have not reached my goal. I have only one week before I will gain enlightenment. Then I will repay your kindness and come to teach you in the near future." Thus, his mother was the first person for whom Gautama broke his vow of silence. Completing his six years of meditation, Siddhartha arose from that place, setting out on foot for what would come to be known as Bodh Gaya, or the Diamond Seat. There he came before the great bodhi tree. He knew that this was the place where all the past Buddhas—including Krakucchanda, Kanakamuni, and Kashyapa—had attained enlightenment, on the very seat he himself now approached. In deepest reverence, Gautama bowed before the Diamond Seat and then took his place upon it, leaning his back against the bodhi tree. Upon that throne of enlightenment of the past Buddhas, Siddhartha repeated the greatest historical act of all, achieving complete enlightenment. Gautama had spent six years meditating on the banks of the Niranjana and had come to the Diamond Seat of Bodh Gaya to finish his meditation training.

He entered again into seated meditation at dusk on the night of the full moon. Terrifying hosts of mara devils and evil beings swarmed about him in a jealous frenzy. They threatened him with fearsome apparitions, brandishing terrible weapons and hurling them at him in rage and envy. These demons had great power and were able to destroy whatever they set themselves upon. Yet due to the invincible power of meditation, compassion, and loving-kindness emanating from Siddhartha, they could not defeat him. Now only hours from gaining enlightenment, in a meditation of unassailable stability, he transformed all that was flung at him into celestial flowers; he suffered not the slightest harm. He conquered and subdued all the mara devils during the period of dusk on that night, then continuing on through the middle watch of the night, he remained in the deep samadhi of meditation. Finally, at the following dawn, he gained complete and perfect enlightenment, becoming samyak-sambuddha. Having attained enlightenment, Siddhartha Gautama, now the Buddha, entered into the most sublime and indescribable state of bliss and emptiness, which is the enlightened state. In this profound condition, he gave rise to a great wish, thinking, "How wonderful it would be if all sentient beings could share in this realization that is now my own."

Becoming a Teacher

Buddha wished that it were possible to share his discovery with every being, yet he realized that sentient beings were far too deeply immersed in ignorance to join him there. So he spoke these famous words to himself: "I have found a Dharma that is like nectar; it is noncomposite clear light, profound and peaceful and beyond conceptual elaboration. Were I to explain it, others would not understand, so I shall remain in the forest without speaking." Having said this to himself, he vowed to remain in silence for seven years. The Buddha dwelt in a state of contemplation, abstaining from any teaching role.

Brahma, the great sovereign of the universe, and Indra, the lord of the gods and angels, knew that the great enlightened wisdom of a Buddha was now manifest in this world. Brahma appeared and offered the Buddha a thousand-spoked golden wheel, while Indra offered a rare, clockwise-spiraling conch shell. With these supremely auspicious tokens of veneration, they beseeched him to turn the wheel of Dharma for the benefit of all sentient beings. Buddha Shakyamuni consented. Over the course of his life, he set in motion what are known as the three great turnings of the wheel of Dharma, or the wheel of the teachings.

The First Turning the Wheel

The first turning of the wheel of Dharma took place in the ancient Indian city of Varanasi. Buddha initiated this first turning with his central theme of the four noble truths. This collection of teachings is known as the Theravada, or commonly held precepts.

The Theravada mainly focuses on what are known as the four great seals of the Dharma:

All phenomena are impermanent.

All phenomena are suffering.

All phenomena are selfless.

Nirvana alone is peace.

First, the Buddha tells us that all compounded phenomena—all things that are composed of various elements and factors—are transient, impermanent; they do not last. Second, we are told that all phenomenal experience is of the nature of suffering. Third, the Buddha concludes that there is no self to be found in the phenomenal world. Fourth, the Buddha reveals that nirvana, or liberation, is peace. These four teachings became the primary concerns of the first turning of the wheel of Dharma taught by Buddha Shakyamuni, set in motion in Varanasi.

The Second Turning of the Wheel

From the second turning of the wheel of Dharma came the teachings belonging to the Mahayana, or "Great Vehicle." This turning was initiated in the Indian city of Rajagriha, at a place known as Vulture Peak, a hill said to resemble a flock of vultures. There the Buddha taught the Prajnaparamita, or Perfection of Wisdom, sutras. These sutras are of varying lengths, such as the hundred-thousand-verse sutra, the twenty-thousand-verse sutra, the eight-thousand-verse sutra, and so on. All of these teachings reveal the truth of emptiness, that all phenomena, everything that appears to be, actually lack any inherent, true existence.

The Third Turning of the Wheel

The third and final turning of the wheel of Dharma focused on the subtle, definitive meaning of the Dharma. Though the Buddha expounded a myriad of teachings, he himself contemplated the effectiveness of each of them.

He pondered how people would interpret the teachings and tailored his message to suit the minds of his listeners. Because of this, there came to be what are known as the commonly understood teachings, which follow the provisional meaning, and the teachings that reveal the definitive or ultimate meaning. Buddha made the distinction between the ultimate meaning of the Dharma and the commonly held, interpretive meaning. These discourses were given in the ancient Indian town of Vaishali, which became famous in the sutras as the place where a monkey made offerings to the Buddha.

The complete Dharma spoken by Lord Buddha is said to total eighty-four thousand teachings. These serve as direct remedies for the eighty-four thousand emotions or concepts with which sentient beings may be afflicted. Of these, Buddha taught that there are twenty-one thousand defilements related to greed, desire, and attachment that all beings can experience. As an antidote for these obscurations, Buddha taught twenty-one thousand discourses on the Vinaya, the higher training of moral and ethical precepts for laypeople and ordained monks and nuns. Buddha Shakyamuni further distinguished twenty-one thousand types of negativity associated with aversion, anger, and hatred. As a remedy for these afflicted states of mind, he gave the twenty-one thousand teachings of the sutras. As the antidote for the defilements arising based on ignorance, Buddha taught the twenty-one thousand discourses on the Abhidharma. In addition, a further twenty-one thousand talks were given to discuss the defilements of attachment, aversion, and ignorance as they function in common with one another. In this way, Buddha gave direct remedies for all eighty-four thousand defilements experienced by sentient beings.

When considering the three turnings of the wheel of Dharma, one may wonder where and when the Buddhist tantras were taught. The tantras are related to the third turning of the wheel of Dharma.

Oddiyana and King Indrabhuti

During the course of Buddha's life and activity, many of his disciples reached various levels of realization. It is even said that whenever he moved from one place to another, these disciples would fly in the sky, spreading their golden Dharma robes like wings. In this way, they could move from eastern India to the western regions, from south to north. In the western region of India was a kingdom known as Oddiyana. The king of Oddiyana was Indrabhuti, who was the same age as the Buddha. One day, as the king and his ministers were enjoying the palace gardens, a vast flock of monks flew by in the sky above them. Indrabhuti asked the wise elders among his ministers, "Who are they, and how can it be that they fly through the sky like birds?"

A senior minister replied, "Your Majesty, we dwell in western India. I have heard that in eastern India there is the kingdom of the Shakyas, out of which arose a prince known as Siddhartha. He is said to have renounced his kingdom and become an enlightened one. These must be some of his disciples in the skies above."

Astonished, the king exclaimed, "This is remarkable. How can it be? If even the disciples demonstrate such miracles, what a wonder the master himself must be! Might someone go and invite him to come to us?"

The elder minister answered, "There is no need to travel there physically. If those possessed of great faith and devotion make fervent, heartfelt prayers, the Buddha will know and hear their prayers through his omniscient wisdom. If you wish, pray thus, and invite Buddha to come here and teach you."

Hearing this, Indrabhuti composed a famous verse of supplication, acknowledging the Buddha as the leader and guide of all sentient beings, and asking to be included within the Buddha's protective wheel of refuge.

At this time, Buddha Shakyamuni was residing in Rajagriha. He summoned various disciples, such as the Bodhisattvas Manjushri and Vajrapani, as well as the realized Shravakas and Pratyekabuddhas, all of whom had the ability to fly with him. The Buddha told them that on a coming full moon day he would go to the western kingdom of Oddiyana at the invitation of King Indrabhuti. Those who were able to fly were invited to accompany him there. The Buddha and his disciples arrived at the palace of Indrabhuti along with an assembly of the guardian kings of the four directions, Brahma, Indra, and many of the gods, such as had never been seen before. The king could not believe it when he saw that even the great lords of the celestial realms moved in the Buddha's entourage.

The Buddha asked Indrabhuti, "For what purpose have you invited me here?"

The king replied, "You are a prince of eastern India, and I am a prince of western India. We are even of the same age, and yet you are such a sublime one. Please teach me how to become like you. This is my only request."

Hearing this request, Buddha replied, "If you wish to attain the same state as I, then you must abandon all worldly attachments and all the pleasures of the senses. Without renouncing the qualities of sensual experience and practicing the ascetic way, without this kind of renunciation, it will not be possible to attain liberation."

King Indrabhuti was an extremely astute and intelligent person. He knew that the profound depth of the Buddha's realization must include methods that would allow one to attain liberation without abandoning the qualities of the senses. The king responded, "Lord Buddha, I have been spoiled by living my whole life in such luxurious surroundings. At this stage of my life, how can I give up my queens and elegant lifestyle? Even if I must be born as a fox or a dog that feeds on excrement, I cannot abandon all attachment to sensory pleasures. Neither can I abandon the responsibilities of my kingdom. Please grant me a teaching that does not require me to do so."

Hearing the king's genuine plea, Buddha replied that he did indeed possess such a teaching. He consented to impart the esoteric teachings of the Vajrayana, the Diamond Vehicle of Buddhist tantra, particularly the teaching of the Buddha Guhyasamaja. In addition, he offered the transmission of all the empowerments of the *Anuttarayoga-tantra,* including those of all the major tantric emanations of the Buddha such as Kalachakra, Hevajra, and Chakrasamvara.

As Buddha bestowed these transcendent initiation ceremonies, the king, being possessed of unusually sharp faculties, was actually able to spontaneously accomplish and attain each stage and level of realization transmitted during the course of the empowerments. At each successive stage of empowerment, Indrabhuti instantly gained the same realization that a successful practitioner of that stage would enjoy. At the moment of the supreme phase of initiation known as the fourth empowerment, King Indrabhuti entered the highest level of enlightenment and was able to demonstrate simultaneously all the miraculous displays of a fully enlightened one.

This story from the life of the Buddha clearly shows us that people of keen intelligence may practice the Vajrayana and accomplish its vast benefits. One may follow the example of the Buddha's disciples, such as King Indrabhuti, and enter the Path through the tradition of major Vajrayana initiations that began in Oddiyana.

Dhanyakataka

In the southern region of India not far away was the kingdom of Dhanyakataka, known as the "Place of Heaped Rice." Becuase of the abundance of hermitages and meditation retreats that covered the mountainside, it attracted scholars, yogins, and mendicants from a great variety of spiritual traditions and was a famous dwelling place for those who wished to spend most of their time in meditation and prayer. It was at the magnificent stupa of Dhanyakataka that Buddha Shakyamuni imparted the world-renowned tantra known as Kalachakra. This empowerment attracted the Kulika ruler of Shambhala, a kingdom near Oddiyana, to attend as its honored recipient. The kingdom of Shambala is said to have unique inhabitants; although they are human beings, they are supposedly more intelligent and have far more acute faculties than other beings. They are even said to have wings. The king of Shambhala at that time, Suchandra, traveled to Dhanyakataka to receive the Kalachakra initiation from Buddha Shakyamuni.

ONE COULD GIVE INFINITE DETAILS regarding all the boundless activities of the Buddha, but this will suffice for now. It is merely a brief account of the turnings of the wheel of Dharma to summarize the history of the Buddha's teaching career.

The Three Vehicles

The paths outlined by the Buddha in his teachings are grouped into three principal vehicles. The first, which was described earlier, is the vehicle of the Theravada, or "elders." Known as the Hinayana, or "Small Vehicle," it is mainly focused on the path of renunciation and follows the teaching of the four noble truths.

Mahayana

The quintessence of the second vehicle, the Mahayana ("Great Vehicle") taught by Buddha Shakyamuni, comes down to two central practices: loving-kindness and compassion. Let us try to understand the meaning of these. As an example of loving-kindness, we can reflect on the kindness received from our mother until a feeling of gratitude and appreciation naturally arises. We can reflect that from the day we were born into this world, we were utterly helpless and could have easily been abandoned. Yet our mother protected us from every danger, fed and clothed us, taught us what to do and what to avoid. She gave us everything we needed, sacrificing her own needs for ours. To help loving-kindness grow inside of us, we contemplate the kindness received from her. With this in mind, we give rise to the genuine wish that she be happy and further generate the wish that we ourselves are able to provide her with the causes of happiness. From this benevolent wish, we proceed to cultivate a very creative, positive energy of loving-kindness. In so doing, we both increase our affection for others and strengthen the wish to repay the kindness shown to us by our mother, the wish to amplify her happiness. This is what is known as loving-kindness. Everyone can reflect on this example and then begin to extend the feeling they generate through remembering their mother's kindness to include other living beings.

Similarly, compassion arises when, through appreciating the kindness and love shown by our mother, we feel indebted to her and find it impossible to bear the thought of her suffering and undergoing hardships. We never want to see her experiencing any troubles or difficulties. If such situations befall her, we make sincere efforts to rescue her from even the smallest infirmity, from the most trifling circumstance that might cause her pain. We learn active compassion by empathizing with her sufferings and by truly trying to eliminate whatever is causing them. Active compassion is the wish and intent to relieve others of misery and whatever is causing it.

These two practices are the core of the teachings of the Mahayana, which is the Buddha's second turning of the wheel of Dharma. No matter what esoteric meditations of the Vajrayana we may engage in, we must ground ourselves in the essence of Mahayana Buddhist teaching, the practice of loving-kindness and compassion. This will lead to a point where we are actually able to renounce our own self-interest in favor of cherishing the welfare of others. This is genuine altruism. Even if we are not quite ready or able to adopt such a noble attitude, we train ourselves step-by-step to really consider what will help others as much as we look out for our own welfare. We can try to be an instrument of happiness for other living beings, even in the smallest ways. It is equally important that we never ignore or turn a blind eye to any causes that might bring suffering to others. As long as there is suffering—and it doesn't need to be ours—it still needs to be resolved or healed. One who has this attitude is able to develop an active, or engaged, compassion. If there is happiness in a family or between a couple, this happiness hinges for the most part on how loving, caring, and giving the family members and partners are toward one another. It does not depend on their accumulation of wealth and their material success. It is exactly the same as far as the well-being of a community, as far as the level of happiness in the greater world around us, is concerned. Whether or not a leader can set a good example that others can follow depends for the most part on how much he or she really cares about others. It depends on how giving he or she is able to be when conducting daily affairs. This type of leadership sets a noble standard that people will admire and will naturally wish to emulate. It cannot help but benefit us if we are able to live according to the teaching and practice of loving-kindness toward whomever we share our lives with. Whether we are at home or out in the world, if we show more love and empathy for others, we will find more happiness in our lives. If individuals are able to dedicate themselves to a life of loving-kindness and compassion, they will make a great contribution to the well-being of the world as a whole, to the cause of peace and happiness.

What is called "world peace" only depends on how the citizens of the world behave toward one another. Love and compassion lead to the happiness of individuals, and this will naturally bring about a peaceful world. Although each of us has received the kindness of our mother in this particular lifetime, this does not mean that there is only one person to whom we should feel indebted. The Buddha said there have been countless occasions on which we have been reborn. We ourselves have experienced births in all six realms of existence, in every possible situation, in every possible circumstance. We have had a kind mother in each of these lives, so we are actually indebted to all of those mothers just as much as we are to the mother of our present life. Bearing this in mind at all times can lead us to genuine concern for other beings. Due to our involvement with the karma of this present life, we cannot recognize those around us who were actually our previous mothers. Even so, we can still choose to conduct ourselves so as to repay each of them for all the good they have shown us. This is the way to develop loving-kindness.

There is great variety in how the different religions approach the spiritual path, as well as in their doctrines and their assertions of what is true. But one thing they all have in common is that they promote love and compassion and caring for one another. Without a doubt, the spirit of Christianity is the same as that of Buddhism in promoting and upholding the value of love. The Christian teaching says that God is love, and remembering this, one should show love toward others. This must be the most essential belief of Christians, and they try to practice it in their daily lives. It is no different with Buddhism. The Buddhist teachings guide us in how to treat one another. They teach us to understand and resolve for ourselves the moral and ethical choices we make, since these choices will become the causes for whatever results we ourselves wish to achieve. This practice of mindful attentiveness to our conduct, which is emphasized in the Buddhist teachings, encourages us to cultivate beneficial causes. These good causes arise from our intention to benefit others. Any deed that is performed with a good intention to benefit others will eventually bear fruits of happiness due to the law of cause and effect, or karma. Whether we believe in God or in the law of cause and effect, both teach us to be good people. It is doing good that promotes the happiness of others. When we shun and avoid negative conduct, the suffering of others is also avoided. Both views accept the same fact: we ought not to do things that create causes of unhappiness; rather, we should sow seeds of virtue that become causes for the happiness of others. All religions teach love between oneself and others, and that one ought to be a source of benefit to others rather than a cause of pain.

It is important to see that these teachings of loving-kindness and compassion are not some sort of formal doctrine that we have to profess loyalty to or belief in. They are concerned with the way we live. What determines our happiness or lack of it is what we do with ourselves. We can conduct ourselves in a way that shows care and concern for whatever sufferings we see around us, however small or apparently insignificant. We see suffering in the lives of others, and we wish that they did not have to experience such discomfort and unhappiness. We wish that we might be instrumental in the relief of their suffering. We also wish that they will be happy, and that we can help them to be happy and add to their well-being. For example, in the lives of a couple, if each partner wishes the best for the other and that the other will not have to experience pain and misery, then there will be greater harmony between them. If similar relationships exist between an employer and those who work for him or her, this promotes happiness in those situations where some are in a leadership role and others are following their directions. It is through each of us assuming a share of this basic responsibility to other beings and conducting our relationships based on love and compassion that we are able to make our world a different place. People speak about world peace, but peace only comes about when people extend love toward one another. These are essential points of the Mahayana Buddhist teaching.

Vajrayana

Having understood the basis of Mahayana, one may now ask where the Vajrayana, the esoteric tantric vehicle, fits into Buddhism. Vajrayana, the Diamond Vehicle, is a branch of the Mahayana tradition. If one has developed a good basis of loving-kindness and compassion, one may make use of methods that are the special skillful means of the Vajra-yana. The benefit of these methods is that they provide a far more skill-ful and much swifter means of attaining enlightenment than can be gained by relying on the other vehicles on their own. It is said that even if one follows the Perfection of Wisdom, or Prajnaparamita, of the Mahayana, it will still require three incalculable aeons to attain enlight-enment. On the other hand, resorting to the skillful methods of the Vajrayana makes it possible to attain enlightenment in one lifetime, and a great number of practitioners in India and Tibet have done so. The Vajrayana is available as a special means within the Mahayana to greatly accelerate the path to enlightenment. If one has a heart that overflows with love and compassion as a stable foundation, then resorting to esoteric practices will guarantee rapid spiritual development. In this way, one may gain the capacity to benefit many more sentient beings much more quickly.

ANUTTARAYOGA-TANTRA   Within the esoteric vehicle of the Vajrayana, there are four general levels of tantras or scriptures. The highest, or ultimate, of these four is known as *Anuttarayoga-tantra* ("Highest Yoga tantra"). The Anuttarayoga tantras themselves are classed as father tantras, mother tantras, and nondual tantras. In the nondual category, there are only two scriptural traditions: that of Buddha Hevajra and that of Buddha Kalachakra. To understand a bit about Buddhist tantra, let us consider the tradition of Kalachakra. The empowerment of the Kalachakra tantra has been widely given throughout the world in recent times. As a nondual tantra, it is the quintessence of all the Anuttarayoga tantras.

Kalachakra itself is divided into four types of tantra, giving us an elaborate framework to understand its specifics. First, there is the outer Kalachakra. In large part, these sections are concerned with visualizing and meditating on the Buddha in the form of the meditational deity Kalachakra and chanting his mantra. Second comes the inner Kalachakra, which addresses applying the profound internal meditations on the subtle channels, vital winds, elements, and essential drops that make up the subtle (psychic) body. Third, the secret Kalachakra involves meditating on and within the ultimate meaning of the truth of emptiness. Fourth is "other," or "alternative," Kalachakra, which relates to the study of and meditation on the outer cosmos of our realm of existence. Alternative Kalachakra teaches us how all the physical appearances of this world are the manifestation of our collective karma; it teaches us the causes that bring about this universe. It describes the outer universe and how it directly corresponds with and reflects the inner propensities and karmic vision of all the beings within this universe. Thus, the Kalachakra tantra contains the deepest meanings of four types of tantras all within a single tradition.

Due to its profound meaning and the blessing it carries, it is very good if one can receive the Kalachakra initiation or at least the oral transmission of the mantra of Buddha Kalachakra. As an example of the power and benefits of mantras of the Anuttarayoga tantras, it is said that merely by hearing the sound of the Kalachakra mantra, with the proper attitude and faith, many difficulties and obstacles are removed. If you take the opportunity to recite the Kalachakra mantra during the course of your life, this will allay outer obstacles and create peace within you. Even reciting the mantra once definitely has the power to pacify your afflictions and promote a general sense of happiness and well-being.

5

Khenpo Appey Rinpoche

The Production of Faith

The practical manner for producing faith in the Buddhist teachings is to take refuge. When refuge is taken, one promises to hold as one's guide the shrine or the object that one trusts and accepts to be extraordinary and excellent.

The subject matter of refuge is divided into four categories:

1. The nature of refuge
2. The differentiation of refuge
3. The rules of taking refuge
4. The benefits of taking refuge

1. The Nature of Refuge

The nature of refuge is actually the idea of accepting the shrine or object of refuge to be perfect. Thus, the essence of the refuge is the acceptance of the Triple Gem as the most excellent.

2. The Differentiation of Refuge

This is divided into three main categories:

- The worldly refuge that is taken by ordinary sentient beings
- The refuge of the Hinayana
- The refuge of the Mahayana

Each of these categories is also divided into two parts. The worldly refuge is divided into the object and the mind; the Hinayana refuge into the refuge of the Arhats and the refuge of the Pratyekabuddhas; and the Mahayana refuge into the Mahayana refuge itself and the Vajrayana refuge.

When we look at the three main categories of refuge–those of the worldlings, the Hinayana, and the Mahayana—there is a cause for each of them. The cause of refuge for the worldlings is fear of the suffering in this world of existence and also faith in the Triple Gem or the shrine. For the Hinayana, the causes are the same, except that the emphasis is placed on faith. For the Mahayana, in addition to fear and faith, there is the aspect of compassion. All Mahayana practices are always preceded by the thought of compassion, with the wish of relieving the suffering of sentient beings. The emphasis of taking refuge in the Mahayana is on compassion as the motivating force.

When we consider these three aspects of taking refuge, we should also consider them from the point of view of the object in which the refuge is taken. In the case of worldlings, refuge is taken in relation to the object and to the mind. The worldlings who take refuge in relation to object take refuge in great worldly deities such as Brahma or Indra or even in lower worldly beings such as earth spirits or local spirits. Those who take refuge in this form cannot be categorized as Buddhists.

Those worldlings who take refuge in relation to the mind actually take refuge in the Triple Gem. However, their purpose of taking refuge is solely to relieve their fear and gain certain types of benefits in this life alone. So although they take refuge in the Triple Gem, their type of refuge can never lead to any form of liberation, since their aim is for the sake of this life alone.

Although the Hinayana and the Mahayana have the same object of refuge, which is the Triple Gem, there are slight differences. Hinayana followers accept the Buddha as having only two bodies—dharmakaya and rupakaya—whereas the followers of Mahayana accept the Buddha as having three bodies—dharmakaya, sambhogakaya, and nirmanakaya.

In the Hinayana tradition, taking refuge in the Buddha means to accept the Buddha as the teacher who shows the path to liberation. Refuge in the Dharma refers to the path leading to the cessation of suffering.

The refuge of the Sangha means those ordinary people who renounce this world and take ordination as well as those who show the path of the four noble truths.

In the Mahayana tradition, the Buddha has the three bodies of enlightenment—dharmakaya, sambhogakaya, and nirmanakaya. The Dharma is the sutras or teachings of the Mahayana tradition, and the Sangha comprises those who have gained the stages of enlightenment, such as the Bodhisattvas.

When we consider the time to take refuge, we again look at the three categories of those who take refuge. The worldly person takes refuge from this time until he is able to accomplish the purpose that he has set out. This may be a certain desire or object or some kind of benefit for himself. This is not considered the proper refuge. In the Hinayana tradition, one takes refuge from this time until one dies. So the refuge is taken for this lifetime alone. In the Mahayana tradition, one takes refuge from this time until the stage of full and perfect enlightenment is obtained.

For the worldly person, the purpose of taking refuge is to overcome various fears and to accomplish various desires. The Hinayana practitioner takes refuge in order to gain his own personal liberation, and the Mahayana practitioner does so to gain enlightenment and to bring all living beings to enlightenment.

3. The Rules of Taking Refuge

There are two categories of rules of taking refuge: the general rules and the particular rules. The former relate to the Triple Gem in general. The latter are the specific rules for taking refuge in the Buddha, the Dharma, and the Sangha.

The General Rules of Taking Refuge

The first general rule is to always accompany those who are holy. This means that we should stay near a teacher who has gained some stage of accomplishment or entrance into the Dharma itself. We should also associate with fellow Dharma practitioners. If we are unable to surround ourselves with people who are concerned with the practice of virtue, we should associate with those who are able to help us seek refuge and maintain virtue.

The second general rule is to listen to and study the Dharma. This means we should not listen to any kind of teaching haphazardly. We should study it very carefully. We should study the proper Dharma, which is the teaching of the Buddha, whether it is the Hinayana, the Mahayana, or the Vajrayana. What we should study properly is anything that is in the Tripitaka—Vinaya, Sutra, and Abhidharma. If one has received initiation or consecration of the Vajrayana, then the tantric scriptures should also be studied.

The teachings of the Buddha, however, are very difficult to study in the Sutra form because they are not systemized. To gain a better understanding of the teaching of the Sutra, it is good to study the later teachers such as Nagarjuna, Asanga, Maitreya, and Dharmakirti, who wrote good commentaries on the teachings of the Buddha. For one who studies the tantric teachings, which is also very complicated and difficult to understand, it is good to study the great masters such as Virupa, Indrabhuti, and Ghantapa, who wrote clear explanations of these teachings.

The Dharma that we study should be proper Dharma. According to Sakya Pandita, if the Dharma that we hear has the following six qualities, then we can trust that it is the real teaching of the Buddha:

- It was taught by the Buddha himself.
- It falls within those teachings that were systemized by the various Buddhist councils.
- It has been commented on by great scholars and practitioners.
- It has been meditated on by the great saints or great mahasiddhas of India.
- It has been translated by great translators from Indian to other languages such as Tibetan.
- It has been accepted by all the great scholars.

If a teaching has these six qualities, we can accept it as a real teaching of the Buddha. Though teachings from other schools may be good, they do not lead to the proper result. Therefore, we should not study or meditate upon them.

The third general rule of taking refuge is that we should practice the Buddhist teachings according to what the Buddha taught. We rely on the Vinaya, or moral conduct, teaching of the Buddha to train our speech and our body in proper conduct. We should rely on the Sutra to train our mind and on the Abhidharma to explain the Buddha's teachings and give us a proper understanding of the teachings from a wisdom point of view. This is true whether we practice in the Hinayana or the Mahayana tradition. Those who practice the Vajrayana tradition should rely on the various tantric teachings to understand and practice properly.

We should always remember that before we engage in any activity in our daily life, we should always direct our mind toward the Triple Gem to obtain its blessings. If we are going out, we should think that the Buddha of the various families resides in the direction we are going. By praying to that Buddha and seeking his blessings, we will be able to accomplish whatever we set out to do and be free from any obstacles or hindrances on the way.

For example, if we are going to a certain place within our own district, we can seek the blessings of or pray to the Buddha Vairocana. If we are going east, we can imagine that Buddha Akshobhya resides there. If we are going to the south, we can think that Buddha Ratnasambhava resides in that direction. If we are going west, we can imagine that Buddha Amitabha resides there, and if we are going to the north, that Buddha Amogasiddhi resides there.

Also, before we eat or drink anything, it is important that we should offer the first part of the food to the Triple Gem. There are many different methods of doing this. For example, we can recite many different verses from the sutras. We can also offer actual food to different spirits, as is described in the Vinaya teachings. There is a story of a demoness who had eaten many children. In order to satisfy her, the Buddha promised her an offering of part of the food from followers of the Buddhist traditions.

Actually, when we eat, we can perceive the activity from different perspectives. For example, within the Hinayana tradition, we can think that we are eating to keep our body healthy and maintain it as a vessel to gain the Dharma Path. Thus, it is necessary to eat. According to certain Mahayana traditions, there are many different creatures within our body. We eat not for ourselves alone, but in order to nourish these creatures, so by offering the food to them, we are doing a virtuous deed by eating. If we practice the Vajrayana tradition, we can engage in many teachings, such as the eating yoga practice, when we eat.

When we go to bed, we can use sleep to bring us into the Dharma Path. For example, we can lie down in the lion position that the Buddha Shakyamuni adopted when he entered Mahaparinirvana. Also at bedtime, we should think that we are entering the state of dharmakaya, or the Buddha's mind, and pray that all sentient beings may also gain the same state. When we wake up in the morning, we should immediately pray that all sentient beings will gain the rupakaya, or the form body of the Buddha. In this way, we can transform our sleeping and waking activities into a virtuous path.

No matter what happens to us, whether we have happiness or suffering in this life, we must never abandon our refuge in the Triple Gem. For example, when we are sick, we should recite various sutras, dharanis, or mantras, or take prescribed medicine to overcome the illness. Some people say that we should not recite sutras or prayers or take medicine when we are sick because this would harm our refuge in the Triple Gem, that it is as if we do not have faith in it. However, this is a wrong idea because the Buddha himself said that when we are sick, it is very necessary to take medicine and to recite the sutras.

The Particular Rules of Taking Refuge

When we have taken refuge in the Buddha, we should not see others such as samsaric gods or higher beings or even other people who teach various teachings as our guides. Instead, we should rely only on the Buddha as the true teacher of the path to liberation. Having taken refuge in the Dharma, we abandon harming other sentient beings, and we do not rely on the wrong paths to lead us on the path to liberation. We rely on the Buddha's teaching as the only path to the ultimate result of enlightenment. When we take refuge in the Sangha, we do not keep those who belong to other faiths as spiritual friends and teachers.

We can make offerings to others, even to other shrines, but we should not take refuge in other religious traditions because by doing so, we are destroying our own vows of refuge. We can also associate with other religious practitioners as our ordinary worldly friends but not as spiritual friends, because this will harm our refuge. Similarly, we can make offerings or prostrate to other worldly beings, to great and powerful worldly beings such as Brahma or Indra, or even to powerful local spirits, but we should never take refuge in them, because this will destroy our refuge in the Buddha.

Some people say that not respecting the scriptures of the Buddha—for example, walking over or selling dharma books—is a great fault and will destroy our refuge in the Dharma. This is not correct. Though this is a fault, it is not a method for destroying our refuge in the Dharma.

Some people also say that there is no need to study and understand the teachings of the Buddha. This is actually the way we destroy our refuge in the Dharma, because if we do not study the Dharma, there is no way we can understand it, and if we do not understand the Dharma, it will degenerate. So the greatest fault to our refuge in the Dharma is not to study the Dharma; this is greater then showing disrespect for dharma books.

With regard to taking refuge in the Sangha, the scriptures say that if we do not respect the cloth of the Sangha that the ordained people wear, even if it is just a small piece of cloth, we are destroying our refuge because the cloth is the symbol of the Sangha. Again, this is not correct. It is certainly a fault. But the greatest fault, which really destroys our refuge in the Sangha, is not to show respect to the fully ordained persons or those who teach or spread the Dharma. This is the way we destroy our refuge in the Sangha, not merely through walking over or showing disrespect to a piece of cloth.

4. The Benefits of Taking Refuge

The first of the benefits is destroying the various obscurations that keep us from having proper faith or proper understanding of the Triple Gem. We are able to lessen or overcome the disease or suffering of our body or discomfort of our mind. We are also able to destroy any harm that we receive from other people or even from nonhumans or spirits. All our various sufferings will also be lessened through taking refuge in the Triple Gem. Ultimately, we will be able to overcome all our faults and sufferings.

There is a story to illustrate this idea of how other people or spirits cannot harm someone who has taken refuge. At one time, there was a man who became a monk when he was very old. He did not know any Dharma. One day, a woman went to him to offer a very beautiful piece of cloth and asked him to give her Dharma teachings. The old monk became frightened because he did not know any Dharma. However, having been given the piece of cloth, he had to say something. Thinking aloud, he said, "It is because of my ignorance that I am suffering." The woman thought he was saying that all suffering arises in the world due to ignorance. She thought about it carefully and concluded that what he said was very good. So she meditated on that and was able to understand the first truth of suffering and gained a very great result.

The piece of cloth that the old monk got from the woman became known to many people. At one point, a thief heard about it and wanted to get it from the monk. So he went to the monk's house and stood at the door asking for the cloth. The old monk was afraid to go out, so he told the thief that if he wanted the piece of cloth, he should go to the side window. The thief went to the window, stuck his hands in, and said, "Now give me that cloth."

The old monk replied, "When this piece of cloth was given to me, it was given with two hands. So if you want to take it, you should stick both hands in and I will give it to you."

When the thief stuck both hands in the window, the monk bound them with a rope and tied them to a pillar in the house. Then he went out, took a stick, and started beating the thief. With every stroke that he delivered, he would recite one of the refuge formulas—"I take refuge in the Buddha; I take refuge in the Dharma; I take refuge in the Sangha." He kept hitting and reciting until the thief's legs were nearly broken. He was in great pain, and finally the old monk let him loose.

The thief quickly hobbled off to get away from the monk. Someone saw him and asked him why he was hobbling. The thief said that he had tried to steal a piece of cloth from an old monk who had caught and beaten him, and while beating him, the old monk had recited the refuge formula. The thief said that the Buddha was very great because he had included the entire refuge prayer in three lines. Had he not done that, the thief would have been dead.

The thief had the habit of living under a bridge, and during the night, many nonhuman spirits would cross over it. One night, when they went up to the bridge, they were not able to get across. They felt a strong force holding them back. They were curious and began searching around, and they found the thief under the bridge mumbling something. When they asked him what he was saying, he answered that he was reciting the prayer of taking refuge in the Triple Gem. The nonhuman spirits thought the Triple Gem was so powerful that it could stop them from going over the bridge. They therefore decided to take refuge in the Triple Gem. It is said that they were able to gain rebirth in the higher realms. The thief himself gained great faith in the Triple Gem and took full ordination as a monk in the later part of his life.

Through taking refuge, not only are we able to overcome harm, we are also able to gain various qualities. For example, when we become Buddhists, we gain the qualities of Buddhists. It makes life holy and purposeful. By taking the proper refuge and becoming holy, we become suitable to receive offerings from the samsaric gods and human beings who appreciate the Dharma. We will receive protection wherever we are. As we pass through this life, we have the Triple Gem with us. It will make us happy and confident wherever we may be. In both this lifetime and future lifetimes, we will never be separated from the Triple Gem. This is the temporary result of taking refuge.

The ultimate result is that by taking refuge in the Buddha we will be able to gain buddhahood ourselves. By taking refuge in the Dharma, we will be able to teach the dharma to others. And by taking refuge in the Sangha, many would gather to receive the teachings from us when we gain buddhahood. These are the benefits that we receive. Those who come to us to receive these teachings and those whom we seek out in order to bestow these teachings will benefit by receiving help to gain the stage of full and perfect enlightenment.

6

Jetsun Dragpa Gyaltsen

The Song on How to Rely on Antidotes

Namo gurubhyah.[1]

Because mind's independence is not established,
whatever may be done, at no time is mind happy.[2]
Because dharmas are not understood as mind,
you have no confidence in deluded appearances
being the variety of the completely imputed[3] characteristics.[4]
Now, it is of no use imputing the characteristics of a beggar.
The path of enlightenment[5]—meditation and postmeditation—
everything in that path is the state of mahamudra.[6]
Because one does not understand food as nectar,[7]
acceptance and rejection toward any good or bad food arises;
you have no confidence that real food does not appear.
Now, there is no use in seeking beggar's food with hardship—
whatever food comes into the mouth nourishes the body,
also all of that food is the state of mahamudra.[8]
Because appearances cannot be understood from books,
never reaching the end of conventions,
have no confidence in letters, words, and treatises.
Now, also there is no use in a beggar making explanations of treatises.

The container[9] that holds only the words of oral instruction,
all of that meaning is the state of mahamudra.[10]
Because one does not understand mind as the lord of samsara
   and nirvana,[11]
one is completely attached to the Ngari[12] disciples;
have no confidence in the person whose mind is lost to others.
Now also there is no use in taming the untamed beggar.[13]
The six mindfulnesses are the companions of enlightenment;
they are also the state of mahamudra.
This song of the six states of mahamudra
was sung when the mind was sad,
was sung having applied the antidote to the mind.
A song of Jetsun Rinpoche.

Notes

1. *Namo gurubhyah* literally means "prostration to the guru."
2. The first mahamudra antidote is the antidote to suffering.
3. The "completely imputed" nature, posited by the Mind-Only school, refers to the deluded appearances of the mind.
4. The second mahamudra antidote is the antidote to characteristics.
5. The third mahamudra antidote is the antidote to the Path.
6. *Mahamudra* means "Great Seal."
7. This refers to the Vajrayana practice of eating yoga.
8. The fourth mahamudra antidote is the antidote to food.
9. The container is the student.
10. The fifth mahamudra antidote is the antidote to conventions of words and syllables.
11. Nirvana is cessation, which is the result of the Path.
12. Ngari is in western Tibet, also known as upper Tibet.
13. This is the mahamudra antidote to grasping the extremes of samsara and nirvana.

7

Khenpo Appey Rinpoche

The Enlightenment Thought

By definition, "enlightenment thought" means to promise something with the mind. For instance, if one were thinking of going somewhere today, then one would go according to the idea that one has created in one's mind. If one thinks of going to eat, then one would create that idea or mental thought of eating. This is actually a promise in one's mind.

The idea of promising something with the mind occurs not only in the Mahayana tradition, but in the Hinayana tradition as well. Within the latter tradition, there are three different types of enlightenment thought:

- The thought of gaining the state of an Arhat, or the Arhat enlightenment thought
- The thought of gaining the state of the Pratyekabuddha, or the Pratyekabuddha enlightenment thought
- The thought of gaining the state of full and perfect enlightenment, or the fully enlightened Buddha enlightenment thought

Within the Hinayana tradition, there is the small enlightenment thought, which is dedicated to one's own benefit alone. Within the Mahayana tradition, there is the thought of working for others. This is called the great enlightenment thought, because it is dedicated to the benefit of all living beings rather than just oneself.

Within the Mahayana tradition, there are two main schools of enlightenment thought. One is known as the Mind-Only (Chittamatra) school, and the other is the school of the Middle Way (Madhyamika). The Mind-

Only school originated from the great Bodhisattva Maitreya and was transmitted to the Indian saint Asanga and others, such as Chandragomin. Through them, it was passed on to and practiced in Tibet by the earlier Kadampa school and later by the Gelugpa school. The Middle Way school originated from the Bodhisattva Manjushri and was passed down to Nagarjuna and other great scholars and saints such as Shantideva. When it reached Tibet, it was practiced by the Sakya and other schools.

According to certain teachers even within the Sakya, there are many distinctions between the Mind-Only and the Middle Way schools of enlightenment thought. Some of the differences can be seen in the qualities of the one who bestows the precept of the enlightenment thought, the one who receives it, and the rules that must be followed. According to some other scholars, there is actually no distinction between the two.

The enlightenment thought can be divided into two parts: wishing and entering. Wishing enlightenment thought is the wish to gain the state of full and perfect enlightenment for the sake of all sentient beings. It is a promise to attain buddhahood. Entering enlightenment thought is the promise to engage in the cause of gaining that result. It uses various methods of practicing and gaining the merit and wisdom to achieve buddhahood.

The enlightenment thought can also be divided into two main categories: relative and ultimate. Both the wishing and the entering parts fall under the category of relative enlightenment thought. The ultimate enlightenment thought refers to the nature of ultimate reality, or the wisdom of emptiness, by which one can understand all phenomena to be free from any conceptualization. It is being completely void of any characteristic or being what is known as empty by nature.

According to certain teachers, at the time that the enlightenment thought is bestowed on a person, it is given in the form of a ritual. The moment when one makes the promise to gain buddhahood for the sake of others is known as the ritual taking on of this enlightenment thought. Both the relative and the ultimate enlightenment thought can be given in the form of a ritual, just like taking refuge.

However, Sakya Pandita strongly objected to this view. He said that it is only the relative enlightenment thought that can be given in the form of a ritual. The ultimate enlightenment thought can only arise in the meditation of someone who has gained the first bhumi, or the first stage of buddhahood. At the time of meditation, one gains the realization of emptiness that signifies arrival of the first bhumi. This realization of empti- ness in a state of meditation is known as the awakening of the ultimate enlightenment thought. Hence, according to Sakya Pandita, it can only arise through a meditative experience and can never be given through a ritual or ceremony; it cannot be passed on through words.

According to the teaching of the Bodhisattva Maitreya, we can create the enlightenment thought in five ways:

- Through a spiritual friend who explains what the enlighten- ment thought is and also its benefits
- Through awakening one's gotra and thereby creating the cause for entering into the enlightenment thought
- Through the accumulation of great virtue and merit
- Through studying or listening to the teaching, whereby one knows the benefits of the enlightenment thought, the qualities of the Buddha, and the various teachings of the Mahayana
- Through continuous meditation on the various teachings that one has heard and studied

The performance of the ceremony of the enlightenment thought can be given according to four different traditions. One follows the teaching of the Mind-Only school. This is explained in great detail in a book called The Twenty Verses Concerning the Enlightenment Thought, which was written by Chandragomin. The second tradition comes from the Mid- dle Way school, which will be explained in the next section. The third tradition arises from the great mahasiddhas, such as the one given at the Sakya Lamdre teaching, which comes from Virupa and Naropa. The fourth tradition involves tantric initiation. During the initiation, there is a recita- tion of the Vajrayana Sevenfold Prayer, whereby one receives the Bodhi- sattva, or enlightenment thought, vows.

The Enlightenment Thought According to the Middle Way

The school of the Middle Way divides the rules for taking the enlighten- ment thought into two parts. One is related to wishing and the other to entering.

Wishing Enlightenment Thought

The vows pertaining to the wishing enlightenment thought are given in brief, middle, and extensive forms.

THE BRIEF VOW   The brief form of the enlightenment thought vow is just the wish "I must gain the state of full and perfect enlightenment for the sake of all sentient beings." The thought of never being separated from or discarding that wish represents all the precepts of producing the enlightenment thought.

THE MIDDLE VOW   When we are taking the enlightenment thought, we think we are unable to fulfill the wish to gain the state of full and perfect enlightenment for the sake of all sentient beings. When we have that thought, we must overcome it. The middle form of the enlightenment thought vow is dedicated to overcoming three types of negative thinking:

- To be discouraged at the beginning and believe we are unable to attain enlightenment. We have doubts about our strength, ability, or bravery to accomplish our wish and do not create the proper interest right from the start. This is poor thinking.
- To be discouraged at a later point in time.
- To abandon the enlightenment thought due to fear of worldly existence.

The first instance means that we believe there is such a vast difference between ourselves and the Buddha, who has such great qualities and high realization, that we can never gain such a state, and we thus wish to abandon our enlightenment thought. The whole purpose of the middle form of the vow is to realize that we have this idea obstructing our enlightenment thought and to overcome it. To counteract this lack of strength or confidence, the great Bodhisattva Maitreya said that at every moment in this world, there is someone, someplace, who gains enlightenment. Because of this, there is no reason we cannot gain such a state. Thinking this way helps us overcome our discouragement.

The great Bodhisattva Shantideva said that not only ordinary people, but even small insects such as bugs, which do not even have the state of human existence, are able to gain a state of liberation and omniscience through diligence. If they can do this, why shouldn't we—who have the power to understand what deeds are good and bad, and the power to gain a human birth—not be able to attain enlightenment also? This thinking also helps us overcome initial discouragement.

There is a story to show that through even a small cause we can gain a good result. At one time, there were seven insects on top of a leaf. The leaf was blown into a stream, which carried it out to the ocean. The wind held the leaf in a place where a Buddha image was also floating. Due to the wind and the current, the leaf circled the image three times. Even though the insects did not have any motivation to do this, they were born in the next life as seven women, due to the merit arising from the leaf's circumambulation. In that human life, they were born in a very low caste. They were poor, but they would cut grass and collect wood and sell it. With the earnings from their menial tasks, they made many offerings and performed virtuous deeds. Because of their virtue, they were later born as the seven daughters of a king who lived in the time of the Buddha Kashyapa. During that lifetime, they made many offerings to Kashyapa, who told the story about how they came to be and also predicted that they would eventually gain the state of full and perfect enlightenment. So from a tiny cause that did not even arise through proper motivation, they were able to gain the state of enlightenment.

There was also a layperson who lived in the time of the Buddha Shakyamuni. He decided to become a monk and asked Shariputra to ordain him. Through the supernatural power of his mind, Shariputra looked into the man's past and could see no cause for him to be ordained at that time. Therefore, he told the man that he had no cause or virtue that would allow him to take ordination. The man became upset; he approached the Buddha and told him what had happened. The Buddha said that Shariputra's decision was not correct. Shariputra had supernatural power and clairvoyance and was able to understand the minds of others. However, being an Arhat, his power was limited to a certain time and space, so he was not able to see all the deeds of others completely. Actually, a long time before, the man had been a pig, and one day as he was being chased by a dog, he had run around a stupa three times. In this way, he had gained enough merit to be ordained as a monk. So the Buddha himself bestowed upon him ordination and through his own practice in that very lifetime he gained Arhatship.

At another time, there was a woman who made an offering of rice to the Buddha. He predicted that due to the offering, she would gain many fortunate rebirths in the realms of gods and men, and that she would eventually gain the state of a Pratyekabuddha. The women's husband thought this was absurd and said that the Buddha would lie for just one bowl of rice, saying that someone could attain such great result. So he approached the Buddha, asked him why he had lied, and said that he was making trouble for himself by telling a big lie in return for a small bowl of rice. In return, the Buddha asked him about the fruit tree that the man had in his yard. He asked the man about the size of the seed that had resulted in such a huge tree. The man replied that the seed had actually been very small, even smaller than a mustard seed. The Buddha then said the man could see for himself that he could have a great result from a tiny cause. The man thought about that and agreed. He was convinced of what the Buddha had said, and in that lifetime, he was able to attain the first bhumi.

Similarly, there were cases of people who just offered a small piece of herb to the Buddha, and with that, they created the enlightenment thought and were able to gain the state of enlightenment. There were others who gave a small piece of cloth or just a little drinking water to the Buddha. Even from these small causes, they were able to produce the enlightenment thought and gain the desired result. Therefore, there is no reason that we should be discouraged about never being able to gain the state of enlightenment. If we do not produce the enlightenment thought and realize liberation, then we will have to stay in this world of existence for a very long time. The suffering that arises from having to stay here will be much greater than any suffering we could experience through practicing the Path to gain enlightenment. Since this is the case, there is no reason we should not produce the enlightenment thought.

The second form of negative thinking overcome by the middle form of the vow is to lose interest in the practice and believe that we will never be able to gain the result. For example, sometimes when we perform deeds of giving, we think that we can become rich immediately. Instead, we become poor after giving something, and this causes discouragement. Or if we are practicing the sadhana meditation but do not receive the blessing of the deity, we are disappointed and want to give up the practice. Similarly, we can be discouraged if our efforts—such as rituals or Dharma practices—to help a friend or relative overcome an obstacle and recover from a sickness are not successful and the person dies. This may lead us to abandon our practice.

If someone is very sick and dies even after rituals have been performed to overcome the sickness, it can be due to one of seven different causes. If any of these causes are not corrected, then the person can die. The three main causes of death are as follows:

- The exhaustion of life force
- Previous deeds
- The exhaustion of merits

Death may be caused by one of these or a combination of two or three factors. Hence, seven different causes are possible from the three main ones.

If a person's life force is exhausted, we should do certain rituals or meditate on long-life deities such as Amitayus or Vijaya in order to restore it. If the person's previous bad deeds are causing his death, we should release animals that either are going to be killed or are dying. We can buy and release them so they can live. This will restore or replenish the dying person's karma.

If someone's merit is exhausted, we can replenish it through many means, like making offerings to the Buddhas and Bodhisattvas, reciting scriptures such as sutras, making offerings to the Sangha, making gifts to others, and making food offerings to various spirits of the world. We can also use any method that creates virtue, that replaces nonvirtuous thoughts with virtuous ones, or that obstructs any thought of nonvirtue in the mind. These are different methods to replenish our merit through which we can extend our life also.

If only one of the three factors—life force, karma, or merit—is exhausted, there are methods to replenish it and make sure the person will not die. If two of the three are exhausted, it is a little difficult, but still possible, to avert death. However, if all three are exhausted simultaneously, no method, even those possessed by the Buddha, will be able to avert death at that moment. So if someone dies even after different rituals have been done for him, this is the sign that the person died because all three causes occurred at the same time.

We should also see that three different types of karmic result can arise:

- The fully ripened result, meaning the result of the deed can appear in the present lifetime
- The result that is less powerful than the first and will arise only in the next lifetime
- The result that will not appear until at least three lifetimes after this one or very far in the future

So for a result to arise in this lifetime, a deed must have great power, and to produce a deed of great power, the person (object) to whom we are doing this deed must be someone special, such as a fully enlightened being. The motivation for doing the deed must be incredibly strong, and the article involved in the deed must be a special object. If either of these elements are not strong enough, then the result will arise in the next lifetime; if they are even less powerful, then the result can only arise after three or more lifetimes. Thus, it is very difficult to obtain a result quickly in this lifetime.

Sometimes we see that a person who has been virtuous in his lifetime is experiencing a lot of suffering, while someone who has performed a lot of nonvirtuous acts seems to be experiencing a lot of happiness. We should understand that the experience of suffering and happiness result from the deeds of one's previous life and not this one. Also, some people think that those who follow the Buddha's path will experience great suffering. We should understand that until the state of enlightenment is attained, everyone has to experience suffering. It is said that even the Arhats have to suffer, like Maudgalyayana (who was murdered) and another Arhat who died after eating grass ashes. This means that the practice of Dharma does not exclude us from experiencing suffering. Nonetheless, the methods employed in the Dharma are the best ones to destroy all our suffering completely from the result point of view.

Some new practitioners think that by making a few offerings in one day, they will have a night of good dreams or that something wonderful will happen to them. Some people practice sadhana for one or two days thinking they will meet one of the deities the next day. They may even think that one of the Buddhas will walk into their room and shake their hand to congratulate them on their meditation. For someone who has done just a little bit of virtue, the result cannot come so quickly. He does not have the causes or conditions for the result to arise.

On top of that, it is not good for results to ripen too quickly, because we commit a lot of nonvirtue through our speech and thoughts daily. If the results were to come too rapidly, we would experience a great deal of suffering very quickly. If we perform a little virtue and gain a fast result, the happiness will also disappear quickly. This would create more unhappiness in our mind. So it is actually better for a result to arise a little more slowly and at the proper time. We should not expect it to come too quickly; it has to arise through the proper causes and conditions.

The fact that the result of a practice cannot arise immediately is a sure sign of the infallibility of the law of cause and result. A result must arise from proper causes and conditions; if all the necessary causes and conditions do not occur simultaneously, then the result cannot arise. If we want a result to arise at an improper time, when all causes and conditions have not occurred, then the law of cause and result would not be correct, because the result could arise before the condition. For example, if we plant a seed and think that we should see the flower the same day or the next, this will not happen, because the causes and conditions will not be ready for that result. Also, if we are a little sick and think that we can overcome it immediately by performing a little virtue, it cannot happen; all the necessary causes and conditions will not have occurred.

The third aspect of the middle form of vow is to abandon the enlightenment thought due to fear of samsara. This means we give up our enlightenment though, because we are afraid of having to experience many great sufferings in this world. When someone harms us, we think we cannot return that harm in a peaceful way, and instead we want to harm him in return; that is how we abandon our enlightenment thought. Sometimes, for the sake of all sentient beings, we have to endure this world of existence for a very long time, and we are unwilling to do so. Any of these three thoughts can make us wish to give up our enlightenment thought.

In regard to our great fear of this world of existence and its suffering, we should understand that this world is, by its nature, not real. It has no existence, no true nature of its own. The world that we experience or perceive is just like a magic show. Since it is not real, there is no cause for us to fear it. By understanding the illusory nature of this world, we can overcome our fear of being in it.

If someone harms us, we should understand that by harming him in return, we will only create greater suffering. We must meditate carefully on returning any harm that we receive with compassion or loving-kindness, that through this we will be able to overcome the harm.

We may think that this world of existence lasts for a long time, and as it takes a long time to gain the stage of enlightenment for the benefits of others, we do not wish to stay here all that time. We should understand that "short" and "long" are just conceptualizations of the mind. They have no meaning of their own. The ideas of long or short periods of time are just ideas that we create through our own misconception. In reality, the concept of time is meaningless. By understanding this, we can abandon wrong thought and overcome our wish to give up the enlightenment thought.

We can also overcome this wish by praying to the great Bodhisattvas or deities. For example, one great Indian saint, Dignaga, at one point considered giving up his enlightenment thought. He prayed to Manjushri, who appeared to him. Through Manjushri's blessings, Dignaga kept his vows of enlightenment thought.

THE EXTENSIVE VOW   The third form of the vow of the enlightenment thought, the extensive vow, has three parts:

- The causes of producing the enlightenment thought
- The conditions to increase it
- The methods to overcome its destruction

The causes of the enlightenment thought are thoughts of loving-kindness and compassion.

The conditions for increasing the enlightenment thought are to rely on spiritual friends, to produce great faith in the Buddhas, and to understand the deeds—the nature and influence—of Mara and the ways to overcome them. To produce these conditions, we pray to the Buddhas and Bodhisattvas to help us, so we do not fall under Mara's influence. We also pray that we remember the benefits of the enlightenment thought, the faults of this world of existence, and the faults of nirvana or personal liberation. We also remember the various qualities of the Buddhas and Bodhisattvas, such as their miraculous powers, their supernatural cognition and knowledge. We also meditate on the idea that through the enlightenment thought we are able to bring benefits not only to ourselves, but to others. In this way, we are able to produce the conditions for increasing the enlightenment thought.

Methods to overcome the destruction of our enlightenment thought are necessary because we can destroy it in three ways:

- By losing faith in the Buddhas and gurus, and by creating anger or hatred toward the Buddhas or gurus. To overcome this, we should first create proper faith in the Buddhas and the gurus. Producing faith in the Triple Gem and the gurus obstructs any angry or bad thoughts about them.
- By being jealous of the prosperity of others. When we see others' prosperity, it creates jealousy in our mind, and this jealousy will harm our enlightenment thought. To overcome this, we should think about the prosperity of others with joy; whatever they have, we should be happy that they are able to obtain it.
- By thinking of benefiting only ourselves and no one else. To overcome this improper thought, we should meditate on cherishing others in place of cherishing ourselves.

When we do not know the qualities of the Buddhas or enlightened ones, we have no desire to obtain these qualities, so our enlightenment thought can be destroyed. To overcome this, we must understand Buddhas' and Bodhisattvas' qualities. Having understood them, we should engage in the various practices by which we will be able to attain them.

Entering Enlightenment Thought

What has been described so far are the rules related to wishing enlightenment thought. There are also three forms of the vow for entering enlightenment thought.

THE BRIEF VOW   The brief form for the entering enlightenment thought is basically the idea that we should abandon as much as possible, according to our capacity, all nonvirtuous deeds and accomplish all the virtuous deeds we can. Also, if by chance we perform any nonvirtue in the morning, we should confess it at night, and any nonvirtue that we do in the night should be confessed the next day. Whatever virtuous deeds we do, we should always dedicate the merit arising from them to our cause for gaining the state of full and perfect enlightenment for the sake of all sentient beings.

THE MIDDLE VOW   In regard to the middle form of the vow, there are four black dharmas:

- To deceive the Guru, the Triple Gem, or those who are worthy of receiving offering
- To tell those who practice virtue, especially those who practice the Mahayana path, that what they are practicing is wrong and thus make them regret what they have done
- To criticize the Bodhisattvas
- To deceive or trick sentient beings in this world

If we perform these dharmas, we will forget the enlightenment thought in the next life, and it will be spoiled. However, there are also four white dharmas:

- To not lie
- To call others to enter the practice of virtue, especially the Mahayana path
- To praise or create faith in the Bodhisattvas
- To wish to benefit other living beings

If we perform these dharmas, our practice of the enlightenment thought will continue to grow in the next life.

THE EXTENSIVE VOW   The extensive vow is to meditate again and again on the enlightenment thought, which acts as a cause to produce it. To create the conditions for increasing the enlightenment thought, we should recite any sevenfold prayers that we know three times in the day and three times in the night, as well as engage in the same deeds that the Buddhas or Bodhisattvas have done, deeds of giving and other virtues. Examples of such deeds can be found in the *Jatakas*, or life stories, of the Buddhas and Bodhisattvas.

The method for not spoiling the entering enlightenment thought according to the *Akashagarba-sutra* is to avoid the fourteen root downfalls of the Bodhisattva vows. Should we break the vows, we should confess.

One way to maintain our Bodhisattva vows is through reliance on our yidam, or special deity. The great Indian teacher Dignaga managed to keep his enlightenment thought by relying on Manjushri. Dignaga was born in southern India as the son of a powerful, rich king. When he grew up, he gave up his life as a prince and entered a Buddhist order that followed one of the Hinayana traditions. That tradition held the view that there was a self and that everyone possessed it, but Dignaga had heard that within the Buddhist tradition there was no self.

Nevertheless, being a monk in the monastery, he felt that he should not contradict the abbot who had mentioned the view of the self, because he himself might be wrong. To discover the existence of self, he created four new windows in his room and burned four more lamps at night. He examined his body very carefully to find where the self was. However, he could not find it. At times, he would even take off all his clothes and stand naked in front of a mirror to search his entire body. Some of the monks in the monastery saw him doing this and told the abbot about it.

The abbot called for him and told him that since he had renounced the world, he should act in the proper way and stop doing strange things. Dignaga then explained that he was trying to find the self and was thinking that his impure vision might be obstructing him from seeing properly what the abbot was talking about. So he had made new windows and burned more lamps, hoping to see it. Failing, he thought that his clothes might be obstructing his vision, so he took them off and searched carefully. Since he still could not find the self, he said that maybe the abbot's view of the existence of a self was not proper. The abbot told him that the other monks in the monastery had accepted his view, and as Dignaga was denying it and had a nihilistic view, he felt it would be better for Dignaga to leave.

Dignaga left the monastery and decided to go to the mountains of northern India to meditate. On the way, he met another prince who noticed the sign of a wheel on Dignaga's foot. The prince told him that if Dignaga were to become a king, he would be very powerful. He was willing to give half of his kingdom to Dignaga if the ex-monk would agree to join him. Dignaga told the prince that within the three realms of existence, there was no purpose in him ruling a kingdom or having worldly power.

Dignaga found a cave where he meditated and studied the various scriptures of the Buddha. During his study, he realized that the meaning of the Buddha's teachings were scattered throughout many books. So he decided to write a book to bring all the ideas together in a short, manageable form. Before he commenced his work, he wrote one verse in praise of the Buddha on the wall of his cave and stated his purpose in writing the book. Many wonderful signs such as earthquakes arose, and lights illuminated a wide area surrounding the cave.

In the same region, a Hindu scholar and meditator saw the signs. Being a good meditator, he saw through his supernatural power that Dignaga was writing the text in a cave. He realized that the book Dignaga was writing would cause great harm to the Hindu tradition. So whenever Dignaga went out on his alms round, the scholar would go to the cave and wipe off the verse on the wall. Every time he did that, Dignaga would rewrite it. This happened three times. On the fourth day, when Dignaga wrote the verse, he left a message inviting the person who had erased it to meet him and clarify the reason for doing so. When the Hindu went to the cave, he saw the message on the wall and remained until Dignaga came back.

When Dignaga returned to the cave, they debated on the proper view of ultimate reality. Dignaga won the debate and said that the Hindu scholar should give up his religion and embrace Buddhism. The scholar refused, and through his miraculous power, fire spat from his mouth and burned off Dignaga's hair and beard. Though the fire was so powerful that it burned the trees around them, it could not harm Dignaga, because he had produced the enlightenment thought. The Hindu scholar flew off and disappeared into the sky.

At that point, Dignaga considered that in return for what he had done for the Dharma, his hair and beard had been burnt. He thought that the scholar was only one person, and if there were many such people in the world and that was the kind of return he would get, there was no use in him gaining buddhahood for the sake of all those wretched sentient beings.

He wrote his intention to give up the enlightenment thought on a piece of wood and threw it into the air. He decided that from the moment the wood landed he would give up his enlightenment thought and never work for the sake of sentient beings again. But the piece of wood did not come down. When Dignaga looked up into the sky, he saw Manjushri holding the wood; he asked Manjushri why he was doing that. In return, the Bodhisattva asked him what he was doing, and Dignaga explained what had happened. Manjushri told him that he should not give up his enlightenment thought. He said that he would stay with Dignaga and act as his spiritual friend until he attained the first bhumi. Manjushri also told him that what he was writing was very good, and he should continue because it would be beneficial to many sentient beings.

His Holiness Sakya Trizin

The Nature of the Mind

One of the main teachings of the Buddha is the law of karma, the teaching that our lives are not without cause, that they are not created by other beings or by coincidence, but by our own actions. All the positive things we enjoy, such as loving relationships, long life, good health, prosperity, and so forth are also not given by anybody else. It is through our own positive actions in the past that we enjoy all these good things today. Similarly, all the undesirable things we encounter, such as short life, sickness, poverty, and so on, are not created by any outsider, but by our own actions, the negative deeds we committed in the past.

If we really wish to be free from suffering and experience happiness, it is important to work on the causes. Without working on the causes, we cannot expect to yield any results. Each and every thing must have its own complete cause; things do not appear from nowhere, from the wrong cause, or from an incomplete cause. So the source of all our suffering is our own negative deeds. Negative deeds result from not knowing reality, not knowing the true nature of the mind. Instead of seeing the true nature of the mind, we cling to a self for no logical reason. All of us have a natural tendency to cling to a self because we are so used to it. It is a kind of habit we have formed since beginningless time. However, if we carefully examine and investigate, we cannot find the self. If there is a self, it has to be either name, body, or mind. First, the name by itself is empty; any name can be given to anybody.

So too is the body. We say, "my body" just as we say, "my house, my car, my home, my country," and so forth, as if the body and "I" were separate. But if we examine every part of the body, we cannot find anyplace or anything called "I" or self. It is just many things together that form what we cling to as the body or the self. If we look at ourselves carefully from head to toe, we cannot find a thing called self. The body is not a self, because the body has many different parts. People can remain alive without certain parts of the body, so the body is not the self.

Neither is the mind. We think that the mind may be the self, but it actually changes from moment to moment. The mind is constantly changing, and the past mind is already extinct, already gone. Something that is already gone cannot be called the self. The future mind is yet to arise, and something that is yet to arise cannot be the self. Even the present mind is changing all the time, every moment. The mind of a baby and the mind of an adult are very different; these different minds do not occur at the same time. The mind is constantly changing; at every moment it is changing. Something that is constantly changing cannot be the self.

So apart from name, body, or mind, there is no such thing as the self, but due to long-held habits, we all have a strong tendency to cling to it. Instead of seeing the true nature of the mind, we cling to a self for no logical reason. As long as we do this, it is as if we are mistaking a colorful rope for a snake. Until we realize that it is not a snake but only a rope, we will have fear and anxiety. As long as we cling to a self, we will have suffering. Clinging to a self is the root of all suffering. Not knowing reality, not knowing the true nature of the mind, we cling to a self.

When you have a "self," naturally there are "others." The distinction between self and others depends on positing a self. Just like right and left, if there is a right, there has to be a left. Likewise, if there is a self, there must be others. When we have a self and others, attachment arises to our own side, to our friends and relatives, and so forth, and hatred arises toward others with whom we disagree, toward people who have different views and different ideas than ours. Three main poisons keep us in this net of illusion, or samsara: the ignorance of not knowing and clinging to a self, attachment or desire, and hatred. From these three arise other impurities, such as jealousy, pride, and so forth. When we have these poisons and impurities, we create karma, and when we create karma, it is like planting a seed in fertile ground, which will yield results in due course. We create karma constantly and are caught up in the realms of existence. To be completely free from samsara, we need the wisdom that can cut out its root, the wisdom that realizes selflessness. Such wisdom also depends on method.

Without the accumulation of method, wisdom cannot arise, and without wisdom, we cannot have the right method. Just as a bird needs two wings to fly, we need both method and wisdom to attain enlightenment.

The most important and effective method is based on loving-kindness, universal love, and compassion. From this arises *bodhichitta,* or the thought of enlightenment, which is the sincere wish to attain perfect enlightenment for the sake of all sentient beings. When we have this thought, then we naturally acquire all virtuous deeds.

However, we also need the wisdom that realizes the true nature of all phenomena, particularly of the mind, because the root of samsara and nirvana—indeed, the root of everything—is the mind. The Lord Buddha said, "One should not indulge in negative deeds; one should try to practice virtuous deeds; and one should tame the mind. This is the teaching of the Buddha." The fault lies in our wild mind; because of which we are caught up in samsara, or the cycle of existence. The purpose of the eighty-four thousand teachings of the Buddha is to tame our mind. After all, everything is the mind—it is the mind that suffers, that experiences happiness, that is caught up in samsara, and that attains liberation or enlightenment. So when the true nature of the mind is realized, all other outer and inner things are naturally realized.

So what is the mind? If we try to investigate where the mind is, we cannot find it anywhere. We cannot pinpoint any part of the body and say, "This is my mind." So it is not inside the body, not outside the body, and not in between the body. If something exists, it has to be of a specific shape or color, but we cannot find the mind in any shape or color. So the nature of the mind is emptiness. But when we say that everything is emptiness and doesn't exist, it does not mean that it does not exist conventionally. After all, it is the mind that does all the wrong things; it is the mind that does all the right things; it is the mind that experiences suffering; and so forth. Therefore, of course, there is a mind—we are not dead or unconscious; we are conscious living beings, and there is a continuous stream consciousness. Just like the candlelight that glows, the clarity of the mind constantly shines forth. The characteristic of the mind is clarity. We cannot find it in any form or in any color or in any place, yet there is a clarity that continues unceasingly. This is the character of the mind. Its two aspects—clarity and emptiness—are inseparable, just as fire and its heat are inseparable. The inseparability of the clarity and the emptiness is the unfabricated essence of the mind.

To experience such a state, it is important to go through the preliminary practices first. Through these practices, we accumulate merit. It is best to meditate on insight wisdom. For that, we need to prepare the present mind—that is, our ordinary mind that is constantly distracted by streams of thoughts. Such a busy and agitated mind will not be a base for insight wisdom. So first we have to build a base with concentration, using the right method. Through concentration, we try to bring the mind to a stable state, and on stable clarity and single-pointedness, we then meditate on insight wisdom. Through this, we realize the true nature of the mind. To reach this realization, we require a tremendous amount of merit, and the most effective way of acquiring merit is to cultivate bodhichitta.

So with method and wisdom together, we can realize the true nature of the mind. On the basis of that realization and increasing wisdom, we will eventually reach full realization and attain enlightenment.

⊹⇒ 9 ⇐⊹

An Interview with Sakya Pandita

The Buddhist Essence Teaching

I reverently bow at the feet of the holy guru! The glorious Sakya Pandita wrote the following responses to questions from Nyimo Gomchen, a contemplative filled with faith and spiritual aspiration, who applied himself earnestly to his practice.

Q. *What is the cause of renouncing this life?*

SAKYA PANDITA: It is the awareness that the cycle of existence is devoid of essence.

Q. *What is the contributing condition for such renunciation?*

SP: Seeing the faults of the cycle of existence.

Q. *What is the criterion for renunciation?*

SP: Mentally turning away from the eight mundane concerns.

Q. *What is the sign of renunciation?*

SP: Not being affected by the eight mundane concerns, even though one encounters them.

Q. *What is the criterion for attaining enlightenment in one life?*

SP: Liberating one's body from aging and death, and accomplishing the nature of the four bodies of a Buddha.

Q. *What is unspecified [neutral] action?*

SP: Action that cannot produce either good or bad results.

Q. *What is dedication of merit?*

SP: Something that transforms the causal roots of virtue into whatever result one desires.

Q. *What is prayer?*

SP: The yearning for bountiful results [of spiritual practice].

Q. *What is the meaning of "auspicious verses"?*

SP: Special words that produce good results by the blessing of truth.

Q. *In realizing the nature of the mind, is there a complete grasp of the meaning of the three collections of teachings and the four classes of tantras?*

SP: There are two realizations: realizing the emptiness of the mind, and realizing the union of apparent reality and the emptiness of mind. In realizing the emptiness of the mind, one does not fully grasp the meaning of the three collections of teachings and the four classes of tantras. With such realization, one may fully comprehend the Cessation of a Listener (*Shravaka*), but since that cessation falls to the extreme of emptiness alone, one would not grasp the meaning of the Mahayana teachings. This is stated in all the Mahayana sutras and tantras. In realization of the union [of apparent reality and emptiness], there is no blemish of even the most subtle faults. It therefore holds the basis of morality, and the collection of Vinaya is complete. Since the heroic samadhi and all other states of concentration arise [from such realization], the collection of

Sutra is also complete. Since it understands all knowable things, from form to the Omniscient Mind, the collection of Abhidharma is complete. And due to its comprehension of the special outer and inner dependently related events, the four classes of tantra are complete.

Q. *Are the Three Jewels complete in one's own mind?*

SP: In the mere emptiness of the mind and the understanding of that emptiness, the Three Jewels are not complete. In the union of the understanding and emptiness of the mind, the seeds of the Three Jewels are complete. If one properly realizes the meaning of that union, the Three Jewels are manifestly complete.

Q. *Is the supreme accomplishment (siddhi) attained due to the guru or to the meditation deity?*

SP: It does not occur because of either one separately. Rather, it occurs due to the guru, the meditation deity, the Buddhas of the three times, one's own mind, and the realization of the indivisibility of all of samsara and nirvana.

Q. *What makes a person one's true guru?*

SP: The person from whom one correctly receives the four empowerments in accordance with the tantras is one's true guru. A guru from whom one has not received such empowerment—however good a person he might be—is one's guru in name only. For example, the person from whom one receives monastic ordination is one's true abbot, but if one has not been ordained by that person, he is not one's true abbot. And even if he is called "Abbot," he is such in name only. That is the meaning of the following verse:

> Without bestowing empowerment, there is no guru.
> Without monastic ordination, there is no abbot.
> Without precepts, there is no continuum of virtue.
> Without going for refuge, one is not a spiritual person.

Q. *Is it possible for there to be hearing, reflection, and meditation concerning one utterance of the Buddha?*

SP: In relying on one utterance of the Buddha, one may practice hearing, reflection, and meditation. Such an utterance is an enlightened activity of a Tathagata.

Q. *Among all the teachings of the Buddha, which are profound?*

SP: With respect to the mentalities of individual disciples, all of the teachings are profound. On the other hand, only the tantric teachings are profound for all disciples.

Q. *Is a person who realizes the emptiness of the mind a Buddha?*

SP: One who has realized emptiness alone is not a Buddha. If one comprehends all knowable things, one is fully enlightened. Furthermore, there are two modes of comprehension: the comprehension that there is no realization of an ultimately (that is, inherently) existent phenomenon; and the comprehension of all distinct, conventionally existent phenomena.

Q. *Do you claim to be a realized person?*

SP: Since I have not ultimately realized any phenomenon, I do not claim to be a realized person. But since I know the five fields of knowledge concerning conventional truth, I claim to be a pandit.

Q. *Among your pupils, are there some who ascertain the nature of the mind?*

SP: I understand that among my pupils there is no one with ultimate realization of the mind, but there are many who are learned in conventionally existent phenomena. The mind being without [an inherent] nature, what is there in the ascertainment of the mind?

Q. *If one does not ascertain the mind, even though one accumulates merit, doesn't that [just] lead to temporary happiness?*

SP: If one does not realize the mode of existence of the mind—the meaning of emptiness—one cannot attain the joy of liberation by means of one's collection of merit. Although that may act as a cause for joy up to the peak of cyclic existence, the collection of merit is not perfected. On the other hand, if one does not have knowledge of knowable objects but only realization of the emptiness of the mind, how can one be a Buddha? If that were possible, there would be Buddhas in the Nirvana of Listeners, for which there is realization of emptiness alone, and there would also be Buddhas in empty space. But how could there be Buddhas there? Thus, the assertion of all the sutras and tantras is that buddhahood occurs through knowledge of all knowable objects and through realization that there is no inherent nature to be realized—that is, knowing that of which there is nothing to be known.

Q. *At what point does one have the certainty of attaining enlightenment?*

SP: Some people realize the emptiness of the mind alone but have not perfected the qualities of the method aspect of the training. Some have such qualities but do not realize the emptiness of the mind. Some have both, but they are not able to guide their practice of the method with their knowledge. Some have the other qualities, but since they lack the lineage of blessing, they are unable to generate the clear appearance. Thus, I fear that buddhahood is far from them. Since I have a number of these attributes, I hope to attain enlightenment, but not by the swift means.

Q. *Who is your root guru?*

SP: My root guru is the great Sakyapa Dragpa Gyaltsen, the Vajradhara, who is the nature of the body, speech, and mind of all the Tathagatas of the three times.

Q. *For what reason is he your root guru?*

SP: He has granted me the four empowerments of the vase and so on; he has shown me the four paths of the Stage of Generation, and so on; he has set forth the dependent relationships of the four bodies, including the emanation body. In short, since he practices in accordance with the

Buddha's teachings in the sutras and tantras, he performs the deeds of a perfectly enlightened being; thus I regard him as my root guru. On the other hand, one who does not grant empowerment according to the Buddha's teachings, does not reveal the Path, and does not set forth dependent relationships but does ascertain the mind is limited in his teachings to those leading to the Cessation of a Listener, regardless of whatever merit he accumulates. Such a person is not fit to be regarded as the root guru of a Mahayana practitioner, for that path is not a Mahayana path. Thus, from the treatise called *Synthesis (sDud pa)* comes, "With Wisdom alone, without the Method, one falls to the state of a Listener." Those who give little emphasis to the method and great emphasis to wisdom slip down to the Nirvana of the Listener.

Q. *Which path to enlightenment is shorter, that of a learned pandit, or that of a kusulu?*

SP: In general, the term *kusulu* is not correct. *Kusali* means "a virtuous person." There are kusalis who do not rely on the Buddha's path, and there are also pandits who do not rely on that path. None of them become Buddhas. There are both pandits and kusalis who are Buddhists. Among them are both pandits and kusalis following the vehicle of the perfections who attain buddhahood, and it takes them three countless aeons to do so—a long time. There are also tantric pandits and kusalis who internally establish certain dependent relationships and thereby swiftly attain enlightenment.

It is said that the task of a pandit is to become learned in the outer and inner fields of knowledge and that a kusali supremely devotes himself to inner practice after discarding all external affairs. To attain perfect enlightenment, one first becomes knowledgeable regarding all knowable objects and cuts through false assumption by means of hearing and reflection. Then, by taking samadhi as one's essential practice, one cuts through false assumptions by means of meditation and thus achieves the dharma of insight. In this way, one gradually attains enlightenment. Therefore, it is necessary to be both a pandit and a kusali. In terms of those approaches taken separately, the pandit is closer to buddhahood. One might object to that, citing the sutra *Mound of Jewels (dKon mchog brtsegs pa)*:

"If one meditates for one moment, the merit from this is greater than that of listening and explaining to others for ten aeons." I think there is no contradiction here. The meaning of that citation is that meditation [has such benefits] if one already knows the object of meditation, but without such knowledge, how could there ever be such benefits? The Vinaya scriptures also state that one should not meditate in a hermitage without having understood the collections of teachings. The *Treasury of Phenomenology (mNgon pa mdzod)* also states, "Endowed with proper hearing and reflection, Devote yourself to meditation." Aryadeva says, "Without relying upon conventional reality, One will not realize ultimate reality. Without realizing ultimate reality, One will not attain Liberation." All the sutras frequently say that by hearing certain points of Dharma, one is liberated from certain obstacles. Therefore, if hearing and reflection liberate one, one is advised to meditate afterward.

It is wonderful that you dwell as a contemplative, and I think it would be good if you continue in your efforts on the path of the tantric method. I realize that there is no realization of the answers to the question of this realized person (that is, yourself). I understand that there is no understanding, and I know that there is nothing to be known.

This concludes my responses to the questions of the contemplative Nyimo Gomchen.

10

Acharya Lama Migmar Tseten

The Five Aggregates

According to the Abhidharma teachings, all things are classified into two groups, conditioned and unconditioned. All conditioned things are then classified into the five skandhas. Here, *conditioned* means those things that are created due to causes and conditions—that is, that are interdependent and cannot arise on their own.

Skandha is translated as "aggregate" or "collection." All conditioned things are included in the five aggregates, because in samsara the five aggregates are the basis of projection of "I" as the subject and "my" as the object. For example, when one refers to oneself as "I am such and such," that refers to the person; when one refers to a thing, such as "my car," that refers to the object. So these dualistic interactions between the five aggregates perpetuate action (karma) and defilement.

If we study conditioned things further, we may find them to be either material or nonmaterial. In the nonmaterial, we find either mental or nonmental. Thus, in the five aggregates we find matter, mind or mental activities, and neither material nor mental things. In these five skandhas, we study all conditioned things.

In Sutra, the teachings given by the Buddha, we may find different synonyms for the conditioned things. Sometimes in the sutras, a synonym for a conditioned thing is *time* (or *period*), in the sense that there are three times—past, present, and future—in which all conditioned things have appeared, are appearing, or will appear. A second synonym is *basis of talk* (or *basis of discourse*), which means that all these conditioned things are bases to which we give different names so that we can talk about them. A third synonym is *separation* (or *renunciation*), in the sense that to achieve complete freedom from suffering, or nirvana, one must renounce attachment to conditioned things. A fourth synonym is *cause* (or *basis*) because all conditioned things are clearly due to causes and conditions.

In the sutras, we also find a few synonyms for defiled things. The first is *defiled aggregate,* which means all those aggregates that are conducive to the increase of defilements. The second is *battle* (or *war*), because the defilements are always injurious to oneself and others. The third synonym is *suffering,* because it is the result of defilement, and the fourth is *origin of suffering,* which refers to defilement as the cause of suffering. The fifth synonym is *world,* which in Tibetan is *jigten;* the literal meaning of *jigten* is "the object of decay." The sixth synonym is *basis of misunderstanding,* which refers to defiled views based on some wrong understanding, and the seventh is *existence,* which refers to the cyclic continuation of birth and rebirth.

The first aggregate is called *rupa skandha* in Sanskrit and may mean "form," "body," or "matter." I prefer to use "matter" here as the most appropriate translation and call this the aggregate of matter, which includes the five sense organs, the five sense objects, and invisible form. The aggregate of matter is defined as "that which is formed with atoms." The sense organs are the eyes, ears, nose, tongue, and body. These organs are atoms put together in different shapes, which can produce respective consciousnesses when met with the sense objects. The sense objects are form, sound, taste, smell, and tangibles.

Form includes the four basic colors of blue, yellow, white, and red, and the eight secondary colors of cloud, smoke, dust, mist, shade, sunlight, lights other than sunlight, and darkness. Because they appear and dissolve quickly, the secondary colors are enumerated to clarify that the first four are substantial. Ordinarily, we think that light and the object on which it falls are the same. To emphasize that they are different forms, the next four are mentioned. Form also includes eight shapes—long, short, square, round, high, low, even, and uneven. Whenever we see a visual object, we see its color and shape. Although there are countless things in the world, the eye can recognize individual items by their color and shape.

The sense object of the ear comprises eight different sounds. First are sounds produced by sentient beings that express meaning and those without meaning; next are natural sounds produced by wind, water, and so on, also with or without meaning. Each of these four sounds are further divided into sweet and harsh categories.

The sense object of the tongue can be divided into six tastes: sweet, sour, salty, pungent, bitter, and astringent.

The sense object of the nose includes four smells. There are good and bad, and both of these can be mild and strong.

The sense object of the body comprises eleven tangibles. The solidity of earth, humidity of water, heat of fire, and motion of air are called cause tangibles, because all the tangibles are based on these four elements. The other seven tangibles—smoothness, roughness, weight, lightness, cold, hunger, and thirst—are called result tangibles, because they are created by an imbalance of the elements. For example, one feels hunger when there is more air and less earth, and feels thirst when there is more fire and less water.

Because form and sound are not consumed by their sense organs, these sense objects can be shared by many eyes and ears. Thus, many people can see the same things and hear the same sounds. Because the other three objects of smell, taste, and tangibles are consumed by their respective sense organs, they cannot be shared. So whatever anyone has smelled, tasted, or touched cannot be shared by another.

Invisible form is the eleventh enumeration of the aggregate of matter. This is upheld only by the realist Vaibhashika school of Buddhism. It interprets self-liberation vows as an example of invisible form. Whenever one takes precepts to discipline one's physical and verbal wrong actions, like killing and lying, one produces an invisible form with the following characteristics. It is with the mind at every moment, even when the mind is distracted or in deep absorption. By nature, this form is either good or bad. It is produced, maintained, and developed by the four elements. Furthermore, it remains continuously with the mind.

The second aggregate is called *vedana* in Sanskrit, and I prefer to translate it as "sensation." This aggregate is defined as "that which dependently experiences the qualities of the objects." According to the experiences based on body and mind, sensation is enumerated into pleasure, pain, happiness, unhappiness, and indifference. The first two are physical experiences, and the next two are mental experiences. The last refers to both physical and mental experiences. All physical experiences come from interactions with outer objects, whereas mental experiences come from different thoughts. All agreeable physical experiences are included in pleasurable sensations, and all agreeable mental experiences are included in happiness. All disagreeable physical experiences are included in painful sensations, and all disagreeable mental experiences are included in unhappiness. While agreeable and disagreeable physical and mental experiences translate into four categories, indifferent physical and mental experiences fall into one, because indifferent sensations are experienced independently. Indifferent sensations do not react like others that are experienced according to the benefit and harmfulness of the object. All sensations can be categorized as agreeable (happiness and pleasure), disagreeable (unhappiness and pain), and indifferent (neutral) by nature. Sensation also comprises six sensations according to the experiences of the six sense organs.

The third aggregate is called *samjna* in Sanskrit, which I prefer to translate as the "aggregate of ideation." This aggregate is defined as "that which grasps the characteristics of the object." Whenever any object appears to a sense organ, in that first moment, there is no grasping. We grasp an object that is past. Whenever we meet a new person, in the first moment, without any known information, we cannot grasp that person. It is only afterward that we form a perception about that person based on his appearance, which is his shape, color, name, or the words he spoke. So we form a mental image of objects based on their appearance and other characteristics. From those mental images or existing knowledge, we make judgments and react based on our defiled condition, which is the formation of the idea by grasping an object's characteristics. Ideation is based on apparent objects or invisible names, words, and known information.

The fourth aggregate is called *samskara* in Sanskrit; I prefer to translate this as the "aggregate of formation." This aggregate is defined as "those conditioned things not included in the other four aggregates." Included here are all the mental activities, except sensation and ideation, as well as the fourteen dissociated formations that are neither mind, mental activities, nor material things. According to *Abhidharmakosha*, forty-four mental activities are included in the aggregate of formation, which is the detailed study of a person's psychology.

The fifth aggregate is called *vijnana* in Sanskrit and is translated as the "aggregate of consciousness," which is defined as "that which is aware of each object." There are six consciousnesses of eye, ear, nose, tongue, body, and mind. According to the study of skandha, ayatana, and dhatu, the mind is called *vijnana, manas,* and *citta,* respectively. Mind is also called *vijnana* in the skandhas to refer to the six consciousnesses only in the present; *mana* and *citta* refer to them at other times.

11

Khenpo Appey Rinpoche

Awakening Buddha-Nature

It is said that in order to practice the Mahayana, one must belong to the *gotra* (lineage) of the Mahayana. According to these teachings, all of us naturally have a gotra. The point is whether this gotra has been awakened in our mind; for some, it has been awakened, while for others, it has not.

There are four signs to show that our gotra has been awakened:

When we have faith in the Triple Gem—the Buddha, the Dharma, and the Sangha

When we have compassion for other sentient beings

When we have abandoned harming others and have patience no matter what arises

When we have a great desire to do virtuous deeds and accomplish virtue

We can define the word *gotra* as "Buddha-nature," or the "cause of buddhahood." It means that all sentient beings, from beginningless time, have the seed of enlightenment. However, there are four categories of unfavorable conditions or obstructions to the awakening of this gotra within us:

When we are completely under the power of the defilements so that whatever we do, we are controlled by hatred and desire. There is no thought of practicing the Dharma.

When we are under the influence of bad friends and teachers. These people will give bad advice and be an evil influence. Under such circumstances, we will not be able to turn our mind to the Dharma. A bad teacher who teaches the wrong path leads us away from the true teaching and obstructs us from going to other teachers who teach the true Dharma.

When we are in poverty, without food, clothing, shelter, and other basic necessities. This completely obstructs us from entering the Dharma.

When we are under the power of others and do not have any independence to think freely for ourselves. A great Indian scholar said that when a person was young, he was under the power of his parents; he was not allowed to think for himself. When he grew to become a young man, he came under the power of his spouse. Later, when he became old, he came under the power of his children or grandchildren. He was never truly free to do what he wished to do.

In all these cases, no matter who we are, we do not have freedom, and this obstructs the awakening of the Buddha-nature within us.

Different Buddhist traditions discuss the idea of gotra in different ways. For example, the Chittamatra (Mind-Only) school teaches that there are three or four types of gotra. We can enter into the gotra of either the Arhats, the Pratyekabuddhas, or the Buddhas and Bodhisattvas. In addition, some say there is a gotra that is devoid of gotra, that some living things have no gotra and that they can never enter into any of these three paths to gain any form of enlightenment. However, the Madhyamaka (Middle Way) school does not accept this idea of people without a gotra. It says that everyone has a gotra. Temporarily, one has the gotra of Arhat, Pratyekabuddha, or Bodhisattva, but ultimately everyone will enter the final path of buddhahood. Nonetheless, the Madhyamaka accepts the idea that this world of existence is endless, inexhaustible. Indirectly, it is tantamount to saying that some people will never get out of this world of existence.

Two stories illustrate the difficulty of awakening the gotra within us. The first is about Angulimala, whose name means "the one who wears the garland of fingers." It happened during the time when the Buddha

Shakyamuni was in the kingdom of Sarvasti, whose king was Kusananji. In that place, there was a great scholar who had many disciples. One day the king summoned the scholar to the palace. The scholar left one of his disciples, Angulimala, behind to keep watch over his house and his wife. Because of his beauty, the scholar's wife greatly desired Angulimala, and when the scholar and his disciples were away, she approached the young man in a very alluring way. However, the boy told her that she was like a mother to him, and he would not have anything to do with her. To avoid her, he ran away.

The woman became very distressed to hear his rejection. She tore her clothes, scratched her body in many places, and beat herself with a stick. When her husband returned home, she complained that Angulimala had done all that to her while his master was away. The scholar believed her and decided to destroy the boy. But he thought that since Anguli-mala was very clever, a special method would be required to destroy him. So the scholar called Angulimala back and told him that it was through his actions that the boy had lost his place in the Brahmin caste and that he would never be able to gain liberation or rebirth in heaven unless he rectified it by killing a thousand people. At first, Angulimala refused to do it because he felt that it could not be right. But the scholar convinced him that he must believe the man who was teaching him how to gain proper understanding of worldly things.

Believing what his teacher said, the boy went out and killed a thousand people. He went back to tell his teacher what he had done, but the scholar replied that he had to show proof by cutting off a finger from each person he had killed, stringing the fingers into a garland, and wearing it around his neck. The boy went out again and killed another 999 people.

At that time, his mother, who had been worried by his absence for many days, went searching for him. When Angulimala saw his mother coming toward him, he thought that he would kill her and make her his thousandth victim. He believed he would then be able to gain his own rebirth in heaven and also put his mother in heaven by killing her. So he drew out his knife and approached her.

The Buddha Shakyamuni, who was in the vicinity, had perceived what was happening through his omniscience. He saw that it was the right moment to place this boy on the Dharma Path and to awaken his enlightenment thought. So the Buddha approached the boy and began to walk in front of him. Angulimala found the Buddha's appearance very wonderful and called to him to stop. He asked the Buddha who he was and how he had the audacity to wander in front of him. The Buddha replied that he was the fully awakened one. He continued walking in front of Angulimala, who asked him to stop; he now intended to kill the Buddha. Shakyamuni said that he was standing still and not moving anywhere; he was always in the place where no one would ever harm anyone else. That was the place where he stayed, and Angulimala must go and stay in such a place. That was the place where he would have the patience never to harm another living being. The Buddha told the boy that by now he should have realized that he had been tricked into following the wrong path, which would lead to great suffering, that he was even about to kill his own mother who had, out of great kindness and compassion, come to help him.

Speaking thus, he was able to tame the boy's mind and convince him that he was on the wrong path. Angulimala took refuge in the Buddha and asked to become a monk, to which the Buddha acceded. Through the Buddha's teaching, which awakened his seed of virtue, Angulimala became an Arhat at that moment. He rose up to the sky and flew to the city of Sarvasti.

There, the king was preparing his army to kill Angulimala because of what he had done. When the soldiers saw their prey coming down from the sky, they were scared and ran away. They reported to the king that Angulimala had come. The king then decided to ask the Buddha for advice regarding the murderer. The Buddha told him that Angulimala had gained the enlightenment of an Arhat and that the king need no longer be afraid of him. The king wondered why, if the Buddha had the great power to help Angulimala gain the state of arhatship, he had not done it before Angulimala had killed all those people.

The Buddha explained by asking the king about the five hundred people who worked for him as bird hunters. He asked why the king did not stop them from killing when he had the power to do so. The king thought that observation was quite right and told all his hunters to stop killing birds from then on; the punishment for breaking his order would be death.

The five hundred hunters got together and decided that the order did not apply to their sons. So they ordered their sons to go out to kill the birds. As they belonged to the gotra of slaughterers, they were not able to give up the idea of nonvirtue. They would force their children to kill when they were not able to do so. This story shows that they were so steeped in their nonvirtues that no matter what was done for them, nobody could stop their nonvirtuous actions and awaken their gotra. However, it is said that the Buddha then performed a miraculous manifestation in front of them and gave them a teaching, and due to that, they were able to correct their thinking and stopped themselves and their sons from further killing. So we can see that through the kindness of the Buddha, it is possible to awaken the gotra. This illustrates the point that there are many people who do not have the power at this time to awaken the gotra of enlightenment within themselves.

The second story is about a young Chinese boy whose family decided to send him to a temple one day. They told him that he was going to a temple that had many different images of the Buddha, Avalokiteshvara, and others, and he should look at them carefully and learn to identify them. However, the boy did not like to do that. In fact, he had a great dislike for any images of the Buddhas or Bodhisattvas. So before entering the temple, he blindfolded himself to make sure that he would never see any of the images when he walked inside. No matter how much his parents tried to force him, he just refused to look.

Later, they thought of a way to overcome this. They put an image of the Bodhisattva Avalokiteshvara inside a vessel, covered it, and put it in front of the boy. They told him that he must open the vessel and see the image of Avolokiteshvara; he should take it out and look at it. The boy was very angry. He took a piece of cloth and tied it around his eyes and ears so that he could not see or hear. Having wrapped his hand with another cloth, he picked up the vessel and threw it away. He had such a great dislike for the Buddha and his teachings that he would do anything possible to stay away, even to the extent of avoiding seeing the Buddha's image. This illustrates the difficulty of awakening the gotra within oneself.

12

Khenpo Appey Rinpoche

The Five Paths to Enlightenment

It is not absolutely necessary to teach the five paths of the enlightened beings as well as the ten stages of enlightenment, because we do not have the level of realization to understand the teaching. However, to explain the path to enlightenment properly, we should know about it. Just as when we wish to travel to some other country, we want to know about its climate, customs, and so on so that we can prepare properly. In the same way, the five paths and ten stages of enlightenment are taught so that we may accustom ourselves to the path we undertake. It is for this reason that it is necessary to teach these aspects of the enlightenment path.

The five paths refer to the path that we must traverse to gain enlightenment.

The Path of Accumulation

The first path that we must travel is the path of accumulation, which is the idea we have when we begin to meditate on selflessness. In other words, the path of accumulation and the meditation on selflessness are merged together.

The five paths are taught differently in the Mahayana and the Hinayana schools. According to the Mahayana teaching, there are three paths of accumulation—the small path, the middle, and the great path. If we meditate on or progress along the small path of accumulation, there is no certainty as to when we will arrive at the second of the five paths (the path of application). If we follow the middle path, there is a definite time when we will reach the second path. And if we follow the great path of accumulation, we will gain the path of application in this lifetime, with our present body.

In stating who is able to gain this first path, the Hinayana teachings say that only a male or female human being of this world can do so. No other living being, such as a god, an animal, or a human being who does not have the proper organs is able to gain this path. According to the Mahayana, other sentient beings in this world besides humans are able to gain the path of accumulation.

There is also a question as to whether it is necessary to have a mind that can be placed in concentration meditation in order to gain this first path. It is said that it is not necessary, because even those within the realm of desire who cannot perform concentration meditation have been able to accomplish this path. Another question is whether it is necessary to have a mind that can go into different states of dhyanas, or meditative trances. It is said that some people whose minds have not achieved any of the dhyanas have gained the path of accumulation. So it is not necessary for the mind to enter either of these states of meditation to accomplish the path of accumulation.

When we are motivated by compassion to take the vows of the enlightenment thought and begin to practice in accordance with it, we have then entered into the path of accumulation and must perform many practices. To carry out these practices, we should have five special qualities. Actually there are many different qualities, but they can be combined into five principal ones.

The first quality is to have proper moral conduct. This means that we maintain the vows that we have taken either as a monk, a nun, or a layperson.

The second quality is to maintain the proper use of our senses through wisdom and method. This means that whatever we are relating with through our senses—such as forms through our eyes or sound through our ears—we see through the door of wisdom that they are really of the nature of emptiness. Here, method means that whatever we do in this life, we are always purifying all our actions into a quality of enlightenment. For example, when we walk down the street, we purify this act by thinking, "As

I walk down this street, may all sentient beings enter into the path of enlightenment," or when we close a door, "May all sentient beings close the door to the lower realms." In this way, we purify the objects that we encounter with our senses.

The third quality is not to have great attachment to food, meaning that we do not become attached to food or eat because we desire it. In other words, we have a proper perception as to why we are eating food. We should think that we eat to benefit or feed the different types of worms in our body, or that we eat to sustain our body and make it a proper vessel for the practice of Dharma. With these thoughts, we have a proper idea of why we are eating and do not create great attachment to the food we have; we also eat in moderation.

The fourth quality is not to sleep excessively. Instead, we should devote some of our waking hours, like the early part of the night and the early part of the morning, to the purpose of meditation. With a stable and steady mind, we might meditate on the impurities of the human body; on the four states of mindfulness of body, sensation, mind, and Dharma; and on the various aspects of the enlightenment thought.

The fifth quality is to have conscientiousness, or awareness of what should be done and what should not be done. This means that we have not only mindfulness, but also awareness. When we are involved in a certain deed or actions, we should know what is a proper deed and what is an improper deed, which has faults and which has benefits. We should know it at the time the deed is being done, not before or after, and then act in accordance with that proper understanding.

These are just some of the qualities we must have in practicing the path of accumulation. It is said that when we reach the stage of the great path of accumulation, we are able to gain certain forms of miraculous or supernatural power by which we can even go to different buddha realms to receive or listen to the teachings of various Buddhas and Bodhisattvas.

The main practices within the path of accumulation are listening to or studying the Dharma and contemplation. There are also some practices pertaining to meditation within this path, but the principal practices primarily deal with study and contemplation. The Sanskrit word for accumulation is *sambhara,* which means that we must practice virtue again and again in order to accumulate the virtue or merit by which we will really gain the path. This is the main practice within the first path of accumulation.

The Path of Application

The second path is the path of application, which refers to the mind that meditates on emptiness or selflessness. At this stage, we do not yet have the actual realization of emptiness or selflessness; however, we have a thought or a concept of selflessness. Actually, when we consider this thought or idea, we work with it, meditate on it. This is known as the path of application. Just as we can meditate on the things we know about a certain place even if we have not been there, we can now work on the meaning behind the realization of emptiness or selflessness even though we have not yet had the realization. This is what we work with at this path of application.

The three paths of application—the small path, the middle path, and the great path—are similar to those of the path of accumulation. When there is no definite time as to when we will gain the next path (the path of seeing), that is known as the small path. The middle path means that there is a certain or definite time when we will gain the next path, and the great path means that we will gain the path of seeing in this lifetime, with our present body.

The path of application can also be divided into four parts: heat, foremost, patience, and the highest Dharma. Based on the accumulation of merit achieved on the first path, we begin to meditate on emptiness. Before we have the realization of emptiness, it is like before we start a fire; heat starts to appear, and as the heat increases, the fire bursts out. In the same way, before we really have the actual realization of emptiness, our meditation is like the heat that arises before that state bursts upon us. It is like a lesser form of meditation on emptiness. When we are able to begin to produce this heat, which will later blaze into the correct meditation on emptiness, it is known as the first stage of the path of application.

When our meditation on emptiness and the heat arising from it increases, even though we still do not have the realization—in other words, when our mind is being steadied in that type of meditation—this is known as the foremost.

Then when we are able to increase our level of meditation and have no fear of the meditation on emptiness, we have patience toward the meditation itself. It has become bearable and not something of which we are afraid any longer. This is known as patience.

When we are able to overcome any form of fear through our meditation on emptiness—meaning we overcome different types of conceptualization that arise to obstruct us from gaining this realization—then we get to the fourth stage, which is known as the highest, or most excellent, Dharma. However, our realization of emptiness is still not achieved at this stage. We have accomplished all the different types of worldly dharmas but not the transcendental Dharma of the state of realization of emptiness. Everything up to this stage has been accomplished.

According to the Hinayana (ordinary) teaching, anyone in this world of existence who is born as a man or woman with proper organs and anyone within the first six heavenly states of the realm of desire is able to gain the path of application. According to the Madhyamaka or Mahayana teaching, there are others who are also able to obtain this path.

It is said that only those who have gained one of the four states of dhyana, which is divided into six types of meditation found in the realm of form, can accomplish or dwell within the path of application. According to the Hinayana, we realize the nature of the four noble truths within this path. Each of the four noble truths has four aspects, such as the aspect of selflessness, resulting in sixteen aspects that are realized at this time.

According to certain Mahayana teachings, such as the Mind-Only school, during the first two parts of the path of application (that is during heat and foremost), there is a realization of nongrasping toward external objects, or of objective reality. At the time of patience and the highest Dharma, there is a state of nongrasping toward internal subjective reality.

Some teachers, such as Nagarjuna, said that when a person meditates while in the path of application, there is no separate arising of realization such as nongrasping of object and nongrasping of subject. Though the realization of emptiness is not complete, the wisdom arising from the meditation on emptiness increases through these four aspects of heat, foremost, patience, and highest Dharma. This actually produces a more stable understanding of the meditation of emptiness, though it is not completely realized.

The Hinayana says that the third path of application, patience, has three aspects—the small, the middle, and the great—but each of the other three paths has only a single aspect. According to the Mahayana, each of the four paths have the three aspects of small, middle and great, so there is a total of twelve different levels or stages within the path of application.

The Sanskrit for the path of application is *prayogamarga*. *Pra* means paramartha, i.e., "ultimate truth" or "ultimate reality." *Yoga* means "to join" or "to unite." So prayogamarga is the path that unites with ultimate reality. In other words, the path of application or uniting is the meditation that will join us with the realization of the stage of ultimate reality, which arises at the third path (the path of seeing). Through the path of application, all the requisites and the joining of them for the realization that will arise at the next stage are accomplished.

The Path of Seeing

The path of seeing is seeing the nature of the four noble truths, realizing the nature of ultimate reality, and awakening within our own mind the Transcendental Wisdom that directly perceives the nature of all phenomena. This path can be classified as three types—the Hinayana type, the Pratyeka Buddhayana type, and the Mahayana type. To accomplish the path of seeing, we must relinquish the approximate cause and then the cause itself. The approximate cause means that if desire is created, it needs to be abandoned, and then we need to destroy the cause of desire. Generally, this cause is classified as what needs to be abandoned in relation to seeing and what needs to be abandoned in relation to meditation.

What needs to be abandoned on the path of seeing are the ten defilements: the six basic defilements of desire, hatred, pride, doubt, ignorance, and wrong view, the last of which comprises the five secondary defilements. Each of these ten relate separately to the three realms of existence—the realm of desire, the form realm, and the formless realm— and to the four noble truths. According to the *Abhidharmasamuchaya*, or the Abhidharma teaching of the Mahayana, there are 112 different aspects to be abandoned; according to the *Abhidharmakosha* of the Hinayana, there are eighty-eight.

According to the Mahayana, at the time of meditation on the path of seeing, the stage of the first bhumi arises; that is, the path of seeing is equated with the first bhumi. What needs to be abandoned can be divided into two parts: the obscuration of the afflictions or defilements, and the obscuration of knowable things. These need to be destroyed in order to gain, first, liberation and then full and perfect enlightenment.

Also at the time of meditation on this path, the realization that arises completely destroys all the obscuration of the defilements. The obscuration of knowable things can be divided into two sections: what should be abandoned in relation to seeing, and what should be abandoned in relation to meditation. The first of these is also destroyed at the time of meditation.

According to the Hinayana, any male or female within this world of existence, as well as any gods within the first six lower heavenly realms, are able to gain the path of seeing. According to the Mahayana, the animals and other beings are also able to attain this path.

To gain this stage, we must first of all be able to gain some form of samadhi; based on that samadhi, we are able to gain realization into the path of seeing. According to the Hinayana, the first dhyana has three parts and the remaining three have one each. So there are six forms of meditation or dhyana we can achieve. We only need to have gained samadhi of one of the six before we can gain realization. However, the Pratyekabuddhayana and the Mahayana say that we must gain meditation of the fourth and highest form of dhyana before we can gain realization.

The Hinayana says that on the path of seeing we realize the four noble truths as the objects of meditation, and based on this, we proceed to realize there is no self in relation to the person. We see that the personal "I" is selfless. In addition to this realization, the Pratyekabuddha also realizes the objective aspect of the selflessness of all phenomena. The Bodhisattva has both of these realizations, as well as a complete realization of emptiness—the subjective aspect of the selflessness of all phenomena, which is the mind that perceives all phenomena. In other words, a complete realization of emptiness.

According to the Hinayana, all phenomena are empty individually. According to the Mahayana, all phenomena, both the personal self and external phenomena, are completely void of any true nature. In other words, the empty nature that completely transcends all conceptualization or mental creation is completely realized on the path of seeing.

The Sanskrit word for the path of seeing is *darshanamarga,* which means "to see something for the first time," to see the truth of the four noble truths and the emptiness of all phenomena in the proper light. The Mahayana says that by obtaining this path, accordingly one gains the first bhumi and becomes a first-stage Bodhisattva, or noble one. The Hinayana tradition does not have the concept of the ten bhumis; however, the realization that arises on the path of seeing turns one into an Arya, or noble person. Unlike the Mahayana, the Hinayana says there are different forms of noble persons who gain different types of realizations.

The Path of Meditation

The fourth path is the path of meditation. Having realized ultimate reality on the path of seeing, one must meditate on it again and again to make it a habitual pattern in one's mind so that it really becomes a part of one's being. There are two types of meditation for this path: worldly and transcendental (or unworldly). In the worldly type, there are meditations on the four dhyanas related to the realm of form and the four dhyanas related to the formless realm. There are seven preparatory steps for each of the dhyanas. When these steps have been accomplished, the respective dhyana, or state of meditation, is accomplished. To make the mind firm and establish a proper state of meditation within it, each, if not all, of these worldly meditations must be accomplished in order to achieve the path. This teaching on the different states of meditation related to the two realms is very important, and many commentaries have been written on it.

The transcendental type of meditation occurs when one accustoms the mind to the realization on the path of seeing. In that path, when the realization of emptiness arises, it arises only during meditation, and the meditator can see it only at that time. However, all the states in the path of meditation have two aspects: when one is sitting in meditation and after one comes out of the meditation. At the time of the path of seeing, the realization of emptiness only arises at the time of meditation and not after.

The transcendental path of meditation seeks to habituate the mind to the realization of emptiness so that it stays in the mind not only during meditation, but also during one's daily life. This is meditated on and can be seen in relation to the three different schools—the Hinayana, the Pratyekabuddhayana, and the Mahayana. According to the common path teaching (i.e., all three schools), fourteen different aspects must be abandoned at this time to accomplish the path of meditation.

It is said that someone who is born in this world of existence as a male or female and anyone who is born within the six lower realms of desire can achieve this path. Within the realm of form and the formless realm, someone who has not fallen into the state of Brahma but has gained a meditative state known as the state of perception, which arises at the fourth dhyana, may also attain the path of meditation.

According to the Hinayana, we must have accomplished the six dhyanas or samadhi in order to gain the path of meditation—the first dhyana (which is divided into three), together with the second, third, and fourth, as well as the first three stages of the meditative state of the formless realm. Someone who has gained samadhi of all these can gain the transcendental path of meditation. According to the Pratyekabuddhayana and the Mahayana, merely attaining the four dhyanas is sufficient.

The Sanskrit word for the path of meditation is *bhavanamarga,* which means habituating the mind again and again. According to the Mahayana, each of the ten bhumis has two aspects: the realization that arises during meditation and the realization that arises after meditation. At the first stage of enlightenment (bhumi) on the path of seeing, only the first aspect is accomplished; one sees the emptiness of all things only during meditation. The subsequent attainment arising from that meditation does not occur until one has gained the path of meditation, which includes the second part of the first bhumi up to and including all ten bhumis. So the meditative states and the subsequent attainments within the ten bhumis are accomplished within the path of meditation.

The Path of No More Learning

The fifth path is called the path of no more learning, or the path of complete accomplishment. This means that the result and path have merged, and the result one is seeking is gained here. For example, if one is practicing the Hinayana path, at this stage, one gains what the tradition defines as the complete path of accomplishment; one becomes an Arhat. If one is practicing the Pratyekabuddhayana and accomplishes this fifth stage, that person is known as a Pratyekabuddha. According to the Mahayana, this stage is known as the stage of buddhahood.

According to the Hinayana, anyone who is born male or female in this world, anyone living in the six lower heavenly realms of the realm of desire, and anyone in the realm of form or formless realm who has not been born as Brahma can attain this path. The Pratyekabuddhayana says one must be a human being. According to the Mahayana, one must not only be a human being, but must also be born in Jambudvipa (the southern continent of this world of existence) and belong to one of the two higher classes of Brahmin or Kshatriya.

The Hinayana says that to gain the path of no more learning one must have attained the six dhyanas and any of the first three meditative states of the formless realm. According to the Pratyekabuddhayana and the Mahayana, one must have gained the fourth dhyana.

It is said that in the path of application, when one arises from the meditation on the highest Dharma, one actually flows into the realization of the path of seeing. In other words, one sees the true nature of all dharmas. In the same way, at the stage of the tenth bhumi, one practices the seeing meditation of the tenth bhumi and accomplishes the attainments that come after that, that the various qualities in relation to these two are meditated upon again and again until the qualities are completely accomplished. When they are completely accomplished, in a natural flow, if one enters into the next stage of meditation, which is known as the samadhi that is like a diamond (*vajra*), and then arising from that stage, one actually gains complete buddhahood.

The path of no more learning is known in Sanskrit as *nisthamarga*, which means that all the qualities of enlightenment are completely gained. There is no further need to study or meditate or accomplish anything.

13

Khenpo Appey Rinpoche

The Ten Bhumis to Enlightenment

The word *stage*, or *bhumi*, means the level of attainments. The teaching on the bhumis is presented differently in the Hinayana and Mahayana traditions. The Hinayana says eight levels of bhumi can be attained. Within the Mahayana, however, the stages of the bhumi are divided into two parts: that of ordinary worldly people and that of the enlightened ones, which comprises the ten stages of the Bodhisattva path.

The reason the Bodhisattva path has only ten stages is that although the realization of ultimate reality arising from each of the ten stages is the same, the quality arising from the subsequent practices is varied. To gain the qualities of these practices, the practitioner must accomplish the ten perfections, which relate to the ten stages of the Bodhisattva path. Also, because the Bodhisattva must take different births and engage in different practices, there are ten qualities to be gained and ten things to be relinquished.

Each of the ten stages of bhumi has something that must be abandoned and something that must be gained. For example, by gaining the first stage of the Bodhisattva path, one is always free from all suffering such as old age, sickness, disease, and especially the five types of fear:

Fear of where one is going to get one's food

Fear of death

Fear of being born in the lower realms

Fear of being criticized or blamed

Fear of the different things that people are talking about

There are many different qualities to be obtained at the various stages, and they can be classified into twelve different attainments. At the stage of the first bhumi, each of the attainments are increased a hundredfold. For example, a person gains the attainment of having a special type of body, and with that body, he can emanate one hundred different bodies at one moment. Also, each of these hundred bodies will have one hundred disciples listening to the teaching; one is able to see one hundred Buddhas at the same time. The person is even able to perform miracles in one hundred different realms, or world spheres, at the same time.

With the second bhumi, the attainments are similar, but the number is increased to one thousand, and with the third bhumi, it increases again to ten thousand. So there is a progression in the number of people one can liberate or how many bodies one can emanate at each stage.

The word *bhumi* literally means "earth" or "ground." Sometimes, it is translated as the ten earths, the ten stages, or the ten grounds. It is used to illustrate the stages of the Bodhisattva because just as the earth is able to support and hold many animate and inanimate things, the ten bhumis are able to maintain the many qualities obtained by the person who gains the different stages of enlightenment.

From the Dharma point of view, the essence of the word *bhumi* means the stages of realization that combine the understanding of the true nature of all phenomena with compassion for all sentient beings. In other words, when the wisdom of the realization of emptiness and compassion are merged, this is the stage of enlightenment.

The first bhumi is known as "the joyful stage," because those who have gained this realization know definitely that they will be able to attain full and perfect enlightenment. They know that they will gain great benefit for themselves and also be able to help many sentient beings through their realization. Thus, their minds become very happy and joyful.

The second bhumi is called "the stainless stage," or freedom from impure moral conduct. The emphasis at this time is on the perfection of moral conduct, through which one is able to gain freedom from faults.

The third bhumi is known as "the issuing of light rays," which refers to being able to teach the Dharma to many people. Such teaching is similar to light rays going out to all the world.

The fourth bhumi is called "making light rays," which refers to the increase in one's realization of Transcendental Wisdom. Although this stage is basically the same as the third, one has a more thorough realization of the ultimate wisdom.

The fifth bhumi is known as "the purification of difficulties," which means that when a person is working for sentient beings, it is generally very difficult because whenever he does good for others, he always gets something bad in return. When one tries hard to work for other sentient beings, one has to face many problems. However, the Bodhisattva who has attained this stage and has effortless, purified activities does not encounter any difficulty working for sentient beings.

The sixth bhumi is called "direct manifestation." This refers to the stage of the real perfection of wisdom. One actually comes face-to-face with wisdom at this time and directly perceives that the wisdom and one's mind are merged.

The seventh bhumi is known as "going to a far distance," which means that the practitioner has gotten past all the grasping toward duality, past the discriminating mind that is always judging different things as male, female, white, blue, and so on. At this stage, one has gone beyond all the discrimination and the mind does not grasp at the subject/object duality anymore, so it has gone a great distance.

These first seven stages are called the impure stages of the Bodhisattva because there is still a form of grasping in the mind during each of them.

The eighth bhumi is known as "the unshakeable (or unmovable) stage." This means that the enlightened mind no longer needs to conceptualize or create mental thoughts. When the idea of conceptualization has been overcome, the mind is placed in an unshakeable state.

The ninth bhumi is "good intelligence," which means that the mind has gained a pure state of realization or intelligence. The four qualities of transcendental intelligence arise at this point.

The tenth bhumi is known as "the cloud of Dharma." Just as a big cloud filled with water can rain over big areas, the person who has attained this stage has the ability to remember everything about the Dharma. His mind is like a huge cloud that holds all the dharmas and all the different types of samadhi.

⊱ 14 ⊰

Chogyal Phakpa

The Gift of the Dharma
to Kublai Khan

Chogyal Phagpa (1235-1280 C.E.) accompanied his uncle, Sakya Pandita, to the Imperial Court of China. After many years in that country, he was eventually appointed ruler of Tibet and became the personal guru of the Mongol emperor Kublai Khan.

A long-standing custom of Buddhist masters was writing out advice for rulers. In 1271, Chogyal Phagpa composed a short verse for the emperor titled "Divisions of Advice to the King" ("rgyal po la gdams pa'i rab byed" in Tibetan), which is called "The Gift of the Dharma to Kublai Khan" here.

Four years later, Chogyal Phagpa revisited the basic text presented here and composed two supplementary texts: a concise topical outline (bsdus don) and a long commentary (rgyal po la gdams pa'i rab tu byed pa'i rnam par bshad pa gsung rab gsal ba'i rgyan) titled "The Ornament Clarifying the Discourses."

The following text sets out the view and tenets of both the Hinayana and Mahayana schools and can be seen as a brief summary of the whole of the Buddha's teaching. It begins with a discussion of civil law; moves to a discussion of the Dharma; covers all the topics of the four tenet systems, as well as the basis, path, and result explained in Mahayana Buddhism; and concludes with a brief discussion of the three kayas.

TO THE INCOMPARABLE ENLIGHTENED ONE, who is endowed with the splendor of fame in name and the splendor of wondrous virtues in actual fact, I offer homage.

Although you, mighty emperor, know already the discourses on worldly and spiritual science, still, as with the songs and music of musicians to which you listen again and again even when you have heard them all before, why shouldn't a poet repeat wise words?

All of the countless teachings of Dharma taught by the Sage for the sake of countless disciples are, indeed, meant to be practiced. But how may this be done?

Just as a man bound by fear and shame would not disobey his king's command, but dwell in right conduct without harming others and, as a result, would ever grow in good fortune and even earn the praises of his king, so too with a person who accepts, in accordance with his ability to accomplish them, the rules of discipline enjoined by the Sage to help beginners on the Hinayana and Mahayana paths. If, after properly receiving vows from an abbot, that person would then guard them because he is bound both by fear of seen and unseen sufferings in worldly existence and by shame whenever he reflects, "The multitudes of Noble Ones who know the thoughts of other beings will be shamed if I break my vows, . . ." as a result, he would become a foundation not only of seen and unseen joys in worldly existence, but of the virtues of perfect liberation; he would also become a worthy object of veneration for men and gods and even receive the praises of Buddhas.

After all, these three realms of existence are just suffering, while nirvana too is just peace. Looking with pity, therefore, on those who wish for either worldly existence or nirvana, it is the Buddha alone who, himself free from sorrow, removes sorrow and who, having himself attained great joy, bestows joy. He has appeared from among beings like ourselves.

The methods he used we can also use. Without timidity and laziness, therefore, you should unwaveringly aspire to win highest enlightenment and feel free to think, "I must surely attain buddhahood." Guard as your own life the vows you have made which, if violated, will cause you to be burned in hells and which, if preserved, will enable you to experience truly wonderful results in proceeding from joy to joy even now.

Since the three sets of vows—of the Hinayana, Mahayana, and Vajra-yana paths—are the foundation from which all virtues may arise, remain, and grow within oneself and others, try from the very first to be firm in their observance.

Become certain that the teaching, which is virtuous in its beginning, middle, and end, and whose words are quite flawless and not contradic-tory to the two logical proofs of valid knowledge, is the unique spiritual way among ways.

Know, too, that the Enlightened One who taught it is endowed with unhindered wisdom and great compassion—since he revealed [the truth] without closed-fistedness—and also with tremendous power.

Because they are his followers and a gathering of beings with virtues similar to his, and because your own sphere of spiritual activity is iden-tical to theirs, know the noble assembly of Bodhisattvas to be the best field for increasing your merit.

Realizing that it is your preceptor who points out and introduces you to these Three Jewels, that he is endowed with the same virtues they have, and that he sustains you with kindliness, always attend and medi-tate upon him with unflagging faith.

Since they are like yourself in having the nature of being endowed with the causes of pain and with a constant state of unsatisfactoriness, and like yourself, moreover, in wishing themselves to be free from un-happiness and its causes, you should unceasingly meditate great com-passion for all living beings.

Recalling the benefits of virtue that you will need in order to attain highest enlightenment and to achieve others' good as well as your own purposes, strive wholeheartedly and with genuine devotion to acquire it. In brief, since a mind endowed with faith, compassion, and devotion is the precursor of all spiritual accomplishments, perform every least virtue with these three present.

Envision the body of the Enlightened One either in front of you or as your own body, and visualize that your dwelling place is a buddhafield wherein all beings are Conquerors surrounded by Bodhisattvas and dis-ciples. Then worship yourself and others with oceans of offerings con-sisting of the enjoyment of the five sense objects.

Realize that your own virtuous preceptor and all the Conquerors are truly equal and nondual in form, activity, and essential nature. At all times, you should envision him in front of you, seated atop the crown on your head, or within the lotus of your heart, and pray to him or meditate upon him as being nondual with yourself.

Of virtue, nonvirtue, pleasure, pain, and all the phenomena of samsara and nirvana, mind is the substratum.

If you were to examine that mind thoroughly from every angle, you would realize that it has neither color nor shape, nor is it single or manifold. It therefore has no nature; it is not arisen, nor does it remain or cease. It is devoid of both center and periphery, and is thus away from all extremes. It has just the nature of space.

Even so, cognition is not stopped. Hence, mind has the nature of nondual cognition and emptiness.

As one's own mind is, so too is the nature of all beings' minds. Understand thoroughly that all phenomena are nondual appearance and emptiness, and place your mind in meditation without grasping.

Through meditating nondually on the two objects [one's preceptor and the Enlightened One] and objectlessness [emptiness], you will attain a superior meditative state of tranquil concentration (*shamatha*), which cannot be disturbed by thoughts.

Joyfully remembering that every act of virtue or nonvirtue increases the strength of one's virtuous or nonvirtuous inclinations, always bring virtues to mind and strengthen them.

You should especially recollect and analyze the support, form, and experience of your meditation whenever you have meditated upon an object. Through examining further the interdependent origin of their causes and conditions, however many they may be, you will attain meditative insight (*vidarshana*) through realizing the true state of their suchness—that is, that no support, form, or experience whatsoever exists.

Following the performance of virtues, you should gather together all the merit acquired through that [meditation and the like] and fully dedicate it to the attainment of perfect enlightenment for yourself and all these countless beings.

Even though transferable merit may not have been acquired at the time you offer prayers, your wishes will nonetheless be fulfilled if you pray for a great purpose to be achieved; mind alone is chief. Every virtue that is adorned by this kind of recollection, dedication, and noble prayer will increase unceasingly and eventually become the cause of great good for oneself and others.

Everything that is experienced and all other conditioned things (*samskritadharma*)—that is, the five aggregates, the senses, sense objects, and sense consciousnesses—are devoid of any nature of their own because they all depend upon causes and conditions.

You should know, therefore, that these external objects, which appear in various forms to and are experienced by mind that is stained by mental impressions, also are not real. They are like magic shows that appear due to a variety of causes; they are also like dreams that occur during sleep.

The "unconditioned dharmas" (*asamskritadharma*) are simply ascriptions. A person would have to be mad to wish to propose meaningless names for them or to indulge in thoughts about them and thereby accept them as "conditioned dharmas."

Never scorn the connection between deeds and their results, for [the teachings on] the interdependent origin of cause and result as it operates in the sphere of relative truth are not deceptive. You will experience the ripening results of your actions.

There are "eternalists" in whose view the substantiality of phenomena is accepted. However, no object whatsoever exists that is devoid of [both] direction [that is, dimension] and time [that is, consciousness]; if you were to analyze the forms of direction and space, you could not possibly find a single entity [that is not reducible to its component parts]. And if a single entity does not exist, whence could "many" appear? As there is no existence other than these, the concept of "existence" itself is an inferior one.

Just as there is no long without short, how could a nature of nonexistence be apprehended when even a nature of existence is not obtained?

Know, intelligent one, that the real also does not consist of "both" [existence and nonexistence), because this possibility has been removed by the rejection [of each individually]. Nor does it consist of being "neither" of the two, because there is no logical proof for this possibility, and in any case, there is no possible "bothness" to which it could be an alternative.

But if we were to conclude that "Mind alone is real since it is formless and thus has no directions," [we would have to admit that] it also becomes plural and false if subject and object are identical, the latter being manifold.

If, however, subject and object are different from one another, how then do objects become objectified and mind subjectified? If the two arise dually, in what way [simultaneously or otherwise] do they appear? Finally, what kind of liberation is achieved merely by rejecting illusory external appearances?

Since the object is not established as real by nature, the subject is not established as real either. The claim that there somehow exists a pure consciousness apart from these two is as extremely wrong as the Sankhya philosophers' notion of a "self" (*purusha*) distinct from the transformations of primal nature (*prakrter vikara*).

Be free from supports, knowing that all phenomena from the first are unarisen, natureless, away from extremes, and like space.

Marvelous and much more wondrous than any wonder is this knowledge that does not relinquish the emptiness of all dharmas nor stop the process of interdependent origination!

Realize that objects are the nonduality of appearance and emptiness, that mind is the nonduality of knowledge and emptiness, and that the paths to liberation are the nonduality of methods and wisdom. Finally, act [in accord with this insight].

The stages of cause, path, and result should be understood thus: the interdependent origination of the relative sphere is like illusion; in the ultimate, the nature of dharmas is emptiness; finally, both are nondual without differentiation.

Thus, if the foundation [morality], preparation [reflection], meditation, conclusion [dedication of merit and recollection], and process of practice taken as a whole are each multiplied by three [in correspondence to the three stages of cause, path, and result], all the paths of virtue are gathered together in fifteen factors.

Whoever strives to perfect these [fifteen] factors in each performance of virtue enjoys the happiness of fortunate states and accumulates oceans of the two collections [merit and transcendent wisdom].

Through the clarity of his meditation, he becomes joined with the Aryan path and increases in transcendent wisdom as a result of his meditation and noble conduct. Then, attaining the goal [of buddhahood] through coursing along the final stages of the Path, he puts an end to all thought constructions by realizing the nature of mind to be pure from the very beginning. [His mind] becomes one with the *dharmadhatu* and is transformed into the *svabhavikakaya*, which is the transcendent wisdom of dharmadhatu and the knowledge of the perfection of renunciation.

For him, the dharmas of worldly existence become transformed through the practice of the Path so that his body becomes the body [of an enlightened one] adorned by [112] marks and signs of perfection. His voice becomes [the voice of the Buddha], endowed with sixty tones; his mind is transformed into transcendent wisdom and is also endowed with omniscience. Passions are transformed into the boundless virtues of the Conqueror and constitute the *sambhogakaya*. His deeds are transformed into the "task-accomplishing wisdom" and the countless kinds of enlightened activity that form the nirmanakaya.

These five wisdoms constitute the perfect realization of the Enlightened One, and inasmuch as he is also endowed with spiritual power, they are unending and uninterrupted. May you also, O emperor, become like him!

Through the merit of offering this gift of Dharma, which summarizes the deep sense of the noble Path, may all living beings with you, O king, as their chief, quickly attain the highest stage of enlightenment.

My own mind too has become encouraged by composing these lines as a gift of doctrine, and so I shall speak further of another matter. Undistractedly hear it, O Lord among Beings!

The time when you should make efforts is now: make firm the good fortune you have, ensure long life and the success of your lineage, and practice right methods to gain liberation.

It is right to make efforts without distraction. At a time when Dharma has not yet set like a sun and a religious king like yourself sits on the throne, how can your mind remain indifferent to the plight of those who wear saffron robes?

Though I am not old, the strength of my body is slight and my mind inclines to be lazy; therefore, I wish to be excused for a while that I may seek Dharma's meaning in solitude.

—Translated by Acharya Lobsang Jamspal and
   Acharya Manjusiddhartha.
   Copyright Victoria Buddhist Dharma Society, 1976.

⊹ 15 ⊱

Khenpo Appey Rinpoche

The Perfection of Moral Conduct

The perfection of moral conduct is the thought to abandon all nonvirtuous deeds. The way to accomplish this is to engage in moral conduct for the sake of liberating all sentient beings and to create the Mahayana view of ultimate reality. When the enlightenment thought and the view of ultimate reality are conjoined with moral conduct, it becomes the perfection of moral conduct. Ordinary worldlings and those of the Hinayana path have moral conduct. However, they cannot perfect it because they do not create the enlightenment thought and the view of ultimate reality.

There are three ways to spoil moral conduct:

Not guarding the moral conduct we have promised to uphold

Following the wrong type of moral conduct, such as that of other religious traditions

Practicing the moral conduct of the Hinayana path, which does not become the cause for gaining full and perfect enlightenment because it does not have the potential for gaining full and perfect enlightenment

If we spoil our moral conduct, the outcome in this lifetime will be that everyone will criticize or talk against us in many ways. Also, we will feel ashamed when we go in front of our teacher, sit with other members of the Sangha, or receive offerings from others, because when we know that our moral conduct is not pure, it creates a kind of cowardice or timidity. We feel very small when we receive an offering. Not only will other people criticize and blame us, but the nonhumans will create obstacles or harm us, the gods who once protected us will no longer do so, and the Buddhas and Bodhisattvas will not be pleased with us.

The effect of spoiled moral conduct on the next life is that we will be reborn in one of the lower realms. Even if we listen and study the Dharma well, it will not stop us from being born in a lower realm, because we have not upheld proper moral conduct. Practicing properly is what will help us avoid the lower realms.

Engaging in the ten nonvirtuous deeds will cause our rebirth in a lower realm. Even if we do not perform the ten major nonvirtuous deeds but engage in some of the minor ones, we may still be reborn in the lower realms. Engaging in the moral conduct of other religions or practices is also a cause of rebirth in the realm of existence. By practicing the moral conduct of the Hinayana, we can gain nirvana, but it is still a personal nirvana, not perfect enlightenment, so it still has faults.

There are four causes of spoiling or destroying moral conduct:

To be ignorant of what the moral conduct is

To not have proper respect for or proper devotion to the rules of moral conduct

To be careless in the maintenance of moral conduct

To engage in various defilements

Of these four, to engage in the defilements is the strongest or most forceful.

There are two methods for overcoming the defilements. We can destroy the defilements one by one as they arise. For example, whenever we are engaged in a certain defilement, such as anger, we counter it at that instant by meditating on loving-kindness or compassion. Through loving-kindness or compassion, we are able to overcome the thought of hatred. Or if desire arises, we can counter that by meditating on the ugliness or impurities of the body. So as each defilement arises individually, we can overcome it with a specific meditation.

We can also destroy the defilements at the root, which means that we meditate on the selflessness of the person. That way, we are able to destroy all the defilements simultaneously before they arise.

The Bodhisattva should engage in three types of moral conduct:

Abandon all nonvirtuous deeds.

Accomplish virtuous deeds.

Work to benefit all sentient beings

To Abandon All Nonvirtuous Deeds

There are two classes of moral conduct for abandoning all nonvirtuous deeds:

The taking of the Hinayana or the pratimoksha vows

The taking of the Bodhisattva vows

There are two classes of Hinayana vows: one for those who renounce the world and one for the ordinary lay practitioner who is not a monk or a nun.

There are five classes of lay practitioner. The first is the layperson who takes the vow of refuge in the Triple Gem. Some people in this class also take the first of the five precepts and promise never to kill any sentient being. Such a person is known as the one-vow layperson. The two-vow layperson also takes the second precept, the vow of not stealing from others. Some people also take the third precept of not lying, and others also take the vows of not performing sexual misconduct and not becoming intoxicated. Someone who has taken refuge and all five of the precepts is known as a complete layperson (*upasaka*). The taking of the five vows also includes upholding the ten virtuous deeds; the complete layperson must promise to abandon the ten nonvirtuous deeds along with the actions of the five precepts.

The second class of lay practitioners, in addition to taking the five basic vows, take the vow of celibacy even though they remain laypeople. Such a person is called a *brahmacharya upasaka*, one who has the pure conduct of a celibate in addition to the other vows.

Lay practitioners in the third class take the eight precepts for their entire lifetime, rather than for one day; they are known as eight preceptors. Both the brahmacharya upasaka and the eight preceptor are different from other laypeople in that they take the vow of celibacy. They are also different from monks or nuns, as they do not take all the vows for full ordination. Members of these classes are therefore called half-renounced or half-unrenounced.

When a layperson, a monk, or a nun takes any of these vows and also has the Mahayana enlightenment thought of wishing to liberate all sentient beings, it is known as the Mahayana pratimoksha vow, or the Mahayana moral conduct vow. If the other vows are not taken with the enlightenment thought of the Mahayana and are simply conjoined with the thought of one's own personal liberation (the Hinayana enlightenment thought), then that is a Hinayana pratimoksha vow.

Whatever practice one does, it is important to begin with a vow. If one does not take a vow, one's practices of virtue will not have the strength or the cause to produce enlightenment or omniscience. For the Bodhisattva path, one can take the vow of either the Middle Way or the Mind-Only school. Or, as just described for the Hinayana pratimoksha practice, one can take the vows of a layperson, a monk, or a nun.

There are three different types of practitioners of moral conduct:

One who has taken the vow of moral conduct and practices accordingly

One who is always engaged in nonvirtuous deeds

One who is somewhere between these two

The person who upholds moral conduct and practices is known as one who is holding the moral conduct. Someone who never practices moral conduct is just like a slaughterer who engages in killing every day. The middle person is one who performs virtuous deeds but who does not take a vow of moral conduct. Without the vow, the practice of virtue is weak and is not a cause for liberation or buddhahood. For example, if the person who has taken the vow of not killing thinks, "I will not kill any other person," every moment that he is engaged in the act of not killing, he is producing virtue because this engagement in the deed of not killing is based on the mind that seeks to abandon nonvirtue. However, if someone does not kill but has not taken the vow of not killing, that by itself is not a virtuous deed, because he does not have a mind that seeks to abandon nonvirtue. Based on that kind of neutral mind, not engaging in nonvirtuous acts does not produce virtue. The person who has taken the vow of abandoning killing, who has the mind to abandon killing, and who avoids killing in his daily life accumulates virtue because he maintains his vow of not killing.

We must therefore have a vow through which we create the thought that we will not engage in nonvirtuous deeds. As long as we continue to avoid such deeds, we are producing virtue.

To train in moral conduct, it is necessary to start from a small thing and then increase it. We can do this based on the object toward which we practice. For example, on the first day, we make the vow to not kill any person. Once we understand that we can accomplish that, we increase the object to include a certain class of animals, then to another class of animals, and so forth. Similarly, if we vow not to steal, we can decide first that we will not steal from our family members. Once we understand that we are able to accomplish this, we vow that we will not steal from our neighbors. We continue to increase the object toward which we are practicing abandonment of the specific nonvirtuous deed.

We can train in avoiding nonvirtuous deeds based on time as well. We vow to avoid them for a short period, then for one day, and then for increasing spans of time. We can also train based on the nature of the vows. We can accept just one vow in the beginning, then increase it to two, then three, and so forth.

If we happen to spoil our moral conduct vow, we should restore it by confessing our nonvirtuous deeds. If we perform a nonvirtuous deed in the morning, then we should confess what we have done before we go to sleep at night. If we perform a nonvirtuous deed at night, then we should confess the next morning before we even take any food. If we are always conscientious about confessing, we will be able to become good Dharma practitioners. The Buddha said there are two types of people who uphold moral conduct—those who never spoil their moral conduct, and those who spoil it and then confess.

To Accomplish All Virtuous Deeds

The second Bodhisattva moral conduct practice is to accumulate virtue, which means to practice moral conduct and abandon the unfavorable conditions or forces that obstruct the accomplishment of virtuous deeds.

For example, if we listen to or study the teachings of the Buddha, this is a virtuous deed. However, the negative force of laziness may obstruct us. Understanding that we are being lazy, we should abandon it and continue in our study. This abandoning of laziness is also a virtuous deed and makes the force of our study much greater.

Similarly, taking refuge in the Triple Gem is a virtuous deed, but experiencing a lack of faith in the Triple Gem may obstruct us. To overcome this lack of faith, we create a proper respect and devotion to the Triple Gem. Overcoming our lack of faith becomes a virtuous deed, which strengthens our refuge and keeps increasing our virtue. Therefore, the accomplishment of virtue means not only doing virtuous deeds but also destroying all the forces that obstruct the performance of those deeds.

To Work for the Benefit of Sentient Beings

In the third Bodhisattva moral practice, working for the benefit of sentient beings, we abandon any unfavorable conditions or obstructing forces that will not allow us to help others. This may even include the abandonment of the first two Bodhisattva moral conduct practices. For example, an ordained person may abandon the four major vows, if by doing so he could accomplish greater benefit for sentient beings; however, by breaking any of the vows, such as refraining from killing, he loses his vow of renunciation.

The perfection of moral conduct involves four qualities and the abandonment of seven different attachments. In relation to the practice of giving, four qualities arise when we practice giving, and through this, we abandon the seven different attachments. The same process is used here and also in the other perfections.

There are great benefits in upholding moral conduct. In this life, for example, we will never regret whatever deeds we do. Also, our mind will be happy and able to produce various states of samadhi, so we will experience the realization of wisdom. Our conduct will also create joy in the hearts of others, so other people will be happy in seeing us; they will praise us and put us on a higher level. We will even become objects of offerings from others. Therefore, many great benefits arise from the maintenance of moral conduct.

The performance of moral conduct in this lifetime will help us gain rebirth in the higher realms of humans and gods. When we have been born in these higher realms, we will possess seven special qualities, such as a higher station, prosperity, wisdom, power, long life, beauty, and freedom from disease.

The ultimate result of moral conduct is the attainment of buddhahood. The manifestation of the qualities of moral conduct in the Buddha's character makes him famous. So fame is a result of the perfection of moral conduct at the time of buddhahood. Also, the Buddha need not hide anything in the behavior of his body, voice, or mind in order to make people think that he is holy; worldly people like us have to resort to hiding certain behaviors to make others think we are good.

To illustrate the point that sometimes we have to ignore the Bodhisattva practices of upholding vows and accomplishing virtue, Rinpoche tells one story about a Brahmin named Karma and another about a ship's captain who possessed great compassion.

A long time ago, when people were able to live thousands of years, there was a Brahmin by the name of Karma who renounced the world and became a monk. He went to live in a forest to meditate and stayed there for forty-two hundred years, meditating diligently and well.

He then went to a nearby town and lived in the king's palace. One day, the daughter of a trader who came to the palace saw him and was very attracted to him. So she went to Karma's room and told him she wanted to marry him. The monk told her that she should not speak in that manner, as he had renounced the world. The girl replied that if he got up and left her, she would kill herself when he took his seventh step. The monk decided that since he had renounced the world and taken his vows, he definitely could not stay with the girl. So he stood up and started to leave.

As he was about to take the seventh step, he thought that if the girl killed herself in his room because he took that step, it would not be good, because people would think it very strange. Moreover, killing herself would be a great harm to her. He felt that she should be an object for his great compassion, even if he had to break his vows and go to the hells as a result. It was better that he should save the girl than to save himself. He thus turned back and accepted her as his wife.

After living with her for twelve years, he again renounced the world and went on to practice for a long time. It is said that he was reborn in a heavenly realm. The idea here is that instead of gaining any type of bad result through a specific deed, he accumulated a great amount of virtue through his wish to benefit someone else. There was no nonvirtue in the act of renouncing his vows, and he was thus able to gain a good result. The Brahmin Karma was the Buddha Shakyamuni in one of his previous lives.

The second story is about a ship's captain. At one time, there were five hundred traders who had gone to many islands to search for jewels and treasures. Having had a successful trip, they began to sail back home. One of the crew saw the jewels that the other traders had collected and conceived a plan to kill all of them and take the jewels for himself. The captain of the ship was a person of great compassion. He came to know the man's intention to kill the other traders, so he tried to think of different methods by which he could stop him. However, no good plan came to mind. The captain thought that if the man were to kill all the traders, the result would be his rebirth in the hells for a long time. Having compassion for the man, the captain decided that if he were to kill the would-be assassin, that man would not need to suffer in the hells, although the captain would suffer instead. With this thought of exchanging his own happiness for the suffering of the others, the captain killed the man.

It is said that instead of being born in the hells, the captain accumulate the same amount of merit as someone who has spent nine aeons practicing virtue. So instead of being a negative deed, the killing became a great deed. As in the first story, the ship's captain was the Buddha Shakyamuni in one of his previous lives.

According to the Hinayana tradition, we should never destroy the four main vows of an ordained person—avoidance of killing, stealing, sexual misconduct, and lying—because by destroying them, we destroy ourselves. However, the Mahayana tradition says that if we are motivated by a proper thought of compassion and by the enlightenment thought, it is acceptable to destroy the four vows if it is necessary to benefit others. There is no fault involved. In fact, it is necessary to act in such a way.

⇥ 16 ⇤

Khenpo Appey Rinpoche

The Perfection of Patience

Rinpoche here discusses the third of the six perfections, the perfection of patience, which means not getting angry even when someone uses harmful actions, thoughts, or speech against us. If this type of patience is conjoined with the thought of saving all sentient beings from this world of existence and with the view of ultimate reality, then it becomes perfect patience.

The obstacles to patience are anger and hatred that arise due to an agitated or disturbed mind. If we do not practice patience, the anger that arises will bring great misfortune in this lifetime, as well as in many lifetimes to come. In this life, our body can become so disturbed that it gets sick, and our mind can become so unhappy that we are unable to think properly. We are not able to sleep well at night and are always consumed by the burning thought of overcoming our enemies. Hatred means we are always thinking of ways to harm our enemy, so our mind is never happy and can even become unbalanced, leading us to madness.

When we have great hatred, we are never trusted by others, who will not like the way we think or act. For example, if we have great hatred in our mind and still give many gifts, the person who receives the gifts will not trust us. The recipient will think that we are harboring hatred toward him, that we must be trying to trick him, that the gifts are not going to be of benefit to him, and that we might actually be trying to destroy him. Also, others who are close to us will not be happy when we are always flaring up in different stages of anger. Even our gifts will not bring them happiness, but mistrust and unhappiness. Anger or hatred does not bring about satisfactory relationships.

Some people think that becoming angry will bring them benefits, but there is never a time or place where this is true. If we practice the Dharma and also have anger and hatred toward other Dharma practitioners, then we are not recognized as Dharma practitioners. For example, if we are with our teacher or with other students and always show anger toward them, they will not think of us as part of the Sangha, but as someone who does not even practice the Dharma.

Even an ordinary householder who is full of hatred or anger will produce great unhappiness among the people around him. No one will trust him. Similarly, if two spouses are always arguing or showing great anger toward each other, their relationship can get so bad that they cannot even speak to each other, but must talk through their children. The situation can degenerate to an extremely low level due to hatred and anger.

The consequences of hatred in future lives are also great. It is said that just one moment of extreme anger can destroy the virtue we have accumulated over aeons. Hatred or anger can also cause us to be reborn in the hell realm.

There are two ways to overcome hatred:

To overcome the cause of hatred

To produce the antidote for the cause of hatred by working on hatred directly once it has arisen

To Overcome the Cause of Hatred

The cause of hatred is an unhappy mind. If our mind is unhappy or dissatisfied, this creates a basis from which hatred can arise. For example, when someone tries to harm us, before hatred arises in us, our mind becomes unhappy. Based on the unhappiness, hatred is produced and then we will take action against that person. So the basic cause of hatred is unhappiness.

To overcome this, whenever our mind is unhappy or dissatisfied, we should remember that the mind is the producer of hatred and that an unhappy mind destroys all our virtue. We are not able to produce or practice any type of virtuous deeds with an unhappy mind, so whatever aims or goals we have, we are not able to accomplish them. In many ways, the unhappy mind is a source of great suffering.

Also, we should think of the many reasons why it is not good to produce an unhappy mind or to fall under its power. For example, if our house is becoming dilapidated and we have a way to renovate it, or if our body becomes sick and we have a way to cure it, then there is no reason to be unhappy, because we can set about rebuilding our house or curing our body. If there is a method to overcome a problem, we should engage in that and not let ourselves fall into a state of unhappiness. However, if there is no method to overcome a problem—for example, if the house has already fallen down or is completely destroyed, or if you are about to die—there is no reason to be unhappy, because nothing can be done about it. The situation is beyond any means of restoration. Since there is no point in being unhappy, we should overcome our unhappiness.

Thus, whatever happens to us in this world, if there is a way to overcome unhappiness, we should do so. But if there is no solution and we can do nothing about it, we should not allow ourselves to fall into unhappiness, because it only produces greater and greater misdeeds and suffering.

The great Buddhist saint Shantideva said that to overcome hatred, we must stop its cause, which is the unhappy mind. We should never allow our mind to become unhappy, because this will produce hatred. If we see our mind becoming unhappy, we must stop it immediately. If we do not, it will only produce hatred, and once hatred arises, there is only one activity we will engage in, and that is bringing suffering to ourselves. Besides destroying or harming ourselves, hatred has no other purpose.

To Overcome Hatred Directly

The second method of overcoming hatred is to work on it directly when it arises. For this, we must practice one of three forms of patience:

Patience with physical illness

Patience through proper examination

Patience through not producing hatred against someone who harms us

Patience with Illness

Patience with physical illness means that we accept suffering. When any suffering arises, instead of becoming angry, we reverse it and become glad. When we practice the Mahayana path, we are always thinking not only to benefit ourselves but also to benefit other living beings. Just as we wish to have happiness and be free from suffering, so do all sentient beings.

With this frame of mind, we think there may be a time when we will experience some suffering while working to gain the state of full and perfect enlightenment for the sake of all sentient beings. If suffering or difficulties should arise, then we should think that we are really engaged in such a great practice or virtue that there is no need to fear any type of suffering. So instead of being unhappy or angry, we should feel joy that we are really accomplishing our purpose of helping to bring happiness to all sentient beings. We reverse the mind of unhappiness by substituting a mind of happiness.

Patience Through Proper Examination

The second method for countering or remedying hatred directly is to practice patience with proper thinking, or proper examination. This can be done from two points of view—the relative and the ultimate.

From the relative point of view, we see that the nature of fire is heat, the nature of water is fluidity, the nature of earth is solidity, and the nature of air is movement. Just as these elements naturally have different characteristics, the nature of this world of existence is suffering. Being part of this world of existence, whose nature is suffering, our nature is to experience suffering as well. We also see that it is the nature of other living beings to harm us due to their selfish desires. Since the nature of this world is suffering, our nature is to experience suffering, and the nature of others is to harm us, then we just have to have patience with them.

We can imagine that if someone were to harm us, it would be because we did something against him in a previous life and he has taken a form in this life to harm us in return. Thus, we are now paying for negative deeds that we performed in previous lifetimes. If we examine the situation in this way, we will see that the person who is harming us is not the cause of our suffering; we are the cause of our own suffering. We are harming ourselves because of our own past bad deeds.

When we are not able to fulfill our wishes, we often harm ourselves directly. There are people who, having failed in business or in love, commit suicide by jumping off a building or shooting themselves. These people do not need anyone to harm them, as they become their own enemies.

The majority of deeds that we do are nonvirtuous, and it is due to these nonvirtuous deeds that we are born in this world to experience different kinds of suffering, such as disease and death. Since we create great suffering through bad deeds that produce more and more suffering, we are the ones who are really creating great harm to ourselves. This being the case, it is no great wonder if someone else also creates suffering for us. We should not be angry with him, because the harm he does to us is a small matter compared to the greater harm we do to ourselves. There is no need to produce hatred or anger toward other people.

If someone does harm us, we should not allow our mind to think of hatred or retaliation. We should not even think that the person is harming us. We should produce a mind of equanimity and not bear any kind of hatred toward or hold a grudge against him. We should think that he is kind in not harming us more than he already has.

On one occasion, the Buddha Shakyamuni wanted someone to go to another place to teach the Dharma. An Arhat disciple volunteered to go, and the Buddha warned that his destination was not a good place as the practitioners were angry people. The Buddha asked him what he would do if the people were to cause trouble. The Arhat said that he would not do anything in return, but would practice patience. Then the Buddha asked what he would do if someone should abuse him. The disciple replied that he would do nothing in return, but would maintain patience. Then the Buddha asked what he would do if they were to throw stones at him. The Arhat said that he would think them kind because they only threw stones at him; they could have killed him. Finally, the Buddha asked what he would do if the people were to kill him. The disciple responded that he would be thankful that they did not lead him to the hells. The Buddha was satisfied and asked the Arhat to proceed on his journey.

Practicing patience through proper examination from the ultimate point of view means that when someone is harming us, we carefully examine the reality of the situation—the one who is harming us is ourself, and the act that is done to us does not actually exist. None of these three of have any reality of their own from an ultimate point of view. They are of the nature of emptiness, so there is no need to produce any thought against anyone.

Patience Through Not Practicing Hatred

In practicing the third category of patience, we do not produce any thought of hatred against the person who harms us. For example, if someone does us an injury, we should not even think that it is a harmful action. We should instead think that the person who is hurting us has been our mother or our child in many past lifetimes. In this way, we produce a thought of loving-kindness toward him instead of hateful thoughts.

We should also think that the one harming us is actually the cause for producing patience. For example, just as we are unable to take the vow of refuge without someone such as an abbot to bestow it, we cannot practice patience without someone causing us harm. We should believe that there is actually no difference between the spiritual friend who gives us the vow of refuge and the person who causes us harm, because both of them enable us to produce virtue. Without someone to hurt us, we will never produce the virtue of patience.

Following this reasoning, we should think that the one who is harming us is really our great benefactor and spiritual friend, helping us to practice the Path, and we should feel great happiness. So when someone injures us in some way, we should produce a mind of great happiness toward him. Just as someone who has been condemned to be executed and at the last moment has his hands cut off instead will feel happy, we should be happy that by practicing patience when someone harms us, we can purify our karma to avoid being born in the hells.

Also, instead of being angry with someone for harming us, we should produce a thought of compassion. For example, if our mother should become unreasonable or even decide to kill us, we should have compassion for her because she is our mother. Someone who is out to hurt us will go through great difficulties to do so. He will have to search for us and then get the necessary weapons. Along with these difficulties, his actions will accumulate a great deal of nonvirtue, which will produce great suffering for him. Thus, we should have compassion for him. Even if we cannot produce compassion, we should never produce a mind of hatred or anger in return for any harm done to us.

We should remember that those who try to hurt us do so because they are under the sway of the defilements of desire, hatred, and ignorance. In actuality, it is not the person who is trying to harm us but the defilements over which he has lost control that are the real causes of harm. Thus, we should produce compassion for him instead of thoughts of hatred.

It is easier to practice patience if we do so gradually, starting with those closest to us, like our own loved ones. Once we can practice patience with them, then we practice with those who are slightly more removed, such as friends or acquaintances. When we have accomplished this, we expand our practice to beings we do not know, such as mosquitoes that bite us, and even further to our worst enemies. So step-by-step we eventually train to have patience with everyone.

We should also practice patience gradually in relation to time. First, we promise ourselves that we will practice for half a day, then for a whole day. If that is too long, we can begin with maybe half an hour and then an hour, before extending to half a day, a day, a week, or a month. We make ongoing resolutions that we are going to practice patience for certain periods and then keep extending these time frames until we practice for our whole lifetime.

Another way to practice patience is by stages related to the type of harm we receive. We should try to extend our act of patience as the type of harm inflicted on us becomes greater. For example, we first have patience with a minor injury like a mosquito bite and extend that to diseases of the body, physical suffering, abuse, and so on.

We should understand that when we study or train in the practice of patience to increase our practice of the Dharma, there will be great advantages and we will be able to accomplish it. If we try to practice for other reasons or motivations, then we will not receive the blessings or be able to accomplish what we wish. For example, if we want to study the Dharma and our motivation is to write books and teach others without understanding the Dharma ourselves, then we will never be able to gain the blessings of the Dharma or gain the Path properly. However, if we practice the different levels of patience with the understanding that we are doing so to gain the path of enlightenment, we will certainly receive the blessings of the practice.

The Four Qualities of Patience

Along with the practice of patience, we should try to achieve the four qualities of patience:

- To overcome the hatred itself
- To gain the realization of emptiness through patience
- To fulfill the wishes of others through patience
- To bring other living beings into the Dharma

If by one act of patience we can combine all four qualities, then it is the best act we can accomplish. For example, if we do not produce any hatred or anger when someone hurts us, then the first quality is accomplished. If this is merged with the thought of emptiness, then it becomes the proper practice of patience. We exhibit the third quality when someone harms us and we do not retaliate. The person is pleased because we fulfill his wishes, and when we do not harm him in return, he is a bit astounded by our reaction. His thought of hurting us actually turns into a thought of joy or happiness toward us; once he is happy with us, he will approach us, and we can then lead him into the Dharma. So if all four qualities are accomplished in this one practice of patience, the practice is complete.

The Seven Attachments

We must also abandon the seven attachments to patience:

- Abandon attachment to hatred, which is the opposite of patience. By abandoning doing so, we are able to maintain patience.
- Abandon postponement, or the idea that when someone harms us

we can harm him in return now and practice patience later. Patience should be practiced at the moment harm is inflicted on us.

- Abandon being satisfied with the amount of patience we are practicing. For example, when someone harms us, we may exercise a little patience, feeling that it is enough and that if we control our patience for just a few minutes, we can return the harm after that. We should never be satisfied with the amount of patience we practice; we should always keep increasing it.
- Abandon the thought that we are practicing patience because we will gain some reward in this lifetime. For example, when someone injures us, we shouldn't think that later he will like us or reward us because we have been patient with him.
- Abandon the thought that we are practicing patience now to have happiness in a future lifetime. We should abandon any thought of reward for performing virtuous acts. We should practice merely for the sake of accomplishing virtue.
- Abandon the thought that we do not need to have patience with little things, that it is allowable to become angry over small or minor events.
- Abandon any thought or conceptualization at the time of practicing patience. For example, we should not practice patience while thinking of becoming an Arhat or thinking about gaining personal liberation.

WHEN WE EXAMINE THE BENEFITS of practicing patience, we will see that there is benefit in this lifetime and in future lifetimes. For example, in this life, when we do not retaliate in word or deed against someone who harms us, we are able to calm that person. We can decrease the violence against us, if not stop it completely. This means that we can overcome all our enemies in this world. They will disappear through our acts of patience, so there is no need to worry in our daily life that someone is going to hurt us. Also, when we die, if we have practiced patience well in this lifetime, we will have no regret and no fear of experiencing death itself.

Our practice of patience will enable us to gain a beautiful body, long life, freedom from sickness, and many rebirths in high positions (such as kings) and in heavenly realms (as gods) in future lifetimes. We will also be free from any form of enemy.

When a person becomes a fully enlightened Buddha, he will have the thirty-two major marks and eighty minor marks of perfection. These are the result of practicing patience and arise from accomplishing its perfection in previous lives. Anyone having these marks will create great joy and happiness in the minds of those who see him.

⊰ 17 ⊱

Khenpo Appey Rinpoche

The Perfection of Diligence

Rinpoche here discusses the perfection of diligence, which is defined as the mind that has a liking to perform virtue. When this mind is joined with the enlightenment thought and the view of ultimate reality, this practice of diligence becomes the perfection of diligence.

Several forces oppose diligence:

- A mind that does not like practicing virtue
- A mind that likes the wrong sort of virtue, such as the virtue of other philosophical or religious traditions
- The virtue that seeks results within the six realms of existence

The consequence of not being diligent or of being lazy is that whatever activity we engage in, we are not able to accomplish our objective. For example, if we are not diligent in worldly business, we can never accomplish our objective. In the same way, if we try to practice the spiritual path without diligence, we can never gain the result we seek. And if we are lazy in our practice, we may lose even the minor results we gained in previous lifetimes.

From the result point of view, if we do not have diligence, we will never be able to attain the ultimate result. The Buddha said that without diligence, we can never accomplish our own purpose, let alone the purpose of wishing to help other sentient beings. One sutra says that without diligence, we cannot accomplish the other perfections of giving, moral conduct, patience, meditation, and wisdom.

Sometimes when we are lazy, we think there must be some kind of demon obstructing us, causing our laziness. The Buddha said that laziness itself is the demon. So when we are engaged in laziness, this is the greatest obstacle to accomplishing the Dharma path.

The Causes of Laziness

Before we look at the methods for overcoming laziness, we must first look at its causes:

- Procrastination, always thinking we can postpone an activity until a later time. This is explained clearly in the *Bodhicharya-vatara* of Shantideva.
- Great attachment to other types of work, such as the worldly activities of business or trade. In other words, finding no desire for or happiness in performing virtue.
- Discouragement. For example, when we perform virtuous deeds or practice the Dharma and we do not see the result right away, this creates a kind of discouragement. We no longer like practicing, so we become lazy.
- Timidity, thinking that we are unable to practice virtue because we do not have enough strength or power.
- Enjoyment of doing nothing; being satisfied with activities such as just lying down and relaxing.
- Attachment to enjoyments such as eating or talking. For example, we may have a liking for good food, so we worry about and spend our time finding food we can enjoy. Or perhaps we like listening to or telling stories about insignificant matters concerning other people.
- Attachment to sleep.
- Attachment to this life to a degree that we do not see the faults of samsara and the consequences of working for this life alone.

When we consider the methods for abandoning or overcoming laziness, we see that most of its causes really arise from our attachment to working for the sake of this life alone. Thinking that this life is so important that we should only work to improve it is really the source of all forms of laziness.

Ways to Abandon Laziness

The best method for overcoming laziness is to meditate on impermanence, to see that this life is actually transitory and will not last long. Rinpoche's own teacher, Deshung Ajam Rinpoche, once said that when we have great attachment to this life, it creates great obstacles for us. He was referring to himself, saying that by being so attached to this life, he too was unable to benefit himself in any way. When we have this type of attachment, we cannot allow the Dharma to enter our mind. We are unable to turn our mind away from worldliness to the Dharma Path, so we cannot benefit ourselves.

If we truly want to practice the Dharma, it is absolutely necessary to abandon thinking about this life alone. For example, there was a Kadampa monk who thought he was practicing the Dharma diligently. One day, when he was circumambulating the temple, a great teacher named Geshe Thumpa went up to him and said that his circumambulation was good practice, but it would really be better to practice the Dharma. The Kadampa monk decided that he would be practicing the Dharma if he recited the scriptures, so he started studying them. Geshe Thumpa again told him that what he was doing was very good, but it would be better if he practiced the Dharma. So the monk thought about Dharma practice and decided that maybe meditation was the correct method. So he started to meditate diligently. Geshe Thumpa said that practicing meditation was good, but it would still be better if he practiced the Dharma.

The monk finally asked Geshe Thumpa how he should practice. The teacher replied that he must give up all attachment to this life. Without that, he could not truly practice the Dharma.

When we think about how we should practice Dharma, we should think of it like calling a meeting of our mind. Within our mind are many thoughts. One of them must be the thought of this life's impermanence. If we do not have this thought, our practice will not be complete, just as a meeting would be incomplete if someone were missing. But when we have that idea of impermanence within our mind, we have everything we need to make the meeting successful.

When we perform activities and our mind is attached to the eight worldly dharmas—such as gain and loss, happiness and suffering, or praise and blame— whatever deed we do can never be virtuous. However, it is impossible for us to abandon the worldly dharmas completely as long as we are in this world of samsara. So if we perform a deed with the understanding that we must reduce or abandon our attachment to the worldly dharmas, we are entering into the Dharma and the deed will benefit us. It is therefore a mistake to be attached to this life, thinking that it is permanent. We should see that it is very short, and we do not know when we will be leaving it. We are only creating obstacles for ourselves by being attached to it.

For example, if we are on a long journey and have traveled for a long distance, we want to rest. When we do, if we think that we should build an entire house and rest there, it is a mistake because we still have a long way to go. Similarly, if we think that we should work for this life alone, it is like stopping and building a house for which there is no purpose, because we will be leaving it soon. So we must consider the impermanence or shortness of this life and not work only for its sake.

The remedy for laziness is diligence, which has two aspects: pure object and perfect accomplishment.

Pure Object

To produce the pure object or practice means that we have the idea of abandoning nonvirtue, the mind as a basis for practicing virtue, and the resolution to use everything—our body, voice, and mind—for the sake of practicing virtue. We should always think that no matter what we do, in addition to practicing virtuous deeds, we should transform all our actions in this life into a pure practice, or virtuous deeds.

For example, when we go to bed, we should pray that all sentient beings may gain the *dharmakaya,* or the ultimate truth of the Buddha. When we wake up in the morning, we should pray that all sentient beings may awaken from ignorance, and when we rise from bed, we should pray that all sentient beings may gain the *rupakaya,* or the enlightened form aspect of the Buddha. If we remember a dream, we should remember that all worldly visions have the same nature as a dream. In this way, we can make even ordinary actions, which by their nature are neither virtuous nor nonvirtuous, into virtuous deeds. There are many examples. When we put on our clothes, we should pray that all sentient beings understand the meaning of shame and exhibit modesty. When we sit down, we pray that all sentient beings will sit on the seat of enlightenment. When we lean back against a chair, we pray that all sentient beings will lean against the tree of enlightenment, and when it is hot, that all sentient beings depart from the heat of the defilements.

One of the sutras even gives many examples of the types of thought we can produce to transform all our actions into pure objects and create great virtue. Rinpoche says that if we can, we should find other teachings about transforming the entire day into a day of virtue, study them, and then put them into practice.

Perfect Accomplishment

Perfect accomplishment means that whatever we do, it must be for the benefit of both ourselves and other sentient beings. These are goals in all the Buddhist paths, although there are slight differences in emphasis. For example, in the Hinayana practice, the emphasis is on achieving benefits for ourselves and the benefit to others is supplementary. The principal benefit is really for our own sake. In the Mahayana practice, the whole purpose is to act for the benefit of others, and our own benefits are supplementary.

In the Mahayana view, when we work for the benefit of others, we can do so from two perspectives—directly and indirectly. For example, if we gather money or articles to give to others, we are working for them indirectly. In handing over the articles, we are working for them directly.

By directly and indirectly working for the sake of others, we will realize our own benefits. For example, through the acts of accumulating and giving, we can gain fame and prosperity in this lifetime and perfect prosperity in a future lifetime. Eventually, we will accomplish the perfection of giving and then the different stages of enlightenment. By working for others, our benefits are also accomplished. When we study the Dharma for the sake of others, this is the indirect method of helping them; understanding the Dharma and teaching others what we have learned is the direct method of helping. Through these efforts, we can become learned in this lifetime, and we can gain wisdom and eventually the perfection of wisdom in future lifetimes.

When we practice virtue, we must have a happy mind, a mind that enjoys what it is doing. If the mind is not happy and does not enjoy what it is doing, then we cannot accomplish virtue. If we are not happy in our job, for example, then we will not do it properly, and this will create suffering for us.

However, if we like what we are doing and our mind is joyful when we practice, then we can accomplish both small and great things. For example, if we go on retreat for a week or a month, and our mind is happy, then we will have a successful meditation practice in retreat. Or if we study the Dharma with a happy mind, then we will be able to accomplish it well. Rinpoche says that even if we are crying, if we are happy that we are doing it, then we will have a good cry.

As explained in chapter 16, we achieve the four qualities and abandon the seven attachments with each of the perfections. This is also true for accomplishing diligence. If we practice the Vajrayana path, it is absolutely necessary to have diligence, and proper diligence means that we possess these qualities and accomplish these abandonments.

There are also great benefits in the practice of diligence. In this life alone, we are able to accomplish what we have set out to do. We can gain prosperity and fame, and when we die, we will have no regrets, because we will have worked diligently to achieve our goals. If we are diligent, neither humans nor nonhumans will be able to create obstacles for us in our practice of the Dharma; we will be able to accomplish Dharma and gain knowledge and wisdom even in this lifetime.

Through our diligence in this lifetime, we will quickly be able to abandon thoughts of nonvirtue and accomplish virtuous thoughts in a future lifetime. We will also be able to accomplish whatever deeds we attempt. Thus, we see that all the purities and accomplishments arise from diligence. It is the root of carrying out virtuous deeds. So without diligence, it is impossible to gain any special qualities.

The qualities that arise at the state of buddhahood as a result of practicing diligence are the attainment of the ten powers and the four stages of fearlessness. This shows that the various activities performed by the Buddha for the sake of others simply arise from the practice of diligence.

⊷ 18 ⊷

Khenpo Appey Rinpoche

The Perfection of Meditation

The fifth of the six perfections is the perfection of meditation, or concentration, which means focusing the mind one-pointedly on a single object without letting it wander to another object. When this state of concentration is joined with the thought of leading all sentient beings to the state of liberation and with the view of ultimate reality, this is the perfection of concentration.

The opposing force of concentration is distraction, the wavering or distracted mind. If we concentrate but meditate on the wrong view, we will not gain the desired result. Even if we meditate properly with the proper view and the proper idea of virtue, if we seek the result for this life alone or for our own personal liberation, it is not a complete practice of concentration.

When the mind is distracted, we cannot accomplish anything properly. Just as a stream of water will start to overflow and go in many directions if it does not find a proper conduit, our thoughts will go in different directions and we will achieve no benefit if our mind is distracted. And just as water will always flow downward like a waterfall if it does not have a canal to follow, our mind will always turn in a negative direction, always seeking nonvirtuous thoughts or actions, when it is not directed in a proper way.

It is therefore a great fault to be unable to concentrate properly in this life. If we fail in this way, we will experience a great deal of regret and unhappiness when we die. In our future lives, our mind will still be distracted, and we will not be able to overcome this distraction even if we try to meditate. Just as a stream of water is difficult to stop once it starts to fall over a cliff, it will be very difficult to block the distraction of our mind in our future life. Moreover, if we are unable to block our distraction then, more and more nonvirtuous deeds will arise, and the ever-increasing number of defilements will result in our rebirth in the lower realms again and again.

If we meditate with the wrong view, that will also create many obstacles for us. We must have the proper idea of the methods of meditation, its goal, and the view with which we engage in it—especially the view of ultimate reality—while we are practicing. For example, there was a practitioner who meditated for twelve years on a form of emptiness that was not a proper view of ultimate reality. As a result, he was born as a cat in his next lifetime.

When we are going somewhere and make a mistake by taking the wrong way, it makes our journey longer and more difficult because we must return to our starting point. In the same way, whenever we practice meditation, we must have the proper view so we do not make any mistake on the Path. According to the great Bodhisattva Maitreya, when we see others meditating on the wrong view, we should not want to compete with them. Instead, we should meditate on compassion because they are going the wrong way.

If we meditate only on loving-kindness and compassion, and not on the view of ultimate reality as well, then we can never gain liberation. The meditation on loving-kindness and compassion is a virtuous practice, but it is not complete, because it does not include the view of ultimate reality. Conversely, if we meditate only on ultimate reality, or the state of emptiness, and not on loving-kindness and compassion, our practice is again incomplete; although we can gain a result such as the liberation of the Arhat or the lower path of the Buddhist tradition, we are not benefiting others. To practice properly, both compassion and wisdom, or skillful means and emptiness, must be practiced together.

When we look at the remedies for the distracted mind, we see that there are two: one to overcome the causes of distraction and one to overcome the distraction itself.

Methods to Overcome the Causes of Distraction

Abandoning Attachment to Other People

The mind is distracted because of attachment, especially desire for others and desire for one's own benefit. Therefore, to overcome the distraction, we must destroy or abandon this type of attachment.

There are many problems in having attachment for others. First, it stops us from understanding suffering, the sorrow of this world of existence. Since we do not see the sorrow and sadness, we do not want to abandon this world. Second, parting from others causes us great suffering. Third, we fall under the sway of other people, and instead of using our life in our human body for a good purpose, we waste it by using it to accomplishing another person's desire. Thus, the person to whom we are greatly attached becomes a serious obstacle to our gaining the state of enlightenment.

In addition, the people in this world are hard to please. A small matter can make them happy or angry; it can even make them our enemies. Sometimes, they may like us, and sometimes they may not. Even when you do something nice for another person to please him, he may turn around and be displeased by your action. Instead of being happy, he may become angry, and great hatred may arise in his mind. So pleasing another person is a very difficult task.

Living beings are also difficult to deal with. Those who are less fortunate become jealous of us. Those on the same level as we are become our competitors and work against us. Those in higher positions look down on us due to their perceived superiority. If we praise them, they become proud. If we blame them or criticize them, they become hateful. So whatever the relationship may be and no matter what we do, we are never able to please others completely.

If we are wealthy, then someone will criticize us for what we have. If we are poor, people will criticize us for having nothing. So no matter what position we are in, someone will criticize us. The Buddha said that in this world, everyone has an idea to benefit themselves alone. They only wish to gain their own benefit, and when others are unable to contribute to that benefit, they become very unhappy. Since that is the case, there can never be anyone in this world whom we can actually call a friend.

People are also very fickle. For example, if we have great power, then no matter what we say, others always listen to us. If they can benefit from us, they listen for that reason. If they cannot benefit, they still listen because they respect our power. But once we lose our power, then even if we say something nice to them or have done many good things for them in the past, they will never listen to us again. Instead, they will criticize us. Similarly, when we are wealthy, we have many friends. People are happy to come and please us, to do whatever they can for us, but once we lose our wealth, we will never see their faces again. They will turn their heads away and move on. So it is very difficult, if not almost impossible, to please all the living beings in this world.

The Buddha himself said that people criticized the Buddhist teaching, which is perfect in every way, and during his lifetime, they criticized him as well. So it is a bad mistake to want to make everyone happy, to have them look up to us and be pleased with us. We will never be able to satisfy the minds of everyone in this world, because they are so diverse and are always seeking different things for their own benefit.

At one time, the Buddha's cousin and great enemy, Devadatta, became very sick and was near death. The Buddha went to bless him, and because of these blessings, Devadatta was able to overcome his illness. When he was well, he told the Buddha that he must be a capable doctor, and his knowledge of medicine was the reason he had been able to help his cousin. He said that when the Buddha became old, he would never have any difficulty in obtaining food, a statement that showed a great deal of disrespect for the Buddha.

There also was once a man named Legpekarma, who told the Buddha that a Jain master had gained the state of omniscience, and that no one else in the entire world had that quality. The Buddha replied that the Jain master was going to die of indigestion in seven days' time. Legpekarma went back to the Jain master and told him what the Buddha had said, advising the master to eat very little during the next seven days in order to prove the Buddha wrong. So the Jain master ate hardly any food for six days. However, he miscalculated and thought that the seventh day was actually the eighth. So he had a good meal on the seventh day, died of indigestion, and was reborn as a hungry ghost.

The hungry ghost then met Legpekarma and told him that what the Buddha had said was very great. The Buddha was the omniscient one, and Legpekarma should give up his disbelief, seek the Buddha's blessings, and take refuge in him. Legpekarma still did not like the idea. He had no faith in the Buddha. Later, when he met the Buddha, he told him that he had been wrong and that the Jain master had not died. The Buddha replied that not only had the Jain master died within seven days, but that Legpekarma himself had spoken to the dead man. Legpekarma said the Buddha was mistaken, that the Jain master had been reborn as a hungry ghost in one of the heavenly realms. The Buddha asked him to what hungry ghost he had just been talking, the one who had said that he should go to the Buddha and have faith.

At that point, Legpekarma realized that the Buddha really was omniscient. He became embarrassed and ashamed of having tried to trick the Enlightened One. Nonetheless, although he understood the Buddha had the quality of omniscience and could really see the future and the state of other beings, he still did not develop faith in the Buddha. Even though he saw the Buddha's power, Legpekarma just walked away. So even though the Buddha is completely omniscient and a perfectly enlightened being, he cannot satisfy every living being in this world.

The Buddha also said that we should not have attachment even to our loved ones, our parents, or our close relatives, because eventually we will have to part from them. We have to leave this life alone; no one can help us, not even those who have helped us in this lifetime. In addition, it is inappropriate to feel hatred or anger toward enemies, because everyone in this world is always changing. Thus, even our friends and loved ones can sometimes become our enemies, and this will also be the case in the next lifetime.

The following story illustrates the point that everything changes. Once there was a couple who had a daughter. When the couple passed away, the husband was reborn as a fish, and the wife as a dog. One day, the daughter was sitting by the road, eating a fish and holding a small baby close in her lap. A dog came up and tried to get a fishbone from her, but she hit and kicked the dog. As this was happening, an Arhat walked by. He looked at them, and due to his understanding, he shook his head and thought that the world was a very strange place. The woman was eating her father, beating her mother, and sitting with her enemy resting on her lap. So we can see that we should not form attachments to others in this life.

Abandoning Attachment to Things

The second type of attachment is to worldly objects. To gain different things in this life, we engage in nonvirtue and encounter difficulties. Suffering is always involved in the three phases of acquiring things—trying to gain them, having them, and losing them. For example, when we try to accumulate wealth, we perform a lot of difficult tasks and suffer by engaging in many nonvirtuous actions. Sometimes we speak in a bad or violent manner; we may even cheat or take advantage of others. From every point of view, we create many defilements and, in the process, are unable to practice the Dharma. In addition, even those who are close to us, like our own relatives, can become our enemies, and our original enemies can become even greater opponents. Even people we do not know can become our enemies.

Once we have gained our wealth, we suffer with the fear that we are going to lose it, so we try to protect it in many ways that create more suffering. Our worry about protecting our possessions becomes so great that we become slaves to the wealth we originally wanted. Instead of us owning those possessions, they begin to own us; we have to work for them. In trying to keep our wealth, we also become the slaves of other people and make many enemies. We fear that others may try to take what we have and that they are against us. By always trying to protect our possessions, we perform so many bad thoughts and deeds that we create great defilements, which results in bad rebirths. So we are always engaged in different types of suffering.

When we lose an article, we again experience great suffering because we cannot practice any virtuous deed, and this exhausts our source of virtue. We also become very unhappy and displeased with others, and anger and hatred arise in our mind. More defilements, suffering, and nonvirtuous deeds are created. Thus, losing an article is also a state of suffering.

This does not mean that we have to get rid of everything we own. The objects themselves have no fault. The fault is in our attachment to them, and it is this attachment that we must overcome. So we do not need to throw our car keys away and take a bus home. Similarly, if we are attached to other living beings, it does not mean there is something wrong with them. The fault is in our attachment to them. Other people are all right as they are; we do not have to worry about them. But our attachment to them must be lessened or destroyed. In the same way, we must lessen or destroy our attachment to the articles we possess in this life. Decreasing or abandoning our attachment to them will help us to overcome a distracted mind.

Can we gain some happiness by having possessions in this world? The things we accumulate will bring us a small amount of happiness, but the problems that arise are great. It is like putting honey on the edge of a sharp knife and rubbing the knife against our tongue to taste the honey. The taste of the honey is nice, but it is a small pleasure compared to the consequnce of cutting our tongue off. In the same way, our attachment to different objects or people in this world gives us a little happiness but also causes us great suffering. Nagarjuna said that if we have an itchy rash on our arm, we get some pleasure from scratching it. We will feel better, and happiness arises from that. However, if there were no rash or itchiness to start with, that would be a much greater pleasure. Similarly, if we are attached to articles and people, the happiness that arises is small. But if we have no attachments at all, our happiness will be greater.

Methods to Overcome Distraction Directly

The antidote for a distracted mind is a mind of concentration. In other words, concentration meditation is the method for overcoming distraction. There are three different aspects of concentration meditation:

Worldly Concentration Meditation. There are seven preparatory or preliminary aspects to this meditation, then the four states of dhyana and the four states of the formless realm. This means that four states of meditation arise from the realm of form and four more arise from the formless realm.

Hinayana Concentration Meditation. From the Hinayana point of view, it is first necessary to meditate on the suffering nature of this world of existence, then on concentration, and finally on insight wisdom. From insight wisdom, the meditation is expanded to include the thirty-seven factors of enlightenment.

Mahayana Concentration Meditation. The Mahayana school includes two traditions: the Mind-Only tradition, which was taught according to the great Indian teacher Asanga, and the Middle Way tradition, which was taught by Nagarjuna, Aryadeva, and Shantideva. The following explanation follows the tradition from Shantideva's book, the *Bodhicharyavatara.*

Concentration Meditation According to the Middle Way

The Mahayana method for practicing meditation is to meditate directly on the enlightenment thought. However, to produce the enlightenment thought properly, we must first meditate on loving-kindness and compassion. Though it is not taught in the *Bodhicharyavatara* that the meditation on loving-kindness and compassion must come first, it is necessary.

Meditation on Loving-Kindness

When we meditate on loving-kindness, we should think about the object of our meditation. This object should be someone who does not possess complete happiness. In this world, no one possesses complete happiness except the fully enlightened Buddha; all other living beings have some form of suffering. So our meditation on loving-kindness should be directed toward them. We should meditate on someone for whom we have great love and then equate everyone in this world with that person.

For example, if we use our mother as the object of meditation, we create an idea of loving-kindness toward her and then consider all living beings as similar to her. Alternatively, if we use our child, our brother, our sister, or someone else close to us, we create an idea of loving-kindness toward him or her, then equate everyone with that person.

Loving-kindness means that the person on whom we are meditating should have happiness and the causes of happiness. This happiness should be free from all defilements and all nonvirtues; it is pure happiness. Having the causes of happiness means being free from the performance of nonvirtuous deeds, which are the cause of unhappiness.

In addition, they should have great happiness or great virtue. Great virtue means not only a deed that is free from the defilements, but also one that encompasses the Mahayana motivation of working for the sake of all sentient beings. We meditate on this person—or all sentient beings whom we visualize in front of us—gaining a state of happiness and virtue, as well as the causes of happiness, equal to that gained by the fully enlightened Buddha.

The Buddha himself said that the benefits arising from meditating on loving-kindness are vast and great. If we were to take many worlds filled with jewels and offer them to the enlightened beings, we would accumulate many merits. But even greater than that offering is a moment of meditation on loving-kindness. Thus, loving-kindness has the great benefits of accumulating merit and helping both ourselves and others.

Meditation on Compassion

Next, we should meditate on compassion. We should first understand who should be our object of meditation. According to the teaching of Maitreya, we should consider our object from among ten categories:

- Those who have great desire or attachment to others.
- Those who practice virtue but are obstructed in that practice. For example, those who are trying to practice Dharma but are meeting many obstacles, such as being disturbed by spirits or not being able to accumulate the virtues they have set out to accomplish.
- Those in the lower realms who have great sufferings.
- Those who have great ignorance. For example, those who are always engaged in nonvirtue, such as someone who slaughters chickens.
- Those who believe that this world of existence will bring them happiness and rely on it to do so.
- Those who follow the wrong path, a religious or philosophical path that is not able to help them.

- Those who, having gained the states of samadhi or deep states of meditation, create great obstacles for themselves because of their attachment to the attainments.
- Those who practice the wrong path and think they have gained the state of liberation when actually they have not.
- Those who are treading the Hinayana path.
- Those Bodhisattvas who have not accomplished the two accumulations of merit and wisdom.

Maitreya explained that we can also consider our object in relation to the six classes of people who oppose the six perfections. For example, those who are miserly and obstruct the perfection of giving become our objects of meditation on compassion. Similarly, those who break their vows of discipline, are angry, are lazy, have distracted or agitated minds, and are ignorant may also be our objects.

According to Maitreya, we can combine the objects of our meditation into two groups. The first consists of worldly beings, and the second comprises those who fall within the extreme of nirvana—in other words, those of the Hinayana tradition who strive to gain their personal liberation, have not achieved it, and are unable to work for the sake of other sentient beings. We meditate on them as objects of compassion because they will have great difficulty in attaining the state of full and perfect enlightenment.

We can further divide the first group into two categories. The first is composed of people who are creating causes of future suffering—for example, those who are doing deeds of great nonvirtue to accumulate wealth or gain happiness for themselves. By acting in this improper manner, they are creating the causes for their suffering in the next life or future lives, and they will definitely be born in the lower realms.

The second category comprises those who have the result of suffering itself, meaning people who are manifestly experiencing suffering now. This includes, for example, those in the lower realms like the hells and even those in the higher realms such as the human realm. It also includes the poor, those who fear things like sickness or old age, those who are separated from the people or things they wish to have near, and those who wish to be separated from the people or things they have near. Thus, this second group on whom we can meditate comprises people who are not able to satisfy their desires in any way or are living with bad conditions or suffering.

How do we create compassion? It is said that compassion arises as a result of seeing suffering. By repeatedly observing others who are suffering and meditating on it, compassion for them will arise in our mind. We should carefully examine others' state of suffering and see how they have fallen into the three different types of suffering (the suffering of suffering, the suffering of change, and the suffering of conditioned nature that pervades this world). In addition, we can rely on a spiritual teacher to teach us about the methods for producing compassion. When we see the various states of suffering, meditate on them, and also receive as many teachings as we can from a spiritual friend, it should be easy to produce thoughts of compassion. If we have produced the state of compassion in either a previous life or this one, then it is quite easy to do so again.

The method for meditating on compassion is first to equate everyone with someone for whom we have great love, such as our mother, our child, or someone very close to us. Using this person as an object for our meditation, we produce a thought of compassion toward him or her. It is necessary to use someone for whom we have great affection, because it is easier to produce a thought of compassion for a person who brings feelings of happiness to our mind. If we try to meditate on an enemy or someone who is in a poor state, we may feel revulsion because we do not like their appearance. Because of this, we will not be able to create a mind of compassion.

Compassion means that we produce a thought that everyone should be free from all suffering and the causes of suffering (meaning the production of the defilements and nonvirtues). Defilements and nonvirtues are produced by grasping to the self, believing the self to be real. So here we make a wish that all sentient beings may be free from suffering, and especially from this clinging to the ego or the self, which is the real cause of all other suffering.

What are the benefits of practicing compassion? In one of the sutras, the Bodhisattva Avalokiteshvara asked the Buddha, "What is the single Dharma practice that can be equated to all the practices put together?" The Buddha replied that the one Dharma we should always practice and that is really the combination of all the Dharma practices is that of great compassion. In this one practice, all the Buddhist teachings are practiced together. Since compassion is so great that it was even taught by the Buddha, it is said that whenever we practice Dharma, it should be pervaded by compassion at all times—in the beginning, in the middle, and at the end. Compassion is the source, the real essence of the entire Path.

Meditation on the Enlightenment Thought

Next, we meditate on the enlightenment thought. This is done in two ways: by meditating on how we are the same as others, and by meditating on exchanging our happiness for the happiness of others.

THE SAMENESS OF SELF AND OTHERS   When we meditate on the sameness of ourselves and others, we should think, "I myself will bestow happiness on all living beings in this world," and "I myself will free all sentient beings from all the suffering in this world." When any happiness comes to us, we should think, "May all sentient beings obtain the same kind of happiness that I have obtained now." Whenever we have any kind of suffering, we think, "May all sentient beings be free from the kind of suffering that I am now experiencing." In this way, we equate ourselves with all sentient beings to bestow happiness upon them and to free them from suffering. We should meditate on this idea of sameness again and again until it becomes a strong thought. Once we are accustomed to the idea of equating ourselves with others, we can begin to meditate on exchanging ourselves for others.

EXCHANGING ONESELF FOR OTHERS   We can meditate on exchanging our own happiness for the suffering of others through an extensive method and a short method:

- *The Extensive Method.* Generally, when we see people who are superior to us, we are jealous of them. We think that they mistreat us, that they do not have compassion for us, that they look down on us, that they criticize and blame us for many things. We think that the only reason they do this is because they consider themselves greater than we are. In this way, we create jealousy for those above us. We feel highly competitive toward people who are on the same level as we are. We think that we must compete with them in every possible way so they can never become greater than we are. When we think of people who are lower than we are, we feel great pride because they are inferior and should not be treated equally. We look down on them in many ways.

To practice the exchange meditation (exchanging ourselves for others), we have to reverse or abandon this kind of thinking toward other people. For those of whom we are jealous, we exchange our position with theirs; in a sense, we place ourselves in the higher position and them in the lower one. Having done this, we then create jealousy toward the higher person—now ourselves. When we see the bad consequences the jealousy creates, we want to give up the idea and exchange it; instead of having jealousy, we want to take that jealousy away.

For those toward whom we always feel pride, we exchange positions with our inferiors. We become inferior and place them above us, looking down at us with pride. Just as we were proud when we looked down at them, it is now these other people looking down at us.

We also exchange positions with our equals, people with whom we are always competing. Then we start to compete with ourselves.

With this meditation, we try to benefit other people, because we think of their benefit as our own. This whole method of exchanging ourselves for others is explained in detail in the eighth chapter of the *Bodhicharyavatara*.

- *The Short Method.* The short form of exchanging ourselves for others is to imagine that all the happiness and virtue we have is given to all the living beings in this world, and that we take on all their suffering, nonvirtue, and unhappiness. We wish that all our happiness and virtue will fall on others and that all the suffering, unhappiness, and nonvirtue of others will fall on us. This creates a great meditation of exchanging self for others, and the merit arising from it is incredibly vast. Nagarjuna said that if we could make a form or a shape out of the merit arising from this exchange even for one moment, it would be even larger than the sky of the three realms of existence.

We accomplish the meditation on the enlightenment thought by meditating again and again on always giving our own happiness and benefits to others so they will be able to attain a state of full and perfect enlightenment. Along the way, we also give them all forms of happiness on their path to enlightenment and wish for all their suffering to fall on us.

When we perform the exchange meditation again and again, we will be able to accomplish the real meditation on the enlightenment thought. To do so, we must see the error of working for the benefit of ourselves alone and understand the great benefit of working for the sake of others. This will help us create the enlightenment thought and enable us to accomplish the meditation.

To make sure the thought of enlightenment does not change, we should carefully examine the real purpose and benefit behind it. We will see that over many lifetimes we have been working only for our own benefit, never thinking of helping other living beings, and the only things we have gained in this lifetime are the various types of suffering. We have never been able to obtain the happiness we have always sought. As long as we continue to work for the sake of ourselves alone and seek our own happiness, we will never be able to gain that happiness. Instead, we will only gain more suffering. When we understand that it is only through working for the benefit of others that we can gain any real state of happiness, we will understand the purpose of the enlightenment thought.

To fix the enlightenment thought in our mind, we must always examine the state of our mind. In other words, we should create a spy within ourselves to see what we are doing. So when we look at ourselves and find that we have something that can benefit others, we should give it to them. If we become miserly and think we want it for ourselves, we should snatch away our miserliness, because we know we can benefit others by doing so.

Similarly, when we are jealous, we should overcome our jealousy toward others. For example, when we think that someone else is much happier than we are, we should turn this jealousy against ourselves instead of against the other person. We should think, "I am too happy. I have too much happiness compared to others. I am superior to others." Then we create a thought of jealousy toward our own superiority and happiness rather than those of others.

We should examine and question ourselves to see what we are doing. For example, we should ask ourselves whether what we are doing through our body, voice, and mind is sending us down to the lower realms, or whether we are going on the wrong path. We question ourselves to see how we are acting in this world.

We should also question ourselves to see whether we are practicing properly. If someone harms us, we should not think that the harm is caused by the other person. Instead, we should know that we are experiencing suffering due to our own karma. When we act against others, we should think, "I am now doing something that is not right." We need to examine it carefully, and say out loud to ourselves or others that we have made a mistake so that we can stop ourselves.

If someone should praise us, even if the praise is true, we should exchange our own qualities for those of others. So instead of feeling proud of the qualities we have, we should think of giving those qualities to others and taking on their qualities, even though they are inferior to ours. We should believe that our qualities really belong to other people, and their lesser qualities belong to us.

Even if we do have certain qualities that are special, we should realize that they are not permanent. This is a method for destroying any pride that may arise. Moreover, we should not display or show off our qualities, but hide them. We should not become proud of our good qualities.

In brief, we see that all the suffering we have in this world is caused by trying to gain happiness and benefit for ourselves alone, and we have done this through self-cherishing. The only benefit we have attained from all this effort has been birth inside the six realms of existence. So if we really wish to gain the state of buddhahood, the only way to do it is to work for the sake of others. By putting aside all our self-cherishing and beginning to cherish others as we do ourselves, we will be able to accomplish the Path and gain benefit for both ourselves and others.

According to the Tibetans, the word *meditation* means "habituation." It means to take something and make it into a habit, to habituate or accustom our mind to a certain way of thinking. For example, if we habituate ourselves to the idea of the enlightenment thought, then it becomes an actuality in our mind. The Buddha said that if we were to take just one verse of his teachings and apply ourselves fully to studying it, contemplating it, and meditating on it, it would become a habitual tendency and we would be able to accomplish all his teachings.

To accomplish concentration meditation and make it a real perfection in our mind, we have to accomplish the four qualities of that practice and abandon the seven attachments that create obstacles to it.

When we examine the benefits of meditation, we see that they exist in this lifetime as well as in future lifetimes. In this lifetime, we will be able to place our mind in a one-pointed state of concentration. We will be able to overcome the grosser defilements of desire, hatred, and ignorance; this is like cutting the head away from the body, but we cannot destroy the root of the defilements. We will also be able to stabilize and decrease the agitation in our mind. We will be able to equalize the eight worldly dharmas, such as thoughts of happiness or sadness, and we will never want anything at the expense of others. Instead, we will see everything in a state of equanimity. For example, most of us usually hope for something or fear losing something. By accomplishing meditation, all these hopes and fears are equalized, and we are not swayed to different extremes. We will also be able to bring happiness to our body and joy to our mind. We will gain various states of magical power, such as the ability to fly; supernatural abilities, such as reading the minds of others; and different states of supernatural or higher consciousness. People will like us very much.

If we accomplish meditation in this lifetime, we will have miraculous powers or supernatural consciousness in future lifetimes. It will be easier to attain the different states of meditation or samadhi.

When we reach the state of buddhahood, the four purities—which are some of the qualities of buddhahood—will arise. Purity of body means that the fully enlightened Buddha can be reborn in, stay in, and depart from this world according to his wishes. Purity of the object means that the Buddha can accomplish different miraculous feats to benefit others, such as the ability to manifest things that do not exist or cause things that do exist to disappear. Purity of mind means that the Buddha can accomplish all the states of samadhi that he wishes, and purity of wisdom means that he knows everything there is to know in this world.

Jetsun Rinpoche Dragpa Gyaltsen

The Song of Inquiring About Good Health

I bow at the feet of the lord gurus.
When only explaining the history of the circumstances,
because I have many karmic relationships,
we inquire about health when we meet in the morning and evening,
we inquire about health when we depart to other places,
we inquire about health when we return from other places.
If one's health is good, one is joyful,
but there are few dependent originations of good health,
and there are many bases of disease in the illusory body.
There is much hoarseness in one spoken voice;
there are many sufferings in the clarity of mind—
body and mind are seized by objects of both attachment and aversion;
there is never a time the activities of conceptuality will be completed,
which is the fault with being born in samsara.
If one is liberated from samsara, there is joy,
but there are few dependent originations of liberation from samsara.
Although the natural reality of things
may be nonarising emptiness,
because the dense traces of delusion and
grasping to things is not cut from the root,

within the hollow of samsara's three realms,
the whirlwind of the three and five poisons rises,
at the firewood of the various negative actions,
the great fire of various sufferings burns,
incinerating the tree of one's original mind,
reducing the sprout of bodhichitta to ashes.
That wheel of the suffering of the six realms,
continuously revolves, similar to a wheel of fire.
The rope line of birth, aging, illness, and death
is seized time and again.
In a prison cell from which one cannot be released at any time,
such a prisoner, one's imprisoned mind, is miserable.
Have compassion for those who will not be liberated at any time,
although there is compassion, there is no method to perform;
although there is a method, there is no practitioner.
E maho! Living beings are defiled!
A song of experience of the Palden Sakya's.

—Jetsun Rinpoche Dragpa Gyaltsen.

The Song of Happiness

I request the blessings of the Lord Guru,
whose body is the nature of all Buddhas.
Residing in a secluded place, I thought
"Presently, whatever I am thinking is deluded,
I am not unhappy, so I am happy."
Obtaining the precious human birth difficult [to obtain] is bliss;
meeting with the Mahayana Dharma[1] is bliss;
relying on a true guru is bliss;
meeting with the Vajrayana Dharma[2] is bliss;
being ripened according to the method of tantra is bliss;
protecting the samayas and vows is bliss;
meditating on the yoga of the two stages[3] of the Path is bliss;
practicing the profound conduct is bliss.
There is no harm to the mind by apparent objects;
those essenceless objects are false,

similar to the reflection of form in a mirror;
although one acts with grasping, it is essenceless,
also the three objects (odors, flavors, and tangibles) are similar to that.
Whatever sound is heard is similar to an echo;
although one acts with desire and anger, it is essenceless.
Also mentally determine that whatever is thought is an illusion;
in the state of illusion, there is bliss.
Because illusion is searched, nothing exists to be expressed;
in the inexpressible state, there is bliss.
Although searching for samsara, it is not found,
the nature of that is nirvana;
in the nondual state, there is bliss.
Although searching for suffering, it is not found;
the nature of that is great bliss;
in the state of union, there is bliss.
As samsara cannot be abandoned,
yogins, do not give rise to the thought of abandoning [samsara].
As buddhahood cannot be accomplished,
yogins, do not give rise to the thought of accomplishing
    [buddhahood].
That understanding of the nonexistence of samsara and nirvana
is the view of the inseparability of samsara and nirvana;
in the state of inseparability there is bliss.
Yogins who understand in this way,
although there is nothing to practice, practice diligently!
Although there is nothing to meditate, meditate diligently!
Although there is nothing to protect, protect samaya!
If it is understood in that way, there is bliss.
I also am in that state,
Son, you also should remain in that state.
Having attained unattainable enlightenment,
the buddhahood that cannot be accomplished
exists in one's own mind;
mind is not unhappy, so it is happy.
This is superior upadesha of the Jetsun
and was also requested by Yeshe Dorje;

may the highest enlightenment be obtained
with my effort of writing this.

> —This was written by Jetsun Dragpa Gyaltsen while in good
> health at the Temple of Palden Sakya in the middle month
> of the summer, in the iron female hare year (1171).

The Song of Six Contentments

For we who practice the holy spiritual Dharma,
As a support, contentment is produced by the Three Jewels.[4]
As a residence, contentment is produced by a hut.
As a living companion, contentment is produced by personal deities.
As a conversational companion, contentment is produced by recitation.
As a guard, contentment is produced by the personal deities.
The six contentments[5] were taught by Jetsun Rinpoche.

Notes

1. Mahayana is the Buddhist path based on the Bodhisattva vow, the aspiration to achieve complete buddhahood for the benefit of all sentient beings.

2. Vajrayana is the Buddhist path of special methods based on receiving *abhisheka,* which plants the seed of buddhahood in the five aggregates within a person.

3. These two stages are the yoga of creation, or developing oneself into the form of a deity, and the yoga of completion, or practicing with the inner elements of the body—channels, drops, and energies.

4. The Three Jewels are the Buddha, the Dharma, and the Sangha.

5. It appears that one line of this song is missing in the 1736 Derge edition of the Sakya canon.

↦ 20 ↤

Jetsun Rinpoche Dragpa Gyaltsen

The Song of Praising Place

I go for refuge to the sacred gurus
of the three times and the personal deities.
This is the account of agitated thinking
at the occasion of uncontrolled conceptuality.
Both one possessing faith who wishes to practice Dharma
and one possessing faith who has entered into Dharma—
many wandering thoughts arise
by thinking about those two.

First, there are many kinds of faithful [people] indeed,
but the faith of some is childish prattle,
the faith of some is coarse conduct,
the faith of some is spirits and ghosts,
the faith of some is from the heart.
First, that faith of childish prattle:
having aroused faith, one cuts the hair of the head[1];
having lost faith, one performs worldly Dharma[2];
one comes and goes [to Dharma] many times.
[Practice] is not done having made a proper investigation—
is that not the faith of the childish prattlers?
Some faith is coarse conduct:
first, not investigating the spiritual friend,

entering anybody's door,
not knowing what to practice, one is lost in coarse conduct.
Sometimes, having resided in a secluded place,
seated on the peak of Three Mountains, there is nothing to meditate.
Sometimes, residing at a town crossing,
one is lost in coarse conduct in the midst of the crowd.
One is shameful to the learned and the disciplined—
is that not the faith of coarse conduct?
Some faith is of spirits and ghosts:
having entered into Dharma, performing coarse conduct,
one is an amusement to ordinary beings;
one is [the object] of the critical investigation of superior beings—
a cause of destruction for self and others;
making Dharma an excuse is crazy.
Is that not the faith of the spirits and ghosts?
That faith generated from the heart:
first, arousing clear faith,
with the thought of wishing to practice Dharma;
do not be in an impatient hurry.
In the beginning, seek a spiritual friend,
one who possesses the discipline and vows,
one who has trained in the meaning of the sutras and tantras,
one who possesses bodhichitta.[3]
Wherever he resides, follow closely;
perform conduct according to how he teaches.

Of those who enter into Dharma with faith,
how do some protect discipline?
When there is no listening, there is no essence;
there are some who listen for a whole human life;
without meditating, what use is [listening] for the mind?
Some meditate without hearing;
without hearing, there is nothing to meditate on.
Some, without faith, perform activities[4] and method[5]
What is the use of farming the eight worldly dharmas?
Some, possessing faith, seek a place to practice;

if that is explained in detail, it is like this:
some go to Bodh Gaya,[6]
there are many non-Buddhists at Bodh Gaya,
also there is no accomplishment for them.
There are many dangerous bandits on the road;
when one's throat is cut, one dies with the knife of regret.
Some travel to the glaciers of Kailash[7];
there are many nomads at Kailash,
nomads perform many nonvirtues.
When killed by an avalanche, one dies with the knife of regret.
Some travel to Tsari Tsagong,[8]
that part of the land filled with barbarian Monpas[9];
even the sound of the name "Dharma" does not exist;
when killed by its spirits and ghosts, one dies with the knife of regret.
Like this and so on, those [stories] are innumerable.
Do not search for many places to practice.
Meditate in a secluded place together with conducive circumstances,
possessing the confidence of the two stages.
Wherever one resides is the place of Akanishtha[10];
the friend with whom one is befriended is one's personal deity;
whatever one drinks and whatever one eats is the food of amrita.[11]
Not searching for an outer place to practice
is the profound samaya of Vajrayana;
that cannot be sung as a song, so it is left aside.
My residence, this place, Palden Sakya,
is similar to Akanishtha.
In the east, at Trachung Ganga,[12] the elephant's trunk,
is the home of Lord Akshobhyavajra,[13]
savior of living beings through union.[14]
In the south, at Kha'u Tsangpo,[15] the precious horse,
is the home of Lord Ratnasambhava,[16]
fulfiller of the wishes of living beings.
In the west, at Chumig Dzinkha,[17] the peacock's head,
is the home of Lord Amitabha,[18]
guide of living beings to the Dharma.
In the north, at Phunpo Ri,[19] the garuda's wing,

is the home of Lord Amoghasiddhi,[20]
accomplisher of the benefit of living beings.
White earth[21] like a lion's head,
Palden Sakya, the body of the lion,
is the home of Lord Vajradhara,[22]
fulfiller of the wishes of the living beings of the six realms.[23]
In that way, in the supreme place of Akanishtha,
I, the yogin of Vajradhara, am blissful.
I, the yogin who has cut proliferation, am blissful.
I am blissful because of the hard armor of knowledge mantra.[24]
I am blissful because I possess the treasury of upadesha.[25]
I am blissful because I possess the confidence of the view.
I am blissful because I am surrounded by the fence of samaya.
I am not boasting for myself.
In this way, because it helps everyone,
without wandering all over the place,
without rendering the precious human birth useless,
without rendering the body and life useless;
if one has enough comprehension, stay in seclusion;
if one has not enough comprehension, rely on a guru.
Either way, bring diligence to practice
without wasting faith.
This short song of agitated thinking
is carried by the faithful Yeshe Dorje,
and is also sent to Shunpa Gomton.
Sing mounted on the steed of song!

Notes

1. This refers to the hair-cutting part of the ritual of taking refuge.

2. Worldly Dharma comprises those activities oriented solely to this life.

3. Bodhichitta is the wish to achieve enlightenment for the benefit of all sentient beings.

4. The activities are pacifying, increasing, power, and destruction.

5. The method is the sadhana practices of Vajrayana.

6. The place in India where Shakyamuni Buddha attained complete buddhahood.

7. A sacred Himalayan mountain in western Tibet to which Buddhists, Hindus, and Bonpos make pilgrimages.

8. Tsari Tsagong is in the southeastern region of Tibet, near India.

9. *Monpa* refers to the indigenous tribes inhabiting the area around Tsari.

10. Akanishtha is the pure realm where the Sambhogakaya Buddha resides.

11. Amrita is divine food and drink.

12. A hill to the east of Sakya.

13. Aksobhya is the eastern dhyana Buddha.

14. The union of clarity and emptiness.

15. A river to the south of Sakya.

16. Ratnasambhava is the southern dhyana Buddha.

17. A spring to the west of Sakya.

18. Amitabha is the western dhyana Buddha.

19. A mountain to the north of Sakya.

20. Amoghasiddhi is the northern dhyana Buddha.

21. "White earth," or Sakya, refers to a prominent geographical feature on the side of a hill above the town.

22. Vajradhara here refers to the sambhogakaya (enjoyment body) guru.

23. The six realms are god, titan, human, animal, preta, and hell.

24. Knowledge mantras are those associated with wisdom deities.

25. Upadeshas are profound instructions for practice.

Jetsun Rinpoche Dragpa Gyaltsen

The Song of Eight Practices of Dreams

I prostrate to the gurus.
Town, residence, and market
are the places the wild horse of the mind wanders,
because the rider, insight, is bad and
the bridle, calm-abiding, is weak.
Having no control over the wild horse,
having run and run on the field of bad karma,[1]
one risks falling into the ravine of suffering.
Similar to a wild animal that has been injured,
reside in seclusion and practice.
If many meet, arguments will increase;
if two stay together, idle talk will increase.
Like the bastard of a young woman,
reside in solitude and practice.
First, the monk's sectarian enjoyments,
second, the recognized appointments of the assembly of the Sangha,[2]
third, the offerings of the male and female benefactors;
these three are the food offerings of maras[3];
practice Dharma in the manner of being without desire.
First, great attachment to appearances,

second, great grasping to wealth and possessions,
third, great desire for food and drink;
these three are the dropsy of great meditators;
take the strong purgative medicine of nongrasping mind;
practice Dharma in the manner of a child.
First, intoxication harms mindfulness,
second, meat harms compassion,
third, women harm fame;
these three are the tumor of great meditators;
quickly obtain the moxibustion of renunciation;
practice Dharma in the manner of a madman.
First, performing rituals for the ill,
second, [rituals] increasing the greed of the wealthy,
third, the wrong livelihood of performing predictions[4];
these three are the misguided path of the great meditators;
offerings should be understood as demons;
practice Dharma in the manner of being without acquaintances.
First, the bliss of only calm-abiding,
second, experiencing the taste [of bliss] is similar to ignorance,[5]
third, meditating emptiness without compassion;
these three are the wrong exits of the great meditators;
like the great Garuda[6] soaring in the sky,
practice Dharma in the manner of the union [of method and wisdom].
First, the disciple possessing devotion,
second, the relatives connected by karma,
third, brothers and sisters possessing samaya[7]
should be met with friendliness when they appear.
Presently, without having strong feelings,
practice Dharma in the manner of dream.
The Song of Eight Practices of Dreams.

Notes

1. *Karma* refers to mental, physical, and verbal actions and their results.
2. This is the representative Sangha, meaning all persons holding Buddhist vows.

3. Maras are the forces that bring obstacles to the practice of Dharma.

4. Divination and so on.

5. This line refers to the fault of attachment to the bliss of calm-abiding meditation.

6. Garuda is the king of birds.

7. The practitioners of Vajrayana who have received abhisheka under the same guru.

⇥ 22 ⇤

From the Avatamsaka-sutra

The King of Noble Prayers Aspiring to the Deeds of the Excellent

TRANSLATED BY Tulku Thondup

EDITED BY Harold Talbott

I prostrate to the youthful Manjushri.

Seven Preliminaries to Purify One's Mind

1. PROSTRATING

I prostrate with pure mind, speech, and body to all the lions of mankind [Buddhas] in the three times and ten directions of the world.

By the power of this aspiration of the deeds of the excellent, I manifest bodies as numerous as all the atoms in the world, fully aware of the presence of the innumerable Buddhas; I prostrate to all of them.

I imagine that on each atom as many Buddhas are present as atoms in the universe, seated in the midst of Bodhisattvas, thus filling the whole universe with Buddha-manifestations.

I praise all those Bliss-gones [Buddhas], expressing their oceanlike, inexhaustible virtues with an ocean of melodies and voices.

2. OFFERING

I make offering to the Buddhas with the best of flowers, wreaths, musical instruments, perfume, canopies, lamps, and incense.

I offer to the Buddhas the finest robes and fragrances and incense as high as Mount Meru, all perfectly arranged.

By the power of my faith in the deeds of the excellent and devotion to the Buddhas, I prostrate and present these vast and unequaled offerings to all the Conquerors.

3. CONFESSING

I confess [purify] each and every nonvirtuous deed I have committed with my body, speech, and mind due to desire, hatred, and ignorance.

4. REJOICING

I rejoice in all the meritorious deeds performed by the Buddhas as well as those performed by the Bodhisattvas, Pratyekabuddhas, Arhats, those who are in the Path of Training, those who need no more training, and all the beings in the ten directions.

5. REQUESTING

I entreat the enlightened protectors, who have attained buddhahood and freedom from attachments through stages of enlightenment and who illuminate the worlds of the ten directions, to turn the peerless wheel of Dharma.

6. BESEECHING

With folded hands, I beseech those who intend to enter nirvana to remain in the world for as many aeons as there are particles of dust on earth so they can benefit all beings.

7. DEDICATING

Whatever virtue I may have gained by prostrating, offering, confessing, rejoicing, requesting, and beseeching, I dedicate all of them to the cause of buddhahood [for all beings].

Actual Aspiration

1. ASPIRATION FOR PURE ATTITUDE

May all the Buddhas of the past and present in all the ten directions be made offerings. Those who are yet to come, may their wishes be accomplished and may they swiftly attain the stages of enlightenment.

May the world of ten directions become extensively and completely pure. May it be filled with Buddhas who have gone to the bodhi trees and with the sons [Bodhisattvas] of the Buddhas.

May all the beings in the ten directions always be happy and healthy. May they be endowed with favorable circumstances for achieving the dharmic goals, and may their wishes be accomplished.

2. ASPIRATION FOR NOT FORGETTING BODHICHITTA

May I be able to remember my previous lives while in the training of enlightenment. May I always renounce mundane life in all my successive births and deaths.

May I perfect the deeds of the excellent and always engage in the spotless life of morality continuously without defect, in the footsteps of the Buddhas.

May I be able to spread the Dharma in all languages—those of the gods, nagas, yakshas, kumbhandas, and humans.

[Thus] may I tame [my mind] and steadfastly apply myself to the [six] perfections, never forgetting the enlightenment attitude. May I be free from all the nonvirtuous deeds that might obscure my path.

3. ASPIRATION FOR FREEDOM FROM DEFILEMENTS

May I be free from karma, emotional afflictions, and the influence of Mara while traversing the world, like the lotus unstained by water or the sun and moon moving in the sky without hindrance.

4. ASPIRATION FOR LEADING BEINGS TO HAPPINESS

May I completely alleviate the suffering of the inferior realms in all directions and over the breadth of the land. May I be able to bring happiness to and provide benefits for all beings.

5. ASPIRATION FOR THE ARMOR OF DEDICATION

Having perfected the enlightened deeds, may I be able to serve all beings according to their needs by teaching and pursuing the deeds of the excellent in all future aeons.

6. ASPIRATION TO ACCOMPANY OTHER BODHISATTVAS

May I always associate with companions who share similar practices to mine, and may my aspirations be the same as my practice with my body, speech, and mind.

7. ASPIRATION TO HAVE VIRTUOUS TEACHERS AND TO PLEASE THEM

May I always be associated with well-wishing friends who teach me the deeds of the excellent, and may I never disappoint their minds.

8. ASPIRATION TO SEE AND SERVE BUDDHAS IN PERSON

May I always behold the Buddhas surrounded by Bodhisattvas face-to-face and without tiring in all future aeons. May I always present them with magnificent offerings.

9. ASPIRATION TO PRESERVE THE DHARMA

May I always preserve the holy dharmas of all the Buddhas and illuminate the deeds of enlightenment. May I train in the deeds of the excellent in all future aeons.

10. ASPIRATION TO ACQUIRE INEXHAUSTIBLE TREASURES

Through rebirths in all the states of existence, may I gather endless treasures of merit and wisdom; may I become an inexhaustible treasure of all virtues of skillful means, wisdom, contemplation, and freedom.

11. ASPIRATION FOR VARIOUS MEANS OF ENTERING THE DEED OF THE EXCELLENT

a. Entering into Seeing the Buddhas with their Pure Lands

May I always behold as many pure lands as there are atoms in the world, with inconceivable Buddhas sitting in the midst of Bodhisattvas in each pure land, and may I perform the deeds of enlightenment with them.

May I be able to see everywhere, even on the top of a hair, the ocean of Buddhas of the three times and [ten] directions, with their ocean of pure lands for an ocean of aeons; may I fully enter into the enlightened deeds [in each pure land].

b. Entering into Heeding the Speech of the Buddhas

May I always heed the speech of the Buddhas, of which each word is the pure voice of all the Buddhas and an ocean of languages precisely suited to the needs of all beings.

c. Entering into Hearing the Turning of the Dharma Wheels

May I possess the strength of mind to heed the inexhaustible voice of the Buddhas of the three times as they turn the wheels of Dharma.

d. Entering into all the Aeons

[As Buddha wisdom] knows [or enters] all future aeons, so may I also know them in a single instant. May I know in one instant all that is encompassed in the duration of the three times.

e. Entering into Seeing all the Buddhas in One Instant

May I behold all those who are the lions of men, the Buddhas of the three times, in a single instant.

f. Entering into the Object of Enjoyment of the Buddhas

May I always be able to enjoy [enter] their object of enjoyment with the power of liberation [by seeing them as] illusions.

g. Entering into the Accomplishment of all the Pure Lands

May I accomplish upon each atom the perfect array of the pure lands of the three times; and may I enter into the pure lands of the Buddhas [of each atom] in all directions.

h. Entering into the Presence of the Buddhas

When the future Illuminators of the World [Buddhas] realize the stages of buddhahood, turn the wheel of Dharma, and go beyond sorrow to the profound peace of nirvana, may I always be in their presence.

12. ASPIRATION FOR THE POWER OF ENLIGHTENMENT THROUGH NINE POWERS

May I perfectly accomplish the power of enlightenment through [the nine powers]: the power of miraculous swiftness; the power of the all-sided vehicle [the means for benefiting others]; the power of enjoying all the virtuous qualities; the power of all-pervading loving-kindness; the power of the totally virtuous merits; the power of wisdom that is free from passion; and the powers of knowledge, skillful means, and contemplation.

13. ASPIRATION FOR THE ANTIDOTES THAT PACIFY THE OBSTRUCTIONS

May the forces of karma be utterly purified, the power of emotions be utterly subdued, the power of maras be utterly destroyed, and the power of the deeds of the excellent be perfected.

14. ASPIRATION FOR THE ENLIGHTENMENT ACTIVITIES

May I tirelessly perform the [seven enlightened activities] for oceans of aeons: purifying the ocean of lands, liberating the ocean of beings, realizing the ocean of Dharma, attaining the ocean of wisdom, perfecting the ocean of activities, accomplishing the ocean of aspirations, and ceaselessly serving the ocean of Buddhas.

15. ASPIRATION FOR TRAINING FOLLOWING

a. the Buddhas

May I completely fulfill all the aspirations of enlightened deeds of the Buddhas of the three times by attaining enlightenment through the deeds of the excellent.

b. Samantabhadra

The eldest son of all the victorious Buddhas is Samantabhadra. I dedicate all of these merits so that my deeds may become like his. May my body, speech, mind, deeds, and environment always be pure. May I become equal, in these excellent aspirations, to Samantabhadra.

c. Manjushri

May I tirelessly accomplish the virtuous deeds of the excellent by following the aspirations of Manjushri throughout all future aeons.

16. CONCLUDING ASPIRATION

May there be no limit to my enlightened activities and their virtues. Through countless efforts, may I accomplish all the miracles [the virtues of enlightenment].

Extent of the Aspiration

Just as beings are as limitless as the extent of space, and just as their karma and emotions are limitless, so may the extent of my aspirations be without limit.

The Benefits of Making Aspirations

1. THE BENEFITS OF MAKING ASPIRATIONS IN GENERAL

Having heard this greatest dedication prayer, whoever intensely desires supreme enlightenment and develops faith even once will gain greater merit than offering all the realms of the ten directions, beautified with jewels, to the victorious Buddhas or offering [to them] all the supreme joys of gods and men for as many aeons as there are atoms in those lands.

2. THIRTEEN BENEFITS IN DETAIL

Whoever makes this aspiration of the deeds of the excellent will (1) never again endure hellish rebirth, (2) abandon all evil friends, and (3) soon behold the Buddha of Boundless Light [Amitabha].

They will (4) gain all the endowments, (5) live in happiness, (6) attain precious human rebirth, and (7) soon become like Samantabhadra himself.

(8) Even those who committed the five unredeemable deeds in ignorance will soon be completely purified if they recite this [prayer of] the deeds of the excellent.

(9) They will be endowed with perfect wisdom, (10) beautiful form, excellent signs, a noble birth, and a radiant countenance. (11) Profane and devilish beings will not harm them, and (12) they will be honored in the three realms.

(13) They will quickly reach the bodhi tree and sit there to benefit all beings, attain enlightenment, turn the wheel of Dharma, and tame Mara and all his forces.

3. BENEFITS IN BRIEF

Whosoever preserves, teaches, or recites this aspiration [prayer] of the deeds of the excellent shall ultimately attain perfect buddhahood. May none despair of complete enlightenment.

Dedication of the Merits of this Meritorious Aspiration

1. DEDICATION FOLLOWING THE BODHISATTVAS

As glorious Manjushri knows, as does Samantabhadra, I dedicate all my own merits so that I may train myself by following them.

2. DEDICATION FOLLOWING THE BUDDHAS

As dedication is highly praised by the Buddhas of the three times, I dedicate all these roots of virtue for [perfecting] the deeds of the excellent.

3. DEDICATION FOR THE REALIZATION OF FRUITS

At the moment of my death, may all my [karmic] obscurations be removed that I may see the Buddha of Boundless Light [Amitabha] face-to-face and go to his blissful pure land [Sukhavati].

In the blissful pure land, may I completely realize and fulfill all the aspirations [of the deeds of the excellent] and benefit all beings as long as the universe remains.

4. DEDICATION FOR THE FORETELLING BY THE BUDDHA

Happy in that blessed assembly of Buddhas, may I be reborn in the beautiful, perfect body of a lotus, and may the Buddha Amitabha foretell my enlightenment.

5. DEDICATION FOR SERVING OTHERS

Having received the prophecy, may I thereafter perform great benefits for beings in all the ten directions, by the power of wisdom through my myriad emanations.

Conclusion

By whatever small virtue I have gathered by reciting this aspiration of the deeds of the excellent, may all the virtuous wishes of beings be accomplished instantly.

By the boundless merit gained by the dedication of the deeds of the excellent, may the limitless beings be freed from drowning in the ocean of suffering. May they reach the higher realm of Amitabha.

May this King of Aspirations bring benefits for all the countless beings; may they perfect [the virtues promised] in the scripture uttered by Samantabhadra, and may all the lower realms be emptied.

THE NOBLE KING of the Prayers Aspiring to the Deeds of the Excellent [or the Deeds of Samantabhadra] is completed.

Colophon

Note: The King of Noble Prayers Aspiring to the Deeds of the Excellent (*'Phags-Pa bZang-Po sPyod-Pa'i sMon-Lam Gyi rGyal-Po*) comes from the Gandhavyuha (*sDong-Po bKod-Pa or sDong-Pos brGyan-Pa*) of the *Avatamsaka-sutra* (*mDos-sDe Phal-Bo-Ch'e*) section of Kanjur. Bhadracharya (*bZang-Po sPyod-Pa*) has been translated here as "the deeds of the excellent," but it has two meanings. First, because this text is an aspiration and training to perfect the excellent deeds such as the six perfections, it has been translated as "the deeds of the excellent." Second, because this text was uttered by Samantabhadra (*Kun-Tu bZang-Po*), Bodhisattva to Sudhana (*gZon-Nu Nor-bZang*), and because the essence of this text is to bring the trainee into the enlightened deeds, trainings, and virtues of Samantabhadra Bodhisattva, it has been interpreted as "the deeds of Samantabhadra, or the deeds of the Universally Excellent." I have followed the first meaning except where the Tibetan version of the text clearly states otherwise in particular lines.

Translated by Tulku Thondup and edited by Harold Talbott with the assistance of Lydia Segal and Toni Kenyon according to *'Phags-Pa bZang-Po sPyod-Pa'i sMon-Lam Gyi 'Grel-Ch'ung 'Phags-mChog rNams-Kyi rNam-Par Thar-Pa mTha'-Yas La 'Jug-Pa'i sGo*, a commentary written by Lo-Ch'en Dharmashri (1654–1717) of sMin-Grol gLing and also *'Phags-Pa bZang Po sPyod-Pa'i Tshig-Don Gyi 'Grel-Ba Legs-bShad Kun-Las bTus-Pa*, a commentary written by Grags-Pa rGyal-m Tshan (a disciple of Khyentse Wangpo). For a translation from the Chinese, see *Entry into the Realm of Reality*, trans. Thomas Cleary (Boston: Shambhala Publications, 1989), 387–394.

23

Jetsun Dragpa Gyaltsen

The Song of Bringing the Experience of Practice

NAMO RATNA GURUVE.
With the fortune of meeting the precious human birth,
possessing the faith of fearing birth and death,
possessing the devotion of practicing according to the teachings,
intelligent disciples, keep these in mind.
To bring experience of the practice,
please have great persevering effort;
renouncing attachment, stay on a mountain
and mentally renounce this life.
To arouse qualities in the mental continuum,
please have the pure samaya of the three vows,
diminish the mind's pride and vanity,
and be respectful to everyone.
To receive the blessings of the lord gurus,
please imagine them as real Buddhas,
practice according to their biographies,
and offer prayers continually.
Without leaving the view at understanding,
please determine appearances as mind;
without abandoning samsara or accepting nirvana,

also purify the teacher into the natural state.
Without leaving meditation at the grasping of mind,
please be free from attachment to the bliss of clarity,
cut the root [of grasping] completely at its own place,
and go beyond speech, thought, and objects.
Without leaving conduct in accepting and rejecting,
please liberate dualistic grasping in its own place,
level the heads of the eight worldly dharmas,
and be free from the antidotes of the good realization.
Without hope for a later result,
please have direct realization.
Mix both meditation and postmeditation,
and exhaust your desire for accomplishment.
To perform benefit for other living beings,
please complete making aspirations,
arouse the causes and conditions of dependent origination,
and train in objectless compassion.
This small song of eight requests
is sung to the intelligent.
In this way, realization may be possessed.
While it is not possessed, endure in developing meditation.

Song to Inspire Myself

I prostrate to Manjughosha.[1]
I am gripped by defilement, am faithful to samsaric Dharma,
enjoy talking, am diligent in speaking of the faults of others;
without comprehending my own faults, I compete with the inferior;
turn away from this conduct, which is opposed to benefit!
Be diligent in recalling [the faults] of the dharmas of samsara;
always remember going for refuge
to the Three Jewels day and night;
be diligent in any of the vows of individual liberation you have
     obtained.
In order to hold the lineage of the Bodhisattvas,
be very faithful to bodhichitta,

recite the Seven Limb Prayer[2]
and the Sutra of the Three Heaps[3] during the three times.[4]
Without sleeping, practice yoga [of sadhana] diligently
in the first and last parts of the night.[5]
After arising from the meditation sessions,
practice the path of conduct
as it occurs in the sutras and treatises.
Persevere in the root and branch samayas;
be diligent in offering to the Holy Guru;
protect the minds of all sentient beings.
When waves of negative conceptuality occur,
abandon them by developing the antidotes well.
If you do not inspire yourself,
who else will give you inspiration?
In this way, you will be well inspired!
It is very rare to practice according to the texts;
if one does not refrain from this nonspiritual conduct,
one will not obtain a positive result.
Composing this inspiration to myself,
I request the gurus to tolerate any contradictions.

> —This inspiration, written by the Shakya upasaka Dragpa Gyaltsen,
> is well done.

Notes

1. Manjushri, the Bodhisattva of wisdom.
2. The seven limbs are prostration, offerings, confession, rejoicing in the merits of others, requesting Dharma teachings, requesting the Buddhas not to pass into nirvana, and dedication of merit.
3. A popular sutra for confessing sins, rejoicing, and dedicating merit.
4. Morning, noon, and night.
5. The first part of the night is evening, and the last part is early morning.

⊰ 24 ⊱

An Homage to the Buddha Who Performed Twelve Enlightened Deeds

TRANSLATED BY Tulku Thondup

He who is skillful, compassionate, born in the lineage of the Shakyas,
Undefeatable by others, destroyer of maras,
Whose body is majestic like golden Mount Sumeru,
King of the Shakyas—at his feet, I pay homage.

He who first developed the mind of enlightenment,
[Then] perfected the dual accumulations of merits and wisdom,
And in this age [performed] vast enlightened deeds
And became the protector of beings—to him, I offer praise.

Having fulfilled the needs of gods and having known the time to tame
    [the human realm],
He descended from the god realm, came in the form of an elephant,
And seeing the lineage [of Shakyas],
Entered the womb of Mayadevi—to him, I pay homage.

At the completion of ten months, the son of the Shakyas was
Born in the auspicious garden of Lumbini. At that time,
Brahma and Indra praised him, and his excellent signs

Ascertained him to be in the lineage of enlightenment—to him,
    I pay homage.

The powerful youth, the lion of men, who
Exhibited athletic skills at Anga in Magadha,
Defeated the arrogant competitors,
And became unchallengable—to him, I pay homage.

In accordance with the worldly customs
And to avoid calumny,
He was accompanied by the retinue of queens.
With skillful means, he served the kingdom—to him,
    I pay homage.

By seeing that mundane activities have no essence,
He left home and, traveling through the sky,
Near Namdag Stupa he took [the ordination of]
Renunciation from himself—to him, I pay homage.

Intending to attain enlightenment by efforts,
At the bank of Neranjana, for six years
He practiced asceticism. By perfecting perseverance,
He attained supreme absorption—to him, I pay homage.

In order to perfect his efforts from beginningless time,
At the foot of the bodhi tree in Magadha,
With unmoving cross-legged [posture], by attaining the fully
    enlightened state,
He perfected his enlightenment—to him, I pay homage.

Swiftly watching the beings with compassion
In the supreme places such as Varanasi,
By turning the wheel of Dharma, he led beings
Into the three yanas—to him, I pay homage.

In order to defeat the others' evil opposition,
He tamed the six heretical teachers, Devadatta,

And Mara in the country of Khormojig.
To the Sage who conquered war, I pay homage.

With virtues unequaled in the three worlds,
He exhibited great miracles in Sravasti
And was worshipped by all the gods and human beings.
He who caused the doctrine to develop—to him, I pay homage.

In order to inspire lazy people to Dharma,
In the clean land of Kushinagara,
His vajralike immortal body passed away
And attained nirvana—to him, I pay homage.

As perfection is indestructible,
And as the [object] of future beings to make merits,
He manifested [his remains] with many relics
And left them as eight types of reliquaries—to him, I pay homage.

When he, the chief of men, was born,
He took seven steps on this great earth,
And proclaimed, "I am the supreme [among beings] in this world."
To him, the great wise one of that time, I pay homage.

He who first descended from the Tushita gods' realm,
[Then] entered his mother's womb in the royal state
and was born [as] the Sage in the Lumbini garden;
the Blessed One, god of the gods—to him, I pay homage.

In the [royal] mansion, he was worshipped by eight nurses;
Among the Shakya [youths], he demonstrated his athletic skills;
And in Kapilavastu, he accepted Gopa in marriage;
The unequaled body in the three worldly existences—to him,
   I pay homage.

He who showed sadness [at the four views] at the four gates of the city,
Cut off his hair at the Namdag Stupa,
And practiced asceticism on the bank of the Neranjana;
To him, who is free from obscurations, I pay homage.

In Rajgriha, the Sage subdued a mad elephant;
In Vaishali, a monkey offered him honey;
And in Magadha, he attained enlightenment.
To him, who is shining with wisdom, I pay homage.

At Varanasi, he turned the wheel of Dharma;
At the garden of Jeta, he exhibited the great miracles;
At Kushinagara, he passed away into nirvana.
To him, whose mind is like space, I pay homage.

Thus, by the merit of praising the deeds of
The Blessed One, the master of the doctrine,
May the activities of all beings
Also become equal to your deeds.

May we all become like
The body of the Such Gone [Buddha]
And may we have retinues, life spans, buddhafield,
And excellent signs similar to his.

By the power of praying and offering praise to you,
In the area where we are residing,
May sickness, poverty, and wars be pacified
And may Dharma and auspiciousness increase.

May there be the auspiciousness of the longevity of the doctrine
With Buddhas appearing in the world,
The doctrine shining like the sunlight,
And the development and prosperity of the doctrine holders, teachers,
    and disciples.

Note: The source of the last three verses is uncertain. Kyabje Dudjom Rinpoche writes in Chos-sPhyod *that the second prayer is by Acharya Asura and that, according to some sources, the first was composed by Drikung Kyobpa.*

25

Acharya Lama Migmar Tseten

The History of the Sakya School

The First Tibetan king was Nyatri Tsanpo, who some scholars say was born in 126 B.C.E. His reign clearly marks the origin of Tibet (*Bod*) as a sovereign nation. While not much is known about Tibet during this period, ancient records state that the Tibetans were knowledgeable in medicine, astrology, and many other necessary arts.

Buddhism was introduced to the country during the reign of the twenty-eight king, Lha Tho Tho Ri (born in 254 C.E.).

Nearly four hundred years later, Tibet's next major Buddhist milestone was the coming of the trio of grandfathers and grandsons (*mes dbon rnams gsum*). First was Srong Tsan Gampo (617–650 C.E.), the thirty-fifth king. During his reign, which lasted from 629 until his death in 650, he established royal patronage for Buddhism and built Tibet's first Buddhist temples. He was considered an emanation of the Bodhisattva Avalokiteshvara.

Next was the thirty-eighth king, Trisrong Detsen (740–798 C.E.), who played the most important role in introducing Buddhism to Tibet and was considered an emanation of Manjushri. He invited both the Bodhisattva abbot Shantarakshita and Padmasambhava to visit him. In doing so, he venerated the monastics on one side and the white-robed tantric practitioners on the other side of his court, holding both sanghas to be equal in stature.

Finally, Tritsug Detsen (794–839), also known as Tri Ralpachan, became the forty-fourth king in 817. The youngest son of Tride Srongtsen

228

and a grandson of Trisrong Detsen, he was responsible for finalizing the Dharma terminology used by translators.

The History of the Khon

The Khon trace their origin to a class of gods called *wosel lha* ("gods of luminous clarity"). The *Annals of the Khon Lineage* (*gdung rabs*) cites the fifteenth-century author Ngorchen Konchog Lhundrup:

> The line of emanations of Manjushri,
> The glorious Sakyapa, begins in the country of the gods of
>   luminous clarity.
> There were three brothers, Chiring, Yuring, and Yuse [Use].
> Yuse, having been made a king of humans, fathered four sons.
> His elder brother, Yuring, came to his aid.
> The sons of Yuring and Muza Dembu
> were the group of the seven maza. The six oldest brothers
> with their father returned to the land of the gods.
> The youngest son, Masang Chije,
> and Thogcham Wurmo had a son, Pawo Tag.
> He and his Naga wife, Trama, had a son
> called Lutsa Tagpo Woechan.
> Lutsa and the Mon lady Tsomo Gyal,
> while living together, had a son
> at the divide between slate and grass,
> and so he was named Yapang Kyes,
> a hero who could not be defeated by others.

Manjushri is said to have emitted the three gods of luminous clarity— Chiring, Yuring, and Yuse—to benefit others. It important that these gods are thought to have issued from Manjushri, because all males of the Khon line are also considered emanations of the Bodhisattva and descendents of the three gods.

The three brothers descended to the human realm, where they were asked to rule over human beings. The youngest, Yuse, was elevated to the position of king. He bore four sons, known as the four Se Chi Li brothers. Together, father and sons fought the eighteen major tribes of the Dong, one of the four original Tibetan clans.[1] With the help of Yuse's brother Yuring, they conquered the Dong clan and made its members their vassals.

Yuring married a daughter of the Mu,[2] Muza Dembu. Their sons were the seven Masang brothers, six of whom returned to the country of the gods with their father. The youngest brother, Masang Chije, remained on earth. He married Thogcham Wurmo, the daughter of the Thoglha Woedchan, and they had a son known as Thogtsad Bangpo Tag.

Thogtsad married Lucham Drama, the daughter of a Naga, who bore a son named Lutsa Tagpo Woechan. Lutsa and a Mon[3] lady, Tsomo Gyal, married; their only son was born on the tree line of a mountain, so he was named Yahpang Kyes ("Born at the Divide Between Slate and Grass"). According to Tibetan cosmology, the gods live in the heights of the mountains above the tree line, while human beings live below it.

The Khon in the Imperial Period

Konchog Lhundrup's account continues :

> Then, having slain the Srinpo named Kyareng Khragmey and
> stolen his wife, Yahdrum Silima,
> he [Yahpang] married her.
> They had a son named Khonpar Kye.
> The son of [Khonpar Kye] and a lady of the Tsan, Chambu Dron,
> was handsome and smart, rare in the human lands.
> Named Khonpa Jegung Tag,
> he was known as Khonton Palpoche, who went to Nyantse.

Yahpang fought a Srinpo named Kyareng Khragmey, killed him, and married his wife. Because the child of their union was born as an out-come of a feud between the gods (*lha*) and demons (*srin po*), the boy was named Khonpar Kye ("Born in a Feud"); this is the origin of the Khon's clan name.

Khonpar Kye, the offspring of gods, humans, and demons, married a lady from a lesser class of Tibetan god, the Tsan. Her name was Chambu Dron. Their son was called Khonton Palpoche (the "Khon Teacher Who Increases Wealth") because after being appointed one of the inner min-isters of King Trisrong Detsan's court, he increased the king's wealth.

Khonton Palpoche married Lang Zang Nechung, the sister of a translator named Lang Khampa. Accounts vary as to whether the couple had
two or four sons, but most later scholars believe there were two; the elder
was the great scholar, the Khon Lotsawa Lu'i Wangpo, and the younger
was Khon Dorje Rinchen. Jetsun Dragpa Gyaltsen notes in his *Annals of
the Khon Lineage* (*'khon gyi gdung rabs*), "Khon Lu'i Wangpo Srungs was
the foremost of the seven tested men.[4] His younger brother Khon Dorje
Rinchen became a disciple of Master Padmasambhava and became a
tantrika."

Khon Lu'i Wangpo was ordained by the Bodhisattva Shantarakshita
and given the name Nagendrarakshita (Lu'i Wangpo Srungs). He became a skilled translator, working primarily with the Indian scholars
Devachandra, Jnanagarbha, and Vidyakarasimha, and received instruction from Padmasambhava.

The younger son, Khon Dorje Rinchen, was a direct disciple of Master Padmasambhava; he received many of the Secret Mantra teachings,
and trained for and achieved all types of siddhis. He married a lady of
the Dro, Yanglon Kyid, and they had seven sons.

Five of the brothers left their home in Nyantse and settled in various
parts of western Tibet, but the youngest remained in his father's country.
The sixth son, Sherab Yontan, settled in Drompa in the Yah Valley. He
had two sons, and the elder, Yontan Jungney, was the lineage holder of
the Khon ancestral Dharma teachings.

Yontan Jungney had three sons, and the eldest, Tsultrim Gyalpo, remained in Drompa and maintained the Dharma. He also had three sons;
the eldest and youngest of whom remained in the Yah Valley. The older
brother was named Tsugtor Sherab, or Dorje Tsugtor, and he had seven
sons. Along with Tsugtor Sherab's younger brother, they were known as
the Band of the Eight Khon.

The eldest of these seven brothers, Gethong, had one son called Khon
Balpo, who practiced Vajrakilaya in Tsamo Rong cave. He attained many
siddhis and employed the twelve Tenma as his servants.

Khon Balpo's son was Sakya Lodro, who ruled the Jyaru Valley, upper
and lower Shab, and the ancestral hold of Yah Valley. He had two sons:
Khonrog Sherab Tsultrim and Khon Konchog Gyalpo. The eldest, Sherab
Tsultrim, took the vows of a celibate lay practitioner; his conduct was reputed to be pure, and he had no children. He was skilled in the ancestral

Dharma of the Khon and attained the siddhis of Vajrakilaya. Known for his inconceivable power and ability to perform miracles, he was learned in both the new and old tantras. Having practiced Yangdag and Vajrakilaya, Sherab Tsultrim attained siddhis and was able to show his power to the dharma-protectors Karmo Nyida and Dudgon.

The Founding of Sakya

The story of the Sakya (*sa skya*) school begins with Khon Konchog Gyalpo (1034–1103 C.E.], originally known as the Khon Sakyapa. Born in the wood male dog year, he received empowerments and instruction from both his father and elder brother beginning in his youth, and he became skilled in the ancestral Dharma teachings of the Khon.

Once, when interest in the new tantric translations was high, Khon Konchog Gyalpo and his brother, Sherab Tsultrim, went to a fair in the Dro Valley. During the festivities, many Ngagpas, wearing the costumes and bearing the implements of the twenty-eight Ishvaris,[5] performed a dance associated with Mamo Ekajati.[6] They were accompanied by drums and performed in the center of the crowd.

Upon witnessing this, Khon Konchog Gyalpo told his brother, "Now Secret Mantra has become misguided behavior. From now on, since the signs of attaining accomplishment in the Nyingma school will be rare, I shall conceal the three books we use as treasure." Although he wanted to hide all of the teachings, he had made a promise to the dharma-protectors that kept him from concealing *Yangdag* and *Vajrakilaya*. Later Khon generations have adopted these texts as their main practice and still offer tormas to Dharmapala Karmo Nyida and Dudgon.

Sherab Tsultrim said, "I am an old man. But since you are young, you should train in the new systems of Secret Mantra. Drogmi Sakya Yeshe is now the most learned teacher, so go to him soon."

Khon Konchog Gyalpo received many teachings from the leading translators of his day, first receiving the Hevajra initiation and tantra from Khyin Lotsawa, and when the latter passed away, further teachings from Drogmi Lotsawa. Khon Konchog Gyalpo offered Drogmi seventeen fine horses, herbs, jewels, and so on, receiving the Sung Ngag Rinpoche (the "Precious Oral Instruction"), or the Path and Result teachings in return.

He also received the Guhyasamaja teachings from Go Lotsawa, the cycle of the five tilakas from the Oddiyana Pandita Guhyaprajna, the Chakrasamvara teachings from Mal Lotsawa, and so on. He had faith in many other masters as well, such as Bari Lotsawa, Putrab Lotsawa, the Namkau brothers, Khon Gichuwa, and Kyura Aseng, and completely mastered all of the old and new tantras.

Afterward, he built a shrine to his father and elder brother in the Jag basin in the Zhang region. Inside, he installed an acacia kilaya for blessings. Next, he established a small retreat center in the Trawo Valley (now known as the Sakya Ruins) and stayed there for a few years.

One day, Khon Konchog Gyalpo and his disciples went on a holiday. Looking out from a mountain pass, he saw that Mount Ponpori looked like an elephant lying on its side; its right side had a white, shiny patch, water flowing down, and many other auspicious and positive signs. He thought, "If we build a temple here, there will be vast benefit to the teachings and sentient beings."

The owner of the land, Jowo Dong Nag, gave his permission for a temple to be built. Khon Konchog Gyalpo then asked Gurab (the lord of Zhang Zhung), four villages of monks, and seven villages of gods and men whether they had any objection to the temple and how much they wanted. They all replied, "We seek no payment. Please build your temple."

The master said, "It must be acceptable to later generations," and he set a price of a white mare, a necklace of gems, a lady's fine dress, and so on to be distributed among them.

Khon Konchog Gyalpo was the original founder of Sakya. He widely promoted the teachings of Drogmi, taught many disciples in the Dharma, and passed away at Gorum when he was sixty-nine amid many amazing signs.

The Five Founding Masters of Sakya

In a prophetic declaration from the *Oral Lineage of the Dakini's Clear Space* [*klong gsal mkha' 'gro snyan brgyud*], Guru Rinpoche states,

Kunga Nyingpo, Sakya Lotsawa,
Sonam Tsemo, Dragpa Gyaltsen,
the emanations of the Bodhisattvas of the three families[7] will
    arise in Tsang. . . .
After the Sakya Lotsawa named Kunga,
and the one named Phagpa come,
the people and sentient beings of Tibet will be happy and well.
They will uphold the Buddha's teachings for fifty years,
being emanations of Manjushri.

The birth of the *gongma nga* ("five founding masters") was predicted by many teachers, including Atisha.

Sachen Kunga Nyingpo (1092–1160 C.E.)

The first of the five masters was Sachen Kungpa Nyingpo. Khon Konchog Gyalpo was unable to have a son with his first wife, Dorje Chugmo. When he was fifty-nine, he followed the advice of Kha'u Chenpo and secretly took a second wife, Machig Zhangmo, the daughter of the lord of Zhang Zhung. Through good fortune, they had a son in the water male monkey year (1092) among many amazing signs. They named him Sakyapa Chenpo Kunga Nyingpo.

Sachen Kunga Nyingpo was an emanation of Avalokiteshvara. This was confirmed by the great master Nam Kha'upa Chenpo, who, while in a state of one-pointed concentration in luminous clarity saw Sachen's birth consciousness in a tent made of rainbows in the sky above Machig Zhangmo's valley. The consciousness took the appearance of Kasarpani, the two-armed form of Avalokiteshvara, so the master understood that an emanation of Avalokiteshvara would be born in the Khon clan. For this reason, he encouraged Khon Konchog Gyalpo to take his second wife.

From the time he was young, Sachen could read and calculate. He was learned in scholarly texts, and he understood men and women, animals, the qualities of gems, games, healing, grammar, poetry, composition, and so on. Because of his brilliant ordinary qualities, he made many people happy.

His uncommon qualities were limitless and are divided into two sections in traditional biographies: the qualities of training and the qualities of realization.

He first received the Hevajra empowerment from his father, who passed away when Sachen was eleven years old. On his mother's advice, he then went to study with Bari Lotsawa, who had also been one of his father's gurus.

Bari Lotsawa advised him to practice the sadhana of Manjushri Arapacana. While doing this practice, he encountered obstacles created by the spirit Pekar, so Bari Lotsawa gave him the practice of Acala, along with a water protection rite. After pacifying the obstacles, Sachen practiced for six months in retreat and had a direct vision of Manjushri. It was during this vision that he received the famous Sakya Mind Training teaching "Parting from the Four Attachments," in which all the essential points of the Mahayana path may be seen simultaneously. At this time, he also attained the dharanis of nonforgetfulness and unparalleled analytical wisdom.

When he was twelve years old, he went to Rong Ngur Mig, where he studied *Abhidharmasamucaya* with the teacher Drangti Tharma Nyingpo. Sachen left handprints in stone here that still exist today. After Drangti passed away, he studied logic and Madhyamaka with Drangti's student, Khyung Rinchen Trag, at upper Nyang.

He went back to Bari Lotsawa, from whom he received many teachings, such as the two main systems of Guhyasamaja, Krishnayamari, and the three tantras of the Hevajra cycle. Next, he went to study with the great Khon Gyichu Dralha Bar, from whom he received the three tantras of Hevajra, the teachings on the songs of the eighty-four mahasiddhas, and other instruction.

So by age twenty-nine, he had studied with many of the leading Indian and Tibetan masters of his day.

The account of his meeting with his root guru, Zhangton Chobar, when Sachen was twenty-nine has already been fully recounted by others.[8] From this guru, he received the empowerment of the master of the Lamdre Path and Result teachings, which he kept completely secret for eighteen years at Zhangton's instructions.

When Sachen was forty-seven, he was poisoned while he was staying in Gunthang, and he forgot all the Dharma he knew. He remained in isolation for some time, offering supplications to his guru, and was able to recall a verse here and there.

His guru, Je Gonpa,[9] appeared to him in a dream and taught him all the Dharma he had forgotten, so Sachen was able to recall everything.

After this, he received more teachings from the mahasiddha Virupa, to whom he wrote his famous song of praise. This illustrates the uncommonly close lineage of Lamdre, since Sachen heard all the teachings directly from Virupa in person.

After this, he began to teach Lamdre to select disciples and write out the Vajra verses, which had previously only been given in the oral tradition.

Sachen's partial collected works make up three volumes in the Sakya Kabum and include an important commentary he composed on the complete Laghusamvara root tantra of the Chakrasamvara cycle, called the Rosary of Pearls (*mu tig phreng ba*), and many other texts focusing on various aspects of Vajrayana theory and practice. In a separate collection, he wrote eleven commentaries on the Path and Result teachings, the most famous of which are the Nyagma (*nyags ma*) and the Sey Don ma (*sras don ma*) commentaries.

In addition to these achievements in learning, Sachen was a highly realized person and displayed many signs of accomplishment during his lifetime. In general, his mind was permeated with compassion and lovingkindness. As already mentioned, he saw Manjushri in person and beheld the countenances of Acala and Arya Tara.

Sachen Kunga Nyingpo was a great pracititioner who was never separate from the two stages of creation and completion, engaging in the four modes of benefiting living beings until he was sixty-seven years old. He departed to the pure land during the third sixty-year cycle, on the fourteenth day of Asvina (the tenth month) in the earth male tiger year. At the time, his emanations were in four places: the Sukhavati pure land, the Potala pure land, Oddiyana, and the northern world system Golden.

According to Lama Zhang's prediction, Sachen had three disciples who attained siddhi while in their human bodies. He had seven or eleven disciples, including Jetsun Dragpa Gyaltsen, who attained the stage of patience of the path of application, and fifteen disciples, including Loppon Sonam Tsemo, who attained great heat on the path of application. Thirty-one of his disciples, including Kyara Akyabs, attained medium heat, and countless disciples, including the Khampa Aseng, attained knowledge of signs and attained siddis dwelling in weak heat.

Sachen Kunga Nyingpo married two ladies and had four sons by them. His first son, Kunga Bar, was born to his youngest wife, Lady Jo

Champhurmo. Kunga went to India and became a scholar, but he passed away in Magadha when he was twenty-two.

Sachen's other three sons were born to his other wife, Lady Machig Woedron. The eldest was Sonam Tsemo, who was born when his father was fifty-one. The second son, Dragpa Gyaltsen, was born five years later, and the youngest, Palchen Woedpo, was born three years after that. The latter trained as a physician and was the father of the famous Sakya Pandita, Kunga Gyaltsen.

Lopon Sonam Tsemo (1142–1182 C.E.)

As already stated, Sonam Tsemo was born to Sachen and Machig Woedron in the water male dog year. As soon as he was born, the dakinis wrote, "The emanation of Manjushri, Sonam Tsemo, has been born at Sakya" on the gate of Vajrasana at Bodh Gaya in India.

Sonam Tsemo was extremely handsome, and it is said that he was beyond all childish behavior. He sat cross-legged at all times. When he was twelve, he saw the countenances of the deities Hevajra, Manjushri, Tara, and Acala. He taught the three tantras of Hevajra, the Laghusamvara, and the Jnanasarasamucaya from memory. He also recalled eleven of his Indian pandita rebirths, including that of the important master of the Dombhi Heruka Lamdre lineage, Durgacandra.

When he was seventeen, Sonam Tsemo taught the four tantra divisions from memory, and he was famous throughout Tibet and India as a scholar of all the Vajrayana teachings. He learned all the cycles of his father's Vajrayana teachings and realized them in practice.

In 1161, the year following Sachen's passing, Sonam Tsemo entrusted his thirteen-year-old brother, Jetsun Dragpa Gyaltsen, with the throne of Sakya and departed for Sangphu to continue his studies under the great logician and scholar, Chapa Chokyi Senge. He studied there for eleven years, learning grammar, logic, Madhyamaka, the perfection of wisdom literature; he became very learned in these topics.

Once when he was teaching Lamdre in Utse Nyingpo, he appeared as Manjushri, Virupa, and Avalokiteshvara to the pure vision of the scholars Jepa, Zhujya, and Mogton, respectively. He was a siddha of inconceivable qualities.

Among his major works is a detailed commentary on the *Samputa-tantra*; the earliest known Tibetan commentary on the *Bodhicharyavatara*; and the seminal *General Presentation of the Divisions of Tantra* (*rgyud sde spyi rnams*), the introduction to his trilogy of three comprehensive commentaries written on the textual basis of the Lamdre system (the last two parts were completed by his younger brother, Jetsun Dragpa Gyaltsen, after Sonam Tsemo's passing).

Lopon Sonam Tsemo officially held the throne of Sakya for thirteen years, from ages seventeen to thirty, at which time he passed it to his younger brother, Dragpa Gyaltsen.

As a sign of his great realization, when he was forty years, Lopon Sonam Tsemo manifested the rainbow body—the body of vajra light—to the sound of music and pleasing odors while teaching Dharma on a throne in the middle of an assembly of eighty disciples. These disciples had developed wisdom on the eleventh day of the eleventh month of the water male tiger year (1182).

A lifelong celibate layman, Lopon Sonam Tsemo left no heirs.

Jetsun Dragpa Gyaltsen (1147–1216 C.E.)

Just before Dragpa Gyaltsen was born, a Naga king appeared in a dream to his mother. The boy was born amid auspicious omens in the fire rabbit year. He started talking at an early age and enjoyed spending time alone, was without strong attachments, was diligent in developing qualities, and was beyond childish activities.

When he was eight years of age, he took the vows of a celibate lay practitioner from the Bodhisattva Dawa Gyaltsen, and he was more venerable in his conduct than those who had been ordained. In general, he never drank or consumed meat apart from the samaya substances during the feast offerings. He once recounted a dream in which he had a strong desire to drink alcohol, but he decided this was an activity of mara, so he abstained. After that, he had no desire for it, so neither meat nor alcohol ever touched his lips in daily life.

Having received Saroruhavajra's sadhana tradition of Hevajra when Jetsun Rinpoche was eleven, a year later, he gave a detailed discourse on it that greatly impressed all who heard him. Also when he was twelve, he dreamed of requesting the three tantras of Hevajra, after which he comprehended the true state of all phenomena.

When his father passed away, Dragpa Gyaltsen was called on to give teachings at a great festival of Dharma. He again impressed many disciples with his explanation of the *Hevajra-tantra*.

He had received many teachings from his father, Sachen Kunga Nyingpo. As the holder of the Sakya throne, he also received many teachings from gurus such as Nyan Tsugtor, Zhang Tsultrim Drag, Nyan Wangyal, the Nepali Jayasena, and Lotsawa Palchog Dangpo Dorje. His daily practice encompassed seventy complete mandalas. For example, he would meditate the entire Hevajra practice in the time it took him to ascend his throne when going to teach Dharma. In this way, he was never separate in his body, speech, or mind from the two stages of creation or completion.

In terms of his ability to explain teachings, there was no treatise too difficult for him to clarify, and when he explained even the most difficult texts, his students found them easy to understand. Similarly, he had the ability to remove the doubts and misconceptions of those with whom he debated, since his replies always corresponded perfectly with the Dharma.

Jestun Dragpa Gyaltsen wrote many important commentaries. He finished the trilogy begun by his brother, a complete explanation of the entire ground, path, and result of Hevajra practice called *Precious Wish-Fulfilling Tree* (*rin po che ljong shing*). This text still stands as the definitive statement of the Sakyapa view and practice, and it is one of the true jewels of the Sakyapa tradition. He also wrote the definitive Sakyapa commentary on the *Hevajra-tantra, Endowed with Purity* (*dag ldan*). These two texts, together with Lopon Sonam Tsemo's *General Presentation of the Divisions of Tantra*, form the core of the Sakya school's interpretation of the Vajrayana teachings. They are generally considered to be the full exegesis of Dombhi Heruka's explanatory lineage of the Path and Result, as opposed to the intimate instruction tradition that came down through Krishanapa. Dragpa Gyaltsen also wrote a complete commentary on the *Vajrapanjara-tantra*, so he and his brother contributed complete commentaries on the three main tantras of the Sakya school—the Hevajra, the Vajrapanjara, and the Samputa.

Jetsun Rinpoche also wrote detailed sadhanas and practice manuals for the Khon Vajrakilaya tradition, and he preserved the oral instructions

Padmasambhava gave to Yeshe Tsogyal that had been passed down in the Khon tradition of the Vajrakilaya. Another important cycle of his writings is the *Treasury of the King's Cycle of Medical Treatments* (*gso dpyad rgyal po'i skor mdzod*), which covers every aspect of the healing arts and remains an important treatise of Tibetan medicine today. Finally, he composed one of the earliest accounts of the Tibetan kings, beginning with Nyatri Tsanpo.

All in all, his collected works form four volumes. With additional works that have recently been brought to light, he composed approximately five complete volumes of commentaries, sadhanas, and other writings of all varieties.

In particular, Jetsun Rinpoche wrote several experiential songs, which are presented in this volume, having initially been published by Manjushri Press in the Visions series. These songs are great treasures of the Sakya tradition, especially the Great Song of Experience (*nyams mgur chen mo*), in which Jetsun Rinpoche sets forth the most profound teachings of view and practice that encompass all Tibetan Dharma systems, the profound view of the self-liberated nature of rigpa, and a taste of the inner experience of one of the greatest yogis of Tibet.

He demonstrated many signs of a high level of realization during his lifetimes and through his dreams. He was blessed by meditation deities and was clairvoyant; even gods and nagas came to him to remove their doubts. He possessed such faith that he perceived his root guru as being no different than Vajradhara, and when he was with his teachers, he pleased them by accomplishing their needs of body, speech, and mind and never engaging in meaningless talk around them. When his guru passed away, he spent everything he had, without attachment, to make offerings and so on. For example, he built the temple known as Utse Nyingma. He also built monuments for his grandfather, his father, and his elder brother, and regularly offered one hundred lamps in front of each.

Jetsun Rinpoche had many experiences in his dreams. When he was twenty, he dreamed during a nap that he was reciting the *Litany of the Names of Manjushri* (*Manjushri-namasamgiti*); he awoke still reciting the text. Over the next two years, he had a number of similar dreams relating to his past lives in India.

When he was fifty-six, in the fire male dog year, he had an especially important dream of luminous clarity in which Sachen Kunga Nyingpo appeared and bestowed on him the close lineage of the Path and Result teachings, the special advice clarifying the symbolic meaning:

All the Dharmas I have taught you are included here:
The true nature of bodhichitta,
original dharmata, is made into one's seat.
Grab hold of the wind element,
and develop well the heat of fire with tumo.
The stream of bodhichitta must enter the central channel
and so on, to bring the elements under control.
Having actualized the five wisdoms,
one attains the state of deathlessness.

Jetsun Rinpoche's realization was also recognized by the Kashmiri pandita Sakya Sribhadra, who arrived at Sakya around 1208 and bestowed ordination on Sakya Pandita at that time.

On one occasion, the great Panchen predicted a solar eclipse. Jetsun Rinpoche said, "Please don't say that. It won't happen right now." The junior panditas were very upset, but the eclipse did not occur. Jetsun Rinpoche had prevented it by stopping the winds from moving into the rasana and lalana channels and by causing white and red bodhichitta to enter and mix in the central channel. Panchen said, "That old layman will go to any length just to prove me wrong. So much for that. I understand. That old layman is proud."

Another time, when Jetsun Rinpoche was meditating at Zim Chil Karpo, the great Pandita, who was about to leave Sakya, asked Sapan, "What is your uncle doing?"

Sapan replied, "He is staying in meditation."

Pandita said, "We should go and see him."

The boy answered, "I will go first."

But the Pandita suggested, "Let's go together."

So they went together. Jetsun Rinpoche was making the offerings and praises to the Guhyasamaja deity he had created in front of him. Thinking he should show respect to his visitor, he rose to greet the Pandita, intended to place his bell and vajra on the table but leaving them hanging in the air.

The great Pandita said, "That is really a cause for amazement."

Jetsun Rinpoche humbly replied, "This is nothing amazing at all."

The Pandita then prostrated to Jetsun Rinpoche, but the junior panditas with him complained, saying "It is not appropriate to offer prostrations to a layperson. Even though you did it already, please do not offer him more."

The great Pandita replied, "Jetsun Dragpa Gyaltsen is the true Mahavajradhara. He has seen the mandala of Guhyasamaja." He then made Jestun Rinpoche his crown ornament.

Jetsun Rinpoche was also able to communicate with nonhuman beings, for example, he said to the black naga Kunshe, "I want to build a temple here, so you must take your wealth and go somewhere else."

Searching extensively, the naga answered, "I looked everywhere, and apart from a little space on the shore of the ocean, there is no other place to take it."

Jetsun Rinpoche ordered, "Well, take it somewhere."

"If I were to take the gold alone, it would take a thousand years," complained Kunshe.

"Nevertheless, stay here and make some room," the master insisted.

The naga was moved elsewhere, being led by the Mon Dorje Raja and pushed by Jetsun Rinpoche from behind. The place to which he was relocated is today the stone ruins at eastern Ladrang. Jetsun Rinpoche then built the temple he called Utse Nyingma.

When Jetsun Rinpoche reached sixty-one years of age, he had a dream in which he was in a meadow. Some blue women said to him, "Come to the dakini paradise, Khechari."

Jetsun Rinpoche inquired, "Why must I go to Khechari? Since Buddhas do not exist other than to benefit sentient beings, I am not going to go."

There was a smooth, white stone in front of him, and they urged, "Come forward and step on this, and you will go to Khechari."

But he would not step on the stone.

One evening in the ninth month when he was sixty-seven, Sachen appeared to him surrounded by the eight great Bodhisattvas; on his right was the nine-deity Hevajra mandala and on the left was Shakyamuni surrounded by the eight Arhats, Kaudinya, and so on. Sachen asked, "If you are ordained, who is ordained? If you take empowerment, who receives it?"

Jetsun Rinpoche replied, "If I ordain or receive empowerment, the Lord of Dharma (Sachen) is my abbot and master."

Sachen answered, "You have understood it well according to how it is."

During this dream, Jetsun Rinpoche was able to remove many of his doubts by asking questions.

A year later, many divine emissaries invited him to the pure land of Amitabha, but he sent them away. The next year, though many gods sent him invitations, praising neither the Saha universe[10] nor the pure land, he was neither inclined toward the pure land nor disinclined toward evil destinies. He said, "Those without protection are depending on me, so I won't go," and sent the messengers away.

The messengers said, "By all means, you must go when you reach seventy," and he saw the Sukhavati pure land. In the common people's perception, the ground quaked, sounds were heard, and many miraculous lights appeared.

One evening in his seventieth year, some people saw the host of deities that were inviting him to the pure land, and it is said this was also witnessed by his nephew, Sapan. The next morning, Sapan waited in Jetsun Rinpoche's presence with his head resting on his knees. He had a short dream in which he saw an assembly of deities come from the pure land riding beams of light that filled the sky and surrounded by nets of jewels. They carried a lion throne studded with gems, along with many offerings. They pleaded with Jetsun Rinpoche to come to the Sukhavati, and the master seemed interested. The deities said, "Look at the pure land," and made symbolic prostrations. Sapan saw that the ground was made of sapphires, and there were many beautiful things, such as trees made of jewels.

At that time, when Sapan awoke, having offered a Seven Limb Prayer and meditated on his mandala, Jetsun Rinpoche told Sapan, "I am leaving for the pure land. I won't stay there long, because afterward I shall become a universal emperor in the Golden-Hued world, as I have already explained to you, and purify my buddhafield. After that, in three more lifetimes, I will attain the supreme siddhi of mahamudra in one lifetime without giving up my body in dependence on the dependent origination of Secret Mantra."

Thus the great master left this world for the pure land on the twelfth day of the second Tibetan month in the fire male bird year (1216).

Sakya Pandita Kunga Gyaltsen Palzangpo (1182–1253 C.E.)

Sachen's youngest son, Palchen Woedpo, had two sons with his wife, Machig Garphuma Nyitri Cham. The eldest of these sons was the Dharma Lord Sakya Pandita, named Kunga Gyaltsen. When he was conceived, his mother had a dream in which a jeweled naga looked at her with an unbearable gaze and said, "I shall come to stay in you." She then experienced an excellent state of meditation. When he was born on the twenty-sixth day of the second month of the water male tiger year, the sky filled with lights. His father was thirty-three.

After his birth, due to the activation of his previous traces, he was able to speak some Sanskrit and write in Indian and Tibeten without training. He had been reborn as a pandita in India and protected by Manjushri for twenty-five lifetimes.

In terms of the definitive meaning, the Kashmiri pandita Shakya Sribhadra received a prediction concerning Sakya Pandita from Tara. The physician Biji, the scholar Tsang Nag, and others personally saw him as the emanation of Manjushri, which is clear in his biography. In terms of the provisional meaning, Sakya Pandita was able to comprehend all areas of learning merely by hearing them once.

He took the vows of a celibate lay practitioner from his uncle, Jetsun Dragpa Gyaltsen, and was given the name Kunga Gyaltsen. He received the two systems of Bodhisattva vows and the four empowerments of Mahayoga as well.

From his own father, Sakya Pandita received the Hevajra empowerment and was established in the three vows. When he reached nineteen, he received the teachings of the Abhidharma from the great scholar Vasubandhu while in a state of luminous clarity, and he clearly comprehended every word of the text. Thus, the Sakya school has a special short lineage of Abhidharma that continues to the present day. When Sakya Pandita received it later from the pandita Shakya Sribhadra, there was no difference in meaning at all.

He also had a dream in which he encountered the scholar Dignaga and received the keys to immeasurable texts, and he became omniscient in many subjects, such as logic. He received the Maitreya treatises from Zhudon Dorje Kyab, the Logic cycle from the old lineage of logic from

Majya Changtson and Tsurton Zhon Seng. He also received teachings on the four tenet systems from Tsegpa Wangchug Senge. He was given the Shijey cycle of Padampa Sangye, Dzogchen, Chod, and Kadamapa teachings by Chiwo Lhepa Changchub Wod, and he understood all of them.

When he was twenty-three, Sakya Pandita met one of his most influential teachers, the Kashmiri pandita Shakya Sribhadra, who was accompanied by Sangha Sri, Sugata Sri, and Dana Sri. Sakya Pandita received the five major and five minor sciences, Logic, and so on from them and was proclaimed a pandita.

When Sakya Pandita was twenty-seven, he received full ordination from Shakya Sri, receiving the monastic name Bhadra Sri (or *Palzang* in Tibetan). During this time, he also received the complete teachings maintained by his root guru and uncle, Jetsun Dragpa Gyaltsen. Specifically, when Sakya Pandita requested the profound path of guru yoga, he saw his uncle as Manjushri in person, the essence of all Buddhas, and understood the critical points of all dharmas without error; he thus gained unimaginable samadhi and realization.

He taught all his life. When he was nine, he taught Saroruhavajra's sadhana of Hevajra; at eleven, the Hevajra and Buddhasamayoga tantras; and at twelve, the Vajrapanjara and Samputa. He never ceased giving such explanations until he was seventy years old.

An Indian Vedantin named Harinanda and his five companions came from India to debate Sakya Pandita. Sakya Pandita defeated him and cut the Vedantin's hair, converting him and his followers to Buddhism.

Sakya Pandita wrote many books, the four most important of which are *The Treasury of Reasoning* (*tshad ma rigs gter*) for Buddhist logic; *Clarifying the Muni's Intent* (*thub pa'i dgongs gsal*) for the Mahayana path; *Distinguishing the Three Vows* (*sdoms gsum rab phye*) for removing misconceptions about Vajrayana practice; and his most beloved work— of which most Tibetans have memorized many portions—*The Precious Treasury of Eloquent Sayings* (*legs bshad rin po che mdzod*) for dealing with daily life. In addition, he wrote important treatises and commentaries on grammar, music, medicine, art, poetry, and other subjects. Moreover, he was a skilled translator and was responsible for the final edition of Dharmakirti's Pramanavarttika, as well as other texts. By finding and translating the *Fragment of the Vajrakilaya Root Tantra* (*phur ba'l rtsa rgyud dum bu*), which had been written in Sanskrit on a palm leaf in Padmasambhava's own hand, Sakya Pandita firmly established the validity of the Nyingma *Vajrakilaya-tantra* tradition, the ancestral teaching of the Khon family and one of his own main practices.

When he was sixty, he was invited to China by the Mongolian chieftan Godan Khan. He was unable to refuse this invitation, because it came in the form of a threat to invade Tibet. To protect the Tibetan people from the Mongolians, who had recently invaded and conquered China, Sakya Pandita and his two nephews—nine-year-old Chogyal Phagpa, and Phagpa's five-year-old brother, Chagna—set out for China in 1244. After traveling for five years, they eventually reached the khan's court in China, where Sakya Pandita was to remain for the rest of his life.

One of the famous and amazing events he performed was when the king invited him to an illusory temple that had been created by a Chinese magician. The master caused it to become real through the power of his meditation, and this caused the king and his court to have undivided faith in the Dharma.

In general, Sakya Pandita is the most influential scholar in the history of Tibetan Buddhism. He raised the bar for scholarship and learning, and he initiated the golden age of Tibetan Buddhism. His treatises, though controversial to some extent, are considered authoritative on the subjects of logic, Vajrayana, and Mahayana Buddhism. He manifested outward signs of realization, such as an ushnisha on his crown. After his passing, he went on to become a Buddha called Vimala Sri in the Golden-Hued World.

Drogon Chogyal Phagpa (1235–1280)

Drogon Chogyal Phagpa was born amid excellent signs to Sakya Pandita's younger brother, Zangtsa Sonam Gyaltsen (1184–1239), and his wife, Machig Kunkyi, during the wood female sheep year, when his father was fifty-two years old. He recalled his past lives as Saton Riwa, Langriwa, and others. Chogyal Phagpa was taught the Saroruhavajra sadhana when he was three, and the *Jatakas* when he was eight; when he was nine, Sakya Pandita taught him the *Hevajra-tantra*. To everyone's amazement,

Phagpa gave an explanation of *The Advice for Gathering Accumulations* (*Sambharaparikatha*) by master Vasubandhu that same year, and the pride of scholars was diminished when they heard this explanation from a child. Thinking that an ordinary person could not have such wisdom, they considered him to be an Arya. Thus, he became known to all as Phagpa, which means "Arya."

At nine he traveled north to attend Sakya Pandita. While in Lhasa, Chogyal Phagpa received novice ordination in front of the Jowo statue, and in Kyormo Lung, he received the Getsul vow from Sherab Pal.

He spent all his time attending Sakya Pandita during his travels and residence in China, until at seventeen Chogyal Phagpa left for Mongolia. Sakya Pandita was very pleased with him for having mastered the outer teachings and the inner Vajrayana teachings, and gave him a white conch to proclaim the Dharma and a begging bowl. Having entrusted his students to him, the master said, "The time has come for you to teach, to benefit many sentient beings, and to recall your promise." Then Sakya Pandita passed away, having accomplished all he had intended to do.

Having been invited by the Mongolian Khan, Phagpa established the Khan's faith by performing miracles, such as showing each of the five Buddha families separately by cutting open the five limbs of his body with a sharp sword. Beginning with the Khan, Chogyal Phagpa bestowed the empowerment of Hevajra on twenty-five disciples and brought Vajrayana to the kingdom of Mongolia. The Khan gave Chogyal Phagpa the title of Tishri and thirteen surrounding regions of Tibet as his offering for the empowerment.

At twenty-one, Chogyal Phagpa received full ordination on the border of China and Mongolia from the abbot of Nyethang, Dragpa Senge; the master of ceremonies was Jodan Sonam Gyaltsen. Phagpa received teachings on *Abhisamayalankara* and other texts from the abbot and on Vinaya from the master of ceremonies.

Two years later, he accepted an invitation to the five-peaked mountain and received many teachings on Yamari from Tong Ton. After that, he returned to the Khan's palace, and when a Dharma assembly was convened, he defeated twenty-three Chinese teachers in debates and showed them correct view.

When he was thirty, he returned to the seat of Sakya, having been absent from Tibet since he was nine. He gave many teachings there; he also received many teachings on the outer and inner sciences and an ocean of transmissions and instructions from Nyan Wod Srung, the siddha Yontan Pal, Chim Namkhai Drag, Tsog Gom Kunga Pal, Lowo Lotsawa, Chiwo Lheypa Jowo Sey, and others.

After this, he was again summoned to China by the Khan and arrived there when he was thirty-three. He appointed thirteen positions to manage different responsibilities and was offered the rest of the three provinces of Tibet as an offering for empowerments.

At forty-two, having been in China the second time for nine years, he returned to Sakya. He taught a large Dharma festival and used all of his wealth for this event, holding nothing back. He established the basis for a Dharma college and built shrines for the body, speech, and mind of the Buddhas. He gave donations to all the poor people of the region and demonstrated only positive activities toward sentient beings. He spread the Dharma to Tibet, China, and Mongolia; ordained 450,000 novices and fully ordained monks; and bestowed Vajrayana empowerments on people of fourteen different languages. Moreover, he established countless disciples in ripening and liberation through the blessings of transmission and instruction. He gave commentaries on sutras, treatises, and the stages of practice in Hinayana and Mahayana; answered questions; and wrote many texts that are easy to understand.

In the early morning of the eleventh month of the iron male dragon year, when he was forty-six, having endeavored greatly to benefit others, Chogyal Phagpa sat cross-legged, holding his vajra and bell. He crossed his arms, and amid sounds, amazing scents, and a shower of flowers, he passed away.

Chogyal Phagpa was the last of the five founding masters of the Sakya school. Thanks to his efforts, the school ruled Tibet for close to a century; expanded widely; and became the country's dominant institution of learning for the next two hundred years, producing the most famous scholars in Tibetan history, such as Buton, Dolbuwa, Longchenpa, Rendawa, Tagtsang Lotsawa, Tsongkhapa and his two chief disciples, Rongton, Dagpo Tashi Namgyal, Gorampa, and Shakya Chogden.

Of the five masters, Sachen was considered to be the emanation of Avalokiteshvara; Lopon Rinpoche, Jetsun Rinpoche, and Sapan were regarded as emanations of Manjushri; and Chogyal Phagpa was considered to be an emanation of Vajrapani.

Ngor and Tshar

The two main subschools of the Sakya tradition are the traditions of Ngor and Tshar. The Ngor lineage was founded by Ngorchen Kunga Zangpo (1382–1456 C.E.). He was born in the water male dog year and trained at Sakya and other monasteries. His primary master was the siddha Buddha Sri, and he was one of the main teachers of Gorampa Sonam Senge.

In 1430, when he was forty-eight years old, he founded the main Ngor monastery of Evam Choden near Sakya. He achieved a very high level of realization and passed away in the fire male mouse year, when he was seventy-four.

Ngorchen wrote many important Vajrayana commentaries, and all the main Lamdre teachings passed through him. Other great Ngor masters include Konchog Lhundrup; Panchen Ngawang Chodrag; and more recently, Loter Wangpo, who was the main Sakya disciple of Khyentse Wangpo. The Ngor are also famous for their preservation of the so-called seven mandalas of Ngor: Guhyasamaja, Hevajra, Chakrasamvara, Vajrayogini, Vajrabhairava, Sarvavidya, and Mahakala.

The Tshar lineage was founded by the eclectic master Tsarchen Losal Gyatso (1502–1567 C.E.), who began his Buddhist career as a Gelugpa monk. He was born in the water dog year. He received his novice ordination from the first Dalai Lama, Gendun Gyatso, and trained at Tashi Lhunpo Monastery. Because he had strong faith in the Sakya tradition and in the Sakya master Doringpa, his main teacher, he received a prediction from Vajrayogini in person that caused him to seek out Doringpa, who was residing in the forest surrounding Ka'u Cliff Fortress near Sakya.

Tsarchen reached a high level of realization and passed away at sixty-five, his material body dissolving into the dharmadhatu. He did not found a new monastic order, but the Tshar lineage was established at Rongton Sheja Kunrig's monastery of Nalendra Phanpho. Tsarchen himself had many teachers and many disciples, and there were many great masters in his lineage, including the fifth Dalai Lama, who received both Lamdre and Vajrayogini from Nesar Je in the seventeenth century.

The Doctrines of the Sakya School

The Sakya school teaches the full range of topics proper to the three yanas generally presented in Tibetan Buddhism—that is, Hinayana, Mahayana, and Vajrayana (or Uncommon Mahayana Secret Mantra).

When presenting Buddhist philosophy, it divides tenets into the four divisions of Vaibhashika, Sautrantika, Chittamatra, and Madhyamaka. Like all Tibetan schools, the view of the Sakya School is considered to be Madhyamaka.

Its final view is called "the view of freedom from proliferation" (*spros bral lta ba*), which is clearly defined in Gorampa Sonam Senge's *Differentiation of Views* (*lta ba shan dbyed*). The two other main schools of Tibetan Madhyamaka interpretation are the Other Emptiness school of Dobulwa Sherab Gyaltsan, which originated in the Jonang sect, and Je Tsongkhapa's interpretation of Prasanga Madhyamaka. The Sakya school derives its ultimate Madhyamaka view from the lineage introduced to Tibet by the twelfth-century translator Patshab Nyima Dragpa, who with the pandita Jayananda, established Chandrakirti's Madhyamaka texts as the preeminent Indian interpretation of the Madhyamaka school of Nagarjuna. This eclipsed an earlier Tibetan affection for the Madhyamaka systems of Bhavaviveka and Shantarakshita, which were introduced in the eighth century.

Unlike later Tibetan authorities, such as Tsongkhapa and the Jonang, the Sakya school generally argues for a more conservative interpretation of Madhyamaka, closely following the Indian panditas and resisting novel interpretations.

Lamdre, the Path, and Its Result

The main teaching on which the Sakya tradition structures its practice is a cycle of instructions connected with the *Hevajra-tantra* known as the

Precious Oral Instruction on the Path with Its Result (*gsung ngag rin po che lam dang 'bras bu dang bcas*). This teaching originated with the ninth-century Indian pandita Sri Dharmapala of Nalanda, who practiced Vajrayana for many years. After a series of obstacles and experiences, he met the nirmanakaya emanation of the deity Hevajra's consort, Nairatma, who bestowed empowerment on him and caused him to realize the six bhumis in six days. After his radical conduct became known, he was expelled from his monastery and became a wandering yogin before attaining rainbow body and dissolving into a statue of Avalokiteshvara in south India.

He had two main disciples, from whom the main lines of the Path and Result teachings derive: Dombhi Heruka and Krishnapa.

Dombhi Heruka was very bright and attained full awakening during the empowerment, so he required little instruction and did not remain long with Virupa. His lineage of the Path and Result is regarded as the lineage of the exegesis of the *Hevajra-tantra*.

Krishnapa, on the other hand, was an Indian pandita who remained with and traveled around India with Virupa and whom Virupa had converted. He was not as sharp as Dombhipa, so Virupa gave him a more elaborate instruction, which exists today as the Path and Result Vajra Verses. Thus, Krishnapa's lineage is considered to be the lineage of intimate instruction, or upadesha.

Both of these lineages passed through several masters until they were recombined by the Tibetan Lotsawa Drogmi. Drogmi's life and work are not covered extensively here, since they have been well detailed elsewhere.[11] Suffice it to say that Drogmi was among the most prolific translators of the new period, having translated the *Hevajra-tantra*, the *Vajrapanjara-tantra*, the *Samputa-tantra*, and many other texts. He also brought together many diverse streams of intimate instructions from his twelve-year sojourn in India as a Buddhist monk. For the most part, all of the raw material that later led to the formation of the distinct Sakya presentation of Vajrayana Buddhism—that is, the three tantras—derives primarily from Drogmi.

The Path and Result teachings are based around the vajra verses of Virupa. But these verses primarily deal with advanced completion-stage practices and the experiences of the thirteen stages of awakened tantric practitioners. Much of the rest of the teachings and practice derives from the Sahaja Mahamudra tradition of Saraha and Nagarjuna, which is preserved in a text called *Attained In Front of a Stupa* (*mchod rten drung thob*), and from Kotalipa's *The Inconceivable* (*Acantyakramo-upadeśa*).

The method of the creation stage derives chiefly from Saroruhavajra, also known as Padmakara and Padmavajra, who is reputed to be the Mahasiddha who revealed the *Hevajra-tantra*. The early Sakya masters also relied on Saroruhavajra's liturgy for their practice, but the later tradition has replaced this with the more streamlined six-limb system of Durjayacandra, deriving from the Dombhi Heruka lineage of the Path and Result.

Other instructions include the tumo yoga from Krishnacarya, substantially the same tumo yoga found in the Kagyu tradition's *Six Dharmas of Naropa* and deriving from the same master. Dombhi Heruka's *Sahajasiddhi* instruction, instructions by Indrabhuti, and the instructions of eight other Mahasiddhas were all combined with Virupa's vajra verses into an integrated system of practice for the creation and completion stages of the *Hevajra-tantra*.

There are many branch practices of the Path and Result, guru yogas, practices to remove obstacles, and so on that practitioners gradually adopt as they progress in this system until the ultimate attainment of the rainbow body. The main Indian texts were supplemented by the pure visions of Sachen Kunga Nyingpo, who received further instructions from Virupa as mentioned previously, and these special instructions were concealed and preserved secretly for several generations. Many special points of the Sakya Madhyamaka view are elaborated on in connection with Path and Result teachings, especially in *The Wish-Fulfilling Tree* by Jetsun Dragpa Gyaltsen.

Therefore, the pillar and backbone of the Sakya teachings is the daily practice of the creation and completion stages associated with the Hevajra sadhana. In addition to this daily practice are the Hevajra guru yoga and the Virupa protection practice.

Vajrayogini

The second important practice is a practice cycle whose main home is the famed Sakya collection of the Thirteen Golden Dharmas. This is the very popular cycle of Naropa's Khechari, or Naro Khachod as she is known in Tibet. If Hevajra is the pillar of the Sakya lineage, Vajrayogini is its heart. Lopon Sonam Tsemo told his brother, Jetsun Rinpoche, "Of all the instructions I possess, Vajrayogini is the most profound." Thus, the unique Vajrayogini teachings of Naropa were preserved only in the Sakya school for hundreds of years and did not truly begin to spread to other schools until the fifth Dalai Lama received them from Nesar Je.

The Vajrayogini teachings are Naropa's unique transmission. He received them in a vision of Vajrayogini and passed them solely to his two main Nepalese disciples, the Phamthing brothers, who made their home just below the Asura cave in Pharping near Kathmandu, Nepal. After one generation, these teachings, along with the *Chakrasamvara-tantra*, arrived in Tibet with Mal Lotsawa, a guru of Khon Konchog Gyalpo and Sachen Kunga Nyingpo. The Vajrayogini teachings center around a short sadhana and a set of profound completion-stage instructions, especially the instructions of "the meditation beyond thought."

In general, the teachings have a common and an uncommon form, which differ primarily in details of the guru yoga and completion-stage practices. It has been said that more masters have realized buddhahood in the Sakya lineage through the practice of Vajrayogini than through any other practice. Compared with the Hevajra system, Vajrayogini is extremely easy to practice and understand; for this reason, the Sakya tradition of Vajrayogini has become very popular all over Tibet, regardless of tradition.

Vajrakilaya

The Khon tradition of Vajrakilaya has already been mentioned. It is the only Kama, or Long, lineage of Vajrakilaya teachings that has been continuously practiced until the present day. While the empowerments and practice lineage for the other Kama traditions of Vajrakilaya have been maintained, the Nyingma tradition favors the practice of termas, such as the extensive Kilaya of Rigzin Godem. Another special feature is that the Khon Kilaya, unlike the other Kama traditions of Kilaya, is an Anuyoga system of practice, rather then a Mahayoga system. Thus, it is the only surviving Kama Anuyoga system of Kilaya practice.

Mahakala

The main dharma-protector of the Sakya tradition is the Great Mahakala that derives from the *Vajrapanjara-tantra* who is known in Tibet as Gurgon (Panjaranatha). Panjaranatha Mahakala is practiced as both a dharmapala and a yidam. The lineage of dharmapala practice is a combined lineage of the Mahakala tradition brought to Tibet by several masters.

The first lineage derives from Sri Virupa and comes through Drogmi. The second comes from Pandita Amoghavajra through Bari Lotsawa and is also practiced as a deity. The third comes from the great pandita Sraddhakaravarman through the great translators Rinchen Zangpo, Trag Tengpa, and Mal Lotsawa. This lineage is associated with many wrathful activities. Beyond that, there is the common eight-deity Mahakala and protectors practice that comes from Mal Lotsawa and is the normal protector practice still used in Sakya to this day. The fourth lineage comes from Sakya Sri through Sakya Pandita.

The Lesser Mahakala is the Chaturmukha Mahakala, who is considered to be the protector of the Sakya doctrine and came to Tibet with Nyan Lotsawa. This protector's lineage is associated with the *Guhyasamajatantra* and the explanatory tantra of Chakrasamvara.

Later Scholars in the Sakya Tradition

The amazing scholar-siddhas of the Sakya tradition are too numerous to count, but their impact on the whole Tibetan tradition is critical. The scholar-siddhas of the Sakya tradition such as Yagton, Tagtsang Lotsawa, Rongton, Gorampa, Shakya Chogden, and in modern times, Jamyang Khyentse Wangpo and Loter Wangpo were equally amazing as practitioners and as scholars.

The Sakya tradition has held the banner of learning and realization high in the sky of Dharma since its founding. Sakya masters have supported and nourished scholars of other schools for centuries. For example, the Drugpa Kagyu siddha Yangonpa was a disciple of Sakya Pandita; Longchenpa was a disciple of Lama Dampa Sonam Gyaltsen; Tsongkhapa was a disciple of both Lama Dampa Sonam Gyaltsen and Rendawa Zhonnu

Lodo; and more recently, Kongtrul the Great and Mipham were disciples of Jamyang Khyentse Wangpo.

Notes

1. Dong, sBra, 'Bru, and sGa are the famed *rus chen bzhi* (four great clans). *Chogyal Namkhai Norbu.*

2. The Mu are a class of ancient Tibetan gods.

3. The Mon people are frequently identified with the area of Bhutan.

4. The seven men whom Shantarakshita ordained in order to see whether Tibetans could maintain monastic ordination.

5. Twenty-eight goddesses who frequently appear in Nyingma Mahayoga sadhanas.

6. The chief female dharma-protector of the Nyingma school and the main protector of the teachings of Dzogchen.

7. Avalokiteshvara, Manjushri, and Vajrapani.

8. Cyrus Stearns, *Luminous Lives* (Boston: Wisdom Publications, 2001).

9. Zhangton Chobar.

10. The Saha, or "unbearable," universe refers to our universe with its planets, galaxies, and so on.

11. Stearns, 2001.

BIOGRAPHIES OF THE AUTHORS

Jetsun Rinpoche Dragpa Gyaltsen

Jetsun Rinpoche Dragpa Gyaltsen (1147–1216 C.E.), the third of the three lay founding masters of the Sakya tradition of Tibetan Buddhism, was born in the fire rabbit year to Sachen Kunga Nyingpo and Jomo Machig Oddron. As a young child, he delighted in solitude, diligently practiced virtuous qualities, and never exhibited childish conduct or mundane desires.

He received lay vows from Bodhisattva Dawa Gyaltsen when he was eight years old. His conduct was more disciplined than that of the monks; he never touched meat or alcohol apart from samaya substances in the ganachakra feast offerings.

His principal gurus were his father, Sachen, and his elder brother, Sonam Tsemo. He also received many teachings on the three baskets and four classes of tantras from numerous Tibetan, Indian, and Nepalese masters, such as Nyan Tsugtor Gyalpo, Zhang Tsultrim Drag, Nyag Wang Gyal, Jayasena, the translator Pachog Dangpo Dorje, and the yogi Avadhutipa.

Jetsun Rinpoche began teaching at eleven years of age and, to the astonishment of all, gave instruction in the twenty vows and the extensive Hevajra sadhana after his father passed away. At thirteen, he received the three tantras of the Hevajra cycle in a dream and comprehended the reality of all things. He also sponsored and taught at a great Dharma gathering in memory of his late father, where the entire audience was amazed at his ability to recite the *Hevajra-tantra* from memory. He continued his studies, practice, and teachings in Sakya as commanded by his elder brother, who then departed to continue his own studies at Sangphu in central Tibet.

Jetsun Rinpoche was never separate from the samadhi of the stages of creation and completion. On his way to give teachings, he meditated on Hevajra, and when he settled on his throne, he concluded his practice up to the seal of the lord of his Buddha family. His general offerings represented daily torma offerings, and his Dharma teaching substituted for mantra repetitions. As he returned to his residence, he meditated on Chakrasamvara. Thus, in twenty-four hours, he meditated on seventy different deity mandalas.

As a sign of his attainment, when the Kashmiri pandita Shakya Sribhadra announced an eclipse of the sun, Jetsun Rinpoche performed a yogic practice and the eclipse did not occur. The pandita said, "Jetsun Rinpoche must have gone through every difficulty to prove me wrong." When the pandita went to see him, Jetsun Rinpoche stood up suddenly and left his vajra and bell hanging in space. Because his signs of accomplishment were beyond comprehension, Shakya Sribhadra praised him, saying, "Mahavajradhara Guhyasamaja!" and received the nectar of the teaching. Jetsun Rinpoche became the crown ornament of all the Arya Vajradharas.

At fifty-six, he received the special instruction of the extremely close Path and Result lineage (The Clear Meaning of Signs) from the manifestation of his father's wisdom body at the Tsangkha monastery in Nyemo Rutsam. This occurred at night in the state of clear light.

At sixty-eight and sixty-nine, he blessed and extended his own life by rejecting the invitations of the dakinis from Sukhavati, who came again and again.

Jetsun Rinpoche spread Buddhism through his lectures, debates, and writings. In particular, he liberated many fortunate beings through the Path and Result teachings. He benefited limitless sentient beings throughout his seventy years and died in 1216, the fire rat year.

His main students were his nephews Sakya Pandita and Zangtsa. He also had eight disciples with the last name Dragpa, four disciples who held the teaching of Vajrapanjara, four great Vidyadhara disciples, and many others.

Jetsun Rinpoche predicted that he would be reborn as the son of a Chakravartin king of the Golden-Hued World, where he was to accomplish most of the paths and stages, and at his third rebirth would become a Buddha.

Jetsun Rinpoche Dragpa Gyaltsen was fully conversant in all aspects of Buddhist learning, but for the most part, his writings focused on the Vajrayana systems he received from his father and other teachers. These writings consist of commentaries on tantras, sadhanas, and initiation rituals from the Hevajra and the Chakrasamavara systems, including Vajrayogini.

Sakya Pandita

Sakya Pandita (1182–1251 C.E.) is one of the founders of the Sakya tradition of Tibetan Buddhism and is said to be the emanation of the great Bodhisattva Manjushri. During his lifetime, he attained the first bhumi through his practice of the Vajrayana guru yoga. From then on, he gained higher realizations. He also began to teach and displayed many great activities of the Path. Because of this, he is considered one of the greatest scholars to have lived in Tibet.

To illustrate this, there were many Tibetan scholars prior to Sakya Pandita's birth, but none of them could even gain a mastery of the five major and five minor sciences. The five major sciences cover subjects like construction of images and houses, medicine, Sanskrit, logic, and Buddhist philosophy; and the five minor sciences comprise subjects such as astrology, music, poetry, versification of writings, and lexicography. Sakya Pandita sought out the teachings on the five minor sciences from many Indian scholars, wrote books about them, and established their teaching in Tibet. His fame as a scholar in Tibet and India was so great that to test his scholasticism, six Hindu scholars from India went to debate with him. Sakya Pandita was able to defeat them all, which no one else had been able to do.

In India, the title for a great scholar is Pundit, or Pandita, and it is given to someone who is extremely learned not only in the Dharma, but also in other worldly knowledge and skills. The first Tibetan to be given this title was Sakya Pandita, who received it from the great Indian master Shakya Sribhadra. It was bestowed on him to show that he had indeed gained mastery over the various fields of learning. Until Sakya

Pandita, anyone translating the Buddhist scriptures from Sanskrit into Tibetan had to rely on or work with great Indian Buddhist scholars. Sakya Pandita was the first person who, because of his great knowledge, did not need to rely on someone else to perform translations. Through his own scholarship and mastery of Sanskrit, he was able to translate the texts into the Tibetan language on his own. Other scholars were able to follow in his footsteps later on.

Sakya Pandita was also the first Tibetan to spread the teaching of Tibetan Buddhism outside of that country. When the Mongols ruled China, one of the minor Mongol emperors, Godan Khan, invited Sakya Pandita to spread the Dharma in Mongolia. According to Mongolian history, the founder of the Sakya sect, Sachen Kunga Nyingpo, had been invited to Mongolia to teach the Dharma many years before, but had been unable to do so. According to the Mongolian texts, his grandson, Sakya Pandita, did go and spread the teaching. Sakya's nephew, Chogyal Phakpa, also spread the teaching widely after him. Both the Tibetan and the Chinese texts refer to Sakya Pandita's arrival in Mongolia and his dispensation of the Dharma.

According to Tibetan history, the Buddha's teaching arrived in China even before Sakya Pandita did. It was 110 years after the parinirvana of the Buddha, and both the Hinayana and the Mahayana teachings were taught. It is said that many Chinese within the Hinayana tradition were able to gain the various stages of Arhat enlightenment, and many within the Mahayana tradition were able to practice advanced Bodhisattva practices such as giving of their bodies to others. Even the Vajrayana teaching had spread from India to China, though it was only a small part of the lower tantra and none of the higher tantra. It was only when Sakya Pandita accepted the invitation of Godan and when Chogyal Phagpa later bestowed the Hevajra initiation on Kublai Khan that the higher tantra was introduced into China. From that time onward, the Vajrayana flourished in that country.

It was also through Sakya Pandita, Chogyal Phagpa, and others that the Mahayana was firmly established throughout various parts of China. When Chogyal Phagpa was in China, he acted as personal teacher to the emperor. In his position, he was able to spread the teachings of the Buddha extensively; on one occasion, seventy thousand monks listened to his teachings. After Sakya Pandita and Chogyal Phagpa, the influence of the Sakya sect started to wane. The Kagyu tradition became prominent, but after a number of years, its influence also decreased, and the Gelugpa became popular.

When Sakya Pandita went to Mongolia, there was no written form of the Mongolian language. He created the Mongolian alphabet, which was later revised by scholars. Once the alphabet was created, all the scriptures of the Buddha's teachings, the Tripitaka, the explanatory literature, and other Tibetan teachings were translated into Mongolian.

Sakya Pandita is considered an extraordinary person. For example, prior to his passing into nirvana, many people saw the various marks of enlightenment that had been on the great Shakyamuni's and Nagarjuna's bodies—such as the knob on the top of the head and the turf of hair between the eyebrows—appear on Sakya Pandita.

He wrote many works on various aspects of Buddhist philosophy, as well as on the five major and five minor sciences. He also wrote many commentaries and books on the Dharma. *The Sage's Intent* is basically the teachings of the Mahayana path. It includes the various stages of the Bodhisattva path in relation to some of the great Kadampa teachings, such as the explanation of the various stages that a practitioner must go through from initiation to full and perfect enlightenment.

The teachings in *The Sage's Intent* are based on two verses from a book that was taught by the great Bodhisattva Maitreya. It is said that Maitreya taught five different books to the Indian saint Asanga, one of which is known as the *Mahayana-sutralankara*. It was from this book that Sakya Pandita took two verses and wrote his own book. The Mahayana-sutralankara discusses all the teachings of the Buddha and is divided into ten major sections, but Sakya Pandita condensed them into six sections.

Chogyal Phakpa

Chogyal Phakpa (1235–1280 c.e.) was the fifth founding master of the Sakya order of Tibetan Buddhism. His father was Zangtsa Sonam Gyaltsen, and his mother was Machig Kunkyi. He began giving teachings at the age of three, and scholars were amazed at his knowledge, calling him Phakpa ("the Noble One"). When he was ten years old, he received the monk's vow in front of Jowo Shakyamuni's shrine in Lhasa from his uncle, Sakya Pandita.

At seventeen, Chogyal Phakpa traveled to Mongolia with Sakya Pandita, with whom he studied general Buddhist subjects and many tantric teachings. Before passing away, Sakya Pandita presented him with a white dharma conch (which symbolizes the spreading of Dharma both far and near) and a monk's bowl (symbolizing the establishment of monastic traditions), and asked him to help others by remembering his past vows and resolutions. Chogyal Phakpa arranged an elaborate funeral for his uncle.

The great Mongolian king Kublai Khan invited Chogyal Phakpa, who was then nineteen, to give the Hevajra initiation to twenty-five members of the royal family and introduce them to Vajrayana Buddhism. In return, the king offered him a portion of Tibet, which was then under Mongolian control, and gave him the title Tishri. After this, Sakyas became the spiritual and temporal rulers of Tibet, and Choeyal Phagpa became the first monk or lama in history to rule that country.

When he was twenty-one, he received full ordination from Abbot Nyethangpa Dakpa Senge, under whose guidance he studied several Buddhist subjects. Two years later, Chogyal Phakpa invited Tongton to the "five-peaked mountain" of China to receive many teachings. As that time, he also visited royal courts and, while giving teachings, defeated seventeen heretics. When he was thirty, Chogyal Phakpa returned to Sakya and bestowed many teachings. He also invited numerous masters there, received more teachings, and became the great master of Dharma. At the age of thirty-three, he again traveled to China at the invitation of the king and assigned his responsibilities in Tibet to thirteen deputies. In gratitude for Chogyal Phakpa's initiations, the king bestowed many offerings on him and the people of Tibet. All the offerings were used in the service of the Dharma for constructing and financing religious artifacts, and for the welfare of monks and poor people.

Chogyal Phakpa spread the Dharma in Tibet, China, and Mongolia, and became an abbot of four hundred thousand monks. He gave teachings in many languages and benefited many people. Further, he composed many texts of commentaries, practical instructions, and questions and answers. He passed away at age forty-five.

Ngorchen Kunga Zangpo

Ngorchen was born in the water male dog year (1382). He trained at Sakya and other monasteries, and his primary master was the siddha Buddha Sri. He was one of the main teachers of Gorampa Sonam Senge. In 1430, when he was forty-eight, he founded the main Ngor monastery of Evam Choden near Sakya. He achieved a very high level of realization and passed away in the fire male mouse year (1456). Ngorchen wrote many important Vajrayana commentaries, and all the main Lamdre teachings passed through him.

His Holiness Sakya Trizin

His Holiness Sakya Trizin was born in Tsedong, near Shigatse, in south Tibet on the first day of the eighth Tibetan month (September 7, 1945). "Sakya Trizin" means "holder of Sakya throne." His Holiness is the forty-first Patriarch of the Sakya sect, one of the four main sects of Tibetan Buddhism. He is also a direct descendent of the Khon lineage, an ancient Tibetan religious family that, according to legend, had heavenly origins.

His formal studies started at the age of five, although even before that he had received several empowerments from his father. In fact, he received his first empowerment, one of long life, as soon as he was born.

In the course of intensive studies at Sakya, Ngor, Lhasa, and later in India, he received all the major transmissions of the Sakya Lineage, such as the exoteric and esoteric Lamdre (Path and Its Result) teachings, the Druthab Kuntu (a collection of tantric empowerments and practices), the Vajrayogini instructions, and the Zenpa Zidal. From a young age, he memorized many texts, such as the *Hevajra-tantra*, performed many retreats, and gave numerous empowerments. He also received many teachings from the other traditions of Tibetan Buddhism.

His main gurus were the Ngor abbots; Ngawang Lodro Shenpen Nyingpo; Khangsar Shabdrung; Lama Ngawang Lodro Rinchen; the Venerable Jamyang Kyhentse Rinpoche; the great Nyingmapa yogi Drupchen Rinpoche; Phende Khenpo; Sakya Khenpo Jampal Sangpo; his father, Dezhung Rinpoche; and Chogye Rinpoche.

He formally acceded to the throne of Sakya in early 1959. Almost immediately after the coronation ceremony, he had to leave for India because of the Communist Chinese takeover of Tibet. He stayed first in Sikkim, where he started to learn English, then moved to Darjeeling, where he spent three years mastering philosophical studies under Khenpo Rinchen. Finally, he went to Mussoorie and, in March 1964, founded the Sakya Centre in Rajpur, Dehra Dun. He studied the tantras intensively and received many profound explanations from Khenpo Appey until 1967. He also continued his study of English. From 1971 to 1972, he received the Gyude Kuntu, a major collection of tantras, from the Venerable Chogye Trichen Rinpoche.

At the age of twenty-two, he gave the Lamdre teaching for the first time to a large gathering at Sarnath, Varanasi. In that same year, he also inaugurated the Sakya rehabilitation settlement at Puruwala in Himachal Pradesh, forty miles from Dehra Dun.

His Holiness gave the Druthab Kuntu to a large assembly in Ladakh in 1976. Five years later, he inaugurated the new temple at Puruwala, which is now the seat of the Sakya order. Since then, he has given numerous Lamdre teachings all over the world.

His Holiness has served the Dharma ceaselessly. He has many disciples in India and other countries, and has made several global teaching tours.

His Eminence Chogye Trichen Rinpoche

Chogye Trichen Rinpoche is the most senior Sakya lama and the head of the Tsarpa subschool. Born into the Kushang family in 1920, in the Tsang province of central Tibet, he was recognized as the eighteenth Chogye Rinpoche of Nalendra Monastery by the thirteenth Dalai Lama. At the age of eleven, he received novice vows and was officially enthroned at Nalendra. In these early years, he studied all the basic liturgies and rituals of Nalendra Monastery intensively. His two main root gurus were the fourth Zimwog Tulku Ngawang Tenzin Thrinley Norbu Palzangpo (the other main incarnate lama of Nalendra Monastery) and Dampa Rinpoche Shenphen Nyingpo of Ngor Evam. From these two great teachers, Chogye Rinpoche received all the major and minor teachings of Sakya, such as the two Lamdre traditions, the Greater and Lesser Mahakalas, the four tantras, the Thirteen Golden Dharmas, and Kalachakra.

The name Chogye means "eighteen" and comes from the time of Khyenrab Choje, the eighth abbot of Nalendra, who also belonged to the aristocratic Kushang family. Khyenrab Choje, a great teacher possessing the direct lineage of Kalachakra received from Vajrayogini, was invited to be the abbot by Sakya Trizin Dagchen Lodro Gyaltsen (1444–1495). Khyenrab Choje visited the emperor of China, who was greatly impressed by the tantric scholar from Tibet and bestowed on him eighteen precious gifts. The lineage of Chogye Rinpoches began with Khyenrab Choje. The present Chogye Rinpoche, Ngawang Khyenrab Thubten Lekshe Gyatso, is the eighteenth in the line.

After the Lhasa uprising in the face of the 1959 Chinese invasion, Rinpoche left Tibet for the safe haven of Lo Monthang. Although governed as a Tibetan principality, Lo Monthang (Mustang) is politically a part of Nepal. As the uncle of the current king, Chogye Rinpoche found safe refuge and stayed for some time, giving teachings and performing many ceremonies at the various monasteries. It was then that he wrote the short Hevajra "At the Time of the Path" meditation in verse form. The majority of monasteries in the Lo Monthang area are of the Ngorpa school, and the main monastery was founded in the fifteenth century by Ngorchen Kunga Zangpo.

Later, Rinpoche journeyed to India and lived for several years in Dharamsala, where he met Thomas Merton in November 1968. In 1963, while on a pilgrimage, Rinpoche visited the birthplace of the Buddha in Lumbini, Nepal. Feeling something very special for this holy place, he and the king of Lo Monthang vowed to build a monastery there. After twelve years, the vow was fulfilled. Inscribed on a marble plaque in front of the monastery are the words of Chogye Rinpoche:

Here in the Lumbini Grove is the blessed spot where the Prince Siddhartha was born. This is indisputably proven by the pillar erected by the Emperor Ashoka, on which are inscribed the words, "Here Buddha Shakyamuni was born." The banner of Lumbini's fame has been unfurled in all corners of the world, and it is a shrine worthy of the adoration of all beings. Here in 1963 I and the Mustang Raja resolved to erect a monastery. In 1967 we appealed to H.M. King Mahendra of Nepal, and in gracious response in 1969 we were granted ten kathas of land under the supervision of the Director and Staff of H.M.G. Department of Archeology. Work was begun then, and after six years of untiring labour the monastery was completed inside and outside, including the erection of the main image of Lord Buddha. Then on March 2nd, 1975, coinciding auspiciously with the celebration of H.M. King Birendra's coronation, the monastery was dedicated in a ceremony led by H.M. Government's representative, Prof. Surendra Bahadur Shrestha, Lumbini Zonal Commisioner. Then for the sake of imbuing the monastery with Transcendent Blessings until the end of the aeon, a special consecration ceremony was performed over a three-day period by H.H. Sakya Trizin, head of the Sakya Order, assisted by a group of high ecclesiasts and fifty monks. During the four-day celebration we were deluged by felicitations from many religious and government figures, and all the guests and visitors, exceeding one thousand in number, joyfully participated with ever-deepening reverence for the Lord Buddha and his having taken birth here. In that spirit the celebrations were warmly concluded. It is my fervent prayer that by the merit of these virtuous acts by patrons and clerics alike, may the Buddha's teachings flourish and may all beings ultimately be established in perfect enlightenment.

The main shrine of the new monastery has an eight-foot, gilded statue of Shakymuni Buddha; on his right in a glass case is a statue of Rongton, the original founder of Nalendra Monastery. There is also a statue of Lowo Khenchen, the most famous lama to have come out of Lo Monthang, a major commentator on the works of Sakya Pandita, and a central lineage holder in the Khon tradition of Vajrakilaya. The king of Lo Monthang also donated many statues and religious objects from his palace.

Currently, Rinpoche has two other monastic facilities, both in the Kathmandu Valley. The first is a monastery at the Boudhanath Stupa, and the second is a retreat facility at Parping in the southwestern part of the valley. Rinpoche has taught many of today's high lamas, including His Holiness the Dalai Lama (especially giving teachings on Kalachakra), His Holiness Sakya Trizin, and the late Dudjom Rinpoche. Chogye Rinpoche is regarded as the definitive authority on Kalachakra. Aside from leading several three-year retreats, he spends much of his time in meditation. He normally sleeps sitting up and is said to require only one hour of sleep each night.

Khenpo Appey Rinpoche

Khenpo Appey Rinpoche received his early monastic training and education in the province of Kham in eastern Tibet, where he was born. Later he moved to the Ngor Monastery in central Tibet, where he continued his studies. He was abbot of Dzongsar University in eastern Tibet before fleeing to India during the Communist invasion.

He has resided in India ever since, and until 1967, he was tutor to His Holiness Sakya Trizin there. He and His Holiness Sakya Trizin were the main motivating forces behind the founding of the Sakya College of Buddhist Philosophy in 1972 in Mussoorie, India. Khenpo Appey Rinpoche served as principal and taught at the college for many years, until moving to Nepal to start another Sakya college in Boudhanath. He is the most learned khenpo (abbot) living today and has mastered both sutras and tantras. He has performed many retreats and given countless teachings and initiations.

Tulku Thondup Rinpoche

Tulku Thondup Rinpoche (b. 1939) is the author of many acclaimed books, including *The Healing Power of Mind, Boundless Healing, Masters of Meditation and Miracles,* and most recently, *Peaceful Death, Joyful Rebirth: A Tibetan Buddhist Guidebook.* He was recognized at age four as the reincarnation of Konchog Dronme, a celebrated scholar and adept of Dodrupchen Monastery, a famous learning institution of Tibetan Buddhism in eastern Tibet. In 1980, Tulku Thondup came to the United States as a visiting scholar at Harvard University.

For the past twenty-five years, he has been living in Cambridge, Massachusetts, where he writes and conducts workshops on healing, meditation, and Buddhism. For more about his life and work, please visit www.TulkuThondup.com.

Acharya Lama Migmar Tseten

Acharya Lama Migmar Tseten was born in 1956 in Tibet. He left with his family in 1959 following the Chinese occupation and received his elementary education at a Tibetan primary school in India. In 1970, he joined the Tibetan Institute at Sarnath, where he studied Sutrayana Buddhist philosophy, principally under the late Khenpo Rinchen, as well as Sanskrit, English, and history. He received the Acharya degree and was appointed director of the Sakya Centre and the Sakya Institute in 1981. While serving as director, he continued his studies, receiving transmissions such as the Lamdre from His Holiness Sakya Trinzin, His Eminence Chogye Trichen Rinpoche, and His Eminence Luding Khen Rinpoche. In 1989, he was appointed the teacher at the Sakya Chokhor Yangtse in Massachusetts. He presently serves as the Buddhist chaplain at Harvard University in Cambridge.